NOT ! THE L____ ____ __ A DAUGHTER-IN-LAW

KALBIR BAINS

All rights reserved. © 2017 Kalbir Bains
Cover artwork © Jag Lall

No part of this document may be reproduced, sold, stored in or introduced into a retrieval system, or transmitted, in any form or by any means (electronic, mechanical, photocopying, recording or otherwise), without the prior permission of the copyright owner.

Disclaimer: I have tried to recreate events, locales and conversations from my memories of them. In order to maintain their anonymity in some instances I have changed the names of individuals and places, as well as some identifying characteristics and details such as physical properties, occupations and places of residence. In addition, some names, dates, places, events, and details have been changed, embellished and altered for literary effect.
First printing: 2017.
ISBN-13: 978-1543264067
ISBN-10: 1543264069

British Cataloguing Publication Data
A catalogue record of this book is available from The British Library.

Also available on Kindle from Amazon

AUTHORS NOTE:

Stop! You are holding in your hands a story that is inspired by true events and has peaks of sadness and happiness, yet embraces culture to the fullest. Names and other corresponding details have been altered to protect the privacy and disguise the identities of the individuals mentioned. The issues in this book are cultural issues and not religious issues.

CONTENTS

Prologue: The story before the silence and hurt 13

First comes arranged marriage, and then comes love 15

A brief history of the frogs: Eligible bachelor number one 19

Registering on the matrimonial list 26

Along comes eligible bachelor number two 29

A little insight into my parents' relationship 37

Eligible bachelor number three – three months later 45

Deal or no deal...51

The first official meeting 55

My first ever second meeting 59

Third meeting 62

Fixing the wedding date...75

August, the evening before the shagan 84

September, Harleen's shagan from the Purewal family 91

(Almost) Losing my arm and heart 96

Friendship turns the two Johal families into one...............102

My parents' marriage 106

Back to Maninder and Harleen's relationship....................110

Maninder's birthday 113

Finding the perfect lehenga 116

The ring process with Maninder's parents in Birmingham
and getting his wedding outfit...122

Breaking away from the wedding 131

Christmas Eve with Maninder and the ladies in his
household 134

New Year's Day: three months until the wedding 137

The story of the wedding bands..138

The Purewals join the Johal family for a peaceful meal....142

Who pays for the wedding these days? 148

Modern day dowry lovers 151

Our first Valentine's Day together.......................................154

Collecting my wedding lehenga 156

Mother and Nani Ji see my wedding lehenga for the first

time 158

My Nani Ji and Mother's wedding days............................ 159

The kurmai ceremony 162

The chunni ceremony 164

Return of the gold to the Mother-in-law and another list
completed.. 168

Try to treat others as you would want them to treat you. 170

Punjabi weddings: a bright and colourful event in one's life
.... 173

Our civil ceremony 180

Starting a relationship with your best foot forward.......... 183

The laava de rasam 185

The day after the big fat Punjabi wedding 197

The honeymoon... 199

Returning to the UK and starting my married life as Mrs
Purewal.. 209

Making best friends with one room in the house: the
kitchen 213

Someone I love was never born 221

The phone hacking scandal 242

Opening my letters 252

Round one. Hitting me for the first time after four months
of marriage... 254

Gurleen Visits Milton Keynes 261

Snowdonia – The August bank holiday weekend break.. 266

Gurleen's second visit after I fell ill 269

Our jobless days 271

The birthday party 275

Keeping up appearances in the Purewal family household
.... 284

Jaya's wedding 288

Trip to India.. 292

Our first Diwali together... 301

Round two: Hitting me for the second time 304

October 2008: Maninder's birthday 309

First Christmas with my in-laws... 315

The in-laws vs. the business trip 322

First lohri with my in-laws...325

The desi Big Brother show 329

The tapped phone 332

Booking the first wedding anniversary trip 334

Wedding anniversary in Lovers' Paradise...........................336

Back to Milton Keynes..339

Marriage counselling 341

Holiday to Canada and faking illness to get attention......347

I think I can forge her signature 355

Maninder's cousin's wedding in my hometown 357

Maninder's cousin's dad's passing 359

Issues with my dress...361

Me, the slut...363

Domestic violence: round three and breakfast gate 365

The keys do not fit the lock anymore 377

The homecoming...388

Home again!..391

Epilogue...393

Final word 396

An image and a poem that describe my journey 397

Acknowledgements 398

Kalbir Bains 399

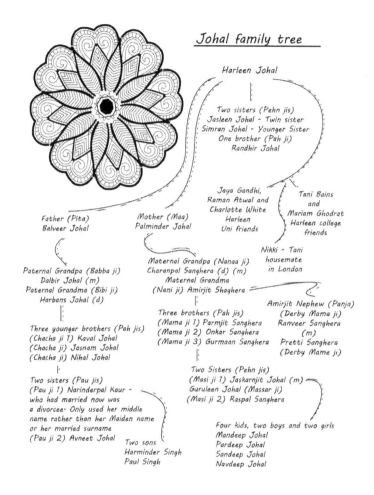

Johal family tree

Harleen Johal

Two sisters (Pehn jis)
Jasleen Johal - Twin sister
Simran Johal - Younger Sister
One brother (Pah ji)
Randhir Johal

Jaya Gandhi,
Raman Atwal and
Charlotte White
Harleen
Uni friends

Tani Bains
and
Mariam Ghodrat
Harleen college
friends

Father (Pita)
Balveer Johal

Mother (Maa)
Palminder Johal

Nikki - Tani
housemate
in London

Paternal Grandpa (Babba ji)
Dalbir Johal (m)
Paternal Grandma (Bibi ji)
Harbans Johal (d)

Maternal Grandpa (Nanaa ji)
Charanpal Sanghera (d) (m)
Maternal Grandma
(Nani ji) Amirjit Shaghera

Amirjit Nephew (Panja)
(Derby Mama ji)
Ranveer Sanghera
(m)
Pretti Sanghera
(Derby Mame ji)

Three younger brothers (Pah jis)
(Chacha ji 1) Kaval Johal
(Chacha ji) Jasnam Johal
(Chacha ji) Nihal Johal

Three brothers (Pah jis)
(Mama ji 1) Parmjit Sanghera
(Mama ji 2) Onkar Sanghera
(Mama ji 3) Gurmaan Sanghera

Two sisters (Pau jis)
(Pau ji 1) Narinderpal Kaur -
who had married now was
a divorcee· Only used her middle
name rather than her Maiden name
or her married surname
(Pau ji 2) Avneet Johal

Two Sisters (Pehn jis)
(Masi ji 1) Jaskarnjit Johal (m)
Guruleen Johal (Massar ji)
(Masi ji 2) Raspal Sanghera

Two sons
Harminder Singh
Paul Singh

Four kids, two boys and two girls
Mandeep Johal
Pardeep Johal
Sandeep Johal
Navdeep Johal

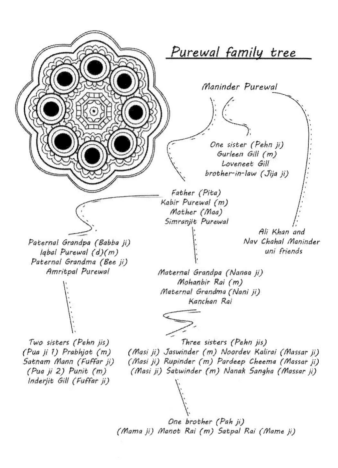

Purewal family tree

Maninder Purewal

One sister (Pehn ji)
Gurleen Gill (m)
Loveneet Gill
brother-in-law (Jija ji)

Father (Pita)
Kabir Purewal (m)
Mother (Maa)
Simranjit Purewal

Ali Khan and
Nav Chahal Maninder
uni friends

Paternal Grandpa (Babba ji)
Iqbal Purewal (d)(m)
Paternal Grandma (Bee ji)
Amritpal Purewal

Maternal Grandpa (Nanaa ji)
Mohanbir Rai (m)
Maternal Grandma (Nani ji)
Kanchan Rai

Two sisters (Pehn jis)
(Pua ji 1) Prabhjot (m)
Satnam Mann (Fuffar ji)
(Pua ji 2) Punit (m)
Inderjit Gill (Fuffar ji)

Three sisters (Pehn jis)
(Masi ji) Jaswinder (m) Noordev Kalirai (Massar ji)
(Masi ji) Rupinder (m) Pardeep Cheema (Massar ji)
(Masi ji) Satwinder (m) Nanak Sangha (Massar ji)

One brother (Pah ji)
(Mama ji) Manot Rai (m) Satpal Rai (Mame ji)

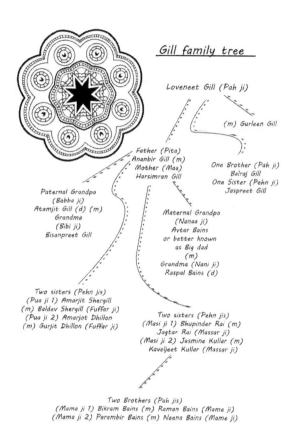

Gill family tree

Loveneet Gill (Pah ji)

(m) Gurleen Gill

Father (Pita)
Ananbir Gill (m)
Mother (Maa)
Harsimran Gill

One Brother (Pah ji)
Balraj Gill
One Sister (Pehn ji)
Jaspreet Gill

Paternal Grandpa
(Babba ji)
Atamjit Gill (d) (m)
Grandma
(Bibi ji)
Bisanpreet Gill

Maternal Grandpa
(Nanaa ji)
Avtar Bains
or better known
as Big dad
(m)
Grandma (Nani ji)
Raspal Bains (d)

Two sisters (Pehn jis)
(Pua ji 1) Amarjit Shergill
(m) Baldev Shergill (Fuffar ji)
(Pua ji 2) Amarjot Dhillon
(m) Gurjit Dhillon (Fuffar ji)

Two sisters (Pehn jis)
(Masi ji 1) Bhupinder Rai (m)
Jagtar Rai (Massar ji)
(Masi ji 2) Jasmine Kullar (m)
Kaveljeet Kullar (Massar ji)

Two Brothers (Pah jis)
(Mama ji 1) Bikram Bains (m) Raman Bains (Mame ji)
(Mama ji 2) Parambir Bains (m) Neena Bains (Mame ji)

(d)=deceased
(m)=Married

PROLOGUE: THE STORY BEFORE THE SILENCE AND HURT

2007. April 22nd. An unremarkable day in my life. So why would I mention it? Because what happened on that day and from that day was far from unremarkable. That day my life changed...

I was in the loft, my bedroom. The door closed, cocooning me away from the madness of my Punjabi family. It was spring; I was cleaning. I was 26, an independent, young professional finally living life. I was in control of my life; it was mine. I had no worries – except one. How had my 'spring clean' gone so tragically wrong?

I have been accused of taking OCD to another level, but that's not fair. My room was the exact opposite of clean. Everything was all over the place – and usually, I had a place for every item of clothing, every pair of shoes, every handbag.

The clocks had gone forward and so had I.

My Mother was on the lookout for a suitable bachelor to take my hand in marriage, and I had never tried to stop her. For me, it was just another option in the lottery that we call love and life. Deep down, I knew it was time to take the next step in life, to ride the romantic rollercoaster. I was ready for Mr. Perfect.

I quickly learnt I had to meet a number of guys recommended by friends and family; *Miley Naa Miley Hum*. ('May we meet or not meet.') Like the saying goes, you have to kiss a lot of frogs before you find your handsome prince ... though in my case, thankfully, I met several frogs I never shared a kiss with.

FIRST COMES ARRANGED MARRIAGE, AND THEN COMES LOVE

Where do I start? Arranged marriages date back as far as biblical times and beyond. Traditionally, these types of unions were political, military and social; they were commonplace amongst the world's royalty and nobility. My parents had an arranged marriage, as did my grandparents and great grandparents; it's part and parcel of life in my culture. Arranged marriage – the union of a man and a woman who may have never met - has been around for many years. The concept hasn't changed greatly over time; however, the practice has become less rigid.

In Elizabethan England, families would often arrange marriages, with both families benefitting through additional wealth or improved social status. Many of the couples would meet for the first time on the day of their wedding, which was usually arranged by the father of the bride, and women hardly ever had a say in who they married. It was a lot like the Punjabi culture back in the day, with women considered second-class citizens. The wedding had to be arranged with the local church and announced three times on three consecutive Sundays before the couple could marry – again a bit like a Punjabi wedding, with its time-consuming rituals. Arranged marriages were also common amongst the lower classes, with parents arranging unions for their children with the offspring of friends and neighbours.

Historically, monarchies have had a (sometimes unwritten) rule that required the monarch and those in the line of succession to marry someone from another royal, or at least noble, family. In most cases, royal families arranged marriages to strengthen their power and influence by forming strategic alliances. They did not take an individual's personal feelings or preferences into consideration. The attitude started to change a few decades ago, with more and more monarchs deciding to marry for love regardless of the status of their spouse, and allowing their heirs to do the same.

One of the chief goals of arranged marriage was to keep the royal bloodline pure. The same can be said in some cultures too. The last arranged marriage that took place in the British Royal Family was between Princes Charles and Lady Diana Spencer. Most members of the Royal Family required the Queen's approval before marrying, at least those who were within a few places of likely succession to the throne. Presumably *Potha* (Grandson) William asked for his *Rani* (Queen) *Dahdi Ji's* (Grandma's) permission before marrying Kate Middleton. As *Rani, Dahdi Ji* said *Haan Ji* and the Royal *ghar wale* and *khaazee* was *rhaazzee*. ('As long as the Queen, her family and the priest said yes and were happy then nothing else mattered.') Now that's how Kate Middleton becomes the *Rani Potri Noo* (Queen's great Granddaughter-in-law) in the modern-day era...

Forced marriages, on the other hand, are not the same as arranged marriages; there is a huge difference. A true 'arranged' marriage is similar to the TV programme 'Blind Date' that Cilla Black used to present. In an arranged marriage you are simply introduced to someone who your family and loved ones think you may be compatible with, and then it's up to the potential couple to decide if they are interested or not. I've always thought Bank Holiday Mondays were created so parents had time to go round to suitable family homes asking for their sons' or daughters' hands in marriage. What else could Bank Holidays have been created for? Well that's what the Punjabi do with their eight extra days' holiday anyway.

Another thing about an arranged marriage is that you have the free will and choice to accept or decline, even after dating for a while. I kept it simple and I knew from meeting a guy once whether I was going to continue through to a second date or not. If I didn't want to, I would politely decline to my mother and let her deal with the rest.

I had no trouble with this concept and, if it is done correctly and honestly, there is a good chance it will succeed. The trouble is that forced marriages, where the partners are matched by families, often for business benefits, are becoming so popular that the term has become inextricably linked with the concept of arranged marriage within certain ethnic groups.

Forced marriage affects men and women all over the world, and across many cultural groups. The British Royal Family has a history of it, as did many members of the British aristocracy in the past.

The difference with forced marriages is that the marriage can be arranged without the betrothed even knowing that it is taking place; the wedding goes ahead without the full consent of both parties. In forced marriages family members can get physical, become forceful or exert emotional pressure. You can also be given a list of duties you owe your parents in return for bringing you up – and one of them could be a duty to marry the person they put forward for you (blackmail, in other words!).

The Asian blackmail system can go to the point where parents will threaten to kill themselves or do something melodramatic if their child doesn't comply. It's a lot like the stories played out in Asian TV dramas. I have seen this first hand through my mother's friend, who kept telling her daughters that she was going to die soon and would love to see them all settled and married. Typical.

I was not the victim of a forced marriage; however, my parents wanted me to meet some eligible bachelors to find me a suitable husband.

A BRIEF HISTORY OF THE FROGS: ELIGIBLE BACHELOR NUMBER ONE

I was introduced to a very 'lucky' man by a close college friend who, up until this point, I thought knew me reasonably well. Harry – short for Harvinder – and I had spoken on the phone twice and arranged to meet outside Birmingham New Street train station on a fresh Sunday morning at 11am. During the week the station is the gateway to Britain's rail network, but on a Sunday morning there aren't as many trains and the station was very quiet as I stood waiting for Harry, after my mother had dropped me off at the station.

(I started calling my mum 'Mother' when I was 12 years old. She'd always been Mum till then but whenever I needed anything from her I would change the tone of my voice and address her as 'Moooooooottttthhhhhheeeeerrrr'. I think this all got too much for her and one day she replied:" I'm not your Mother India." She had clocked on to the fact I only called her 'Mother' when I needed something from her. From that day onwards I decided that I was going to call her Mother all the time so she would never know whether or not I needed something … Pretty good thinking on my part! The truth is that I thought I was being smart at that age. We have all been guilty of that!)

Harry had sounded intriguing during our phone calls; he could hold a conversation, which was a good start. I was a fashion student, full of creative thoughts, and my imagination often got the better of me. Though we hadn't yet exchanged photos, in my mind I had pictured an amazing guy, six foot three tall and handsome (perhaps I was reading too many fairy tales). What need was there for a picture! As I stood waiting for this handsome fella to arrive, my phone rang and his name and number popped up on the screen. As I answered the phone the butterflies in my stomach threatened to make their way up into my throat. In a shy, low voice I said, "Hi Harry."

"Hi, I can see you," he replied. I asked him if he was in the dark blue car ahead of me.

"Look harder," he said. "I'm in the silver car." I could see a silver car over the road, maybe a Peugeot or Nissan. I had not passed my driving test at the time and had zero interest in driving or cars – as long as a car got me from A to B I was happy – so I asked Harry which car he was in. He replied: "I'm in the silver Lotus, sweetheart!"

I started walking towards the car, wondering how the hell this guy could afford it on his salary. He'd told me he was a web designer and had only been working for six months. One of my lovely *Massar Ji* (uncles) always told me there were three types of guys in this big wide world: first, the Mummy *Ji* or Daddy *Ji* boy who is born with a silver spoon in his mouth; second, the drug dealer working under a cloud of illegal activity; and third, the normal guy who works hard and has a normal lifestyle. In my view, a normal guy would own a normal car unless he'd worked long and hard enough to buy something fast and furious! I reckoned Harry must be the silver spoon type – or option two.

I walked over to the car and saw to my surprise that Harry was not my dream man but a short, fat Punjabi from Kent. Well, what can I say? He was an all-rounder! Nor was he given the manners to open the door of his car to a lady. Although I am only five feet seven and a half inches tall, today I was three inches taller thanks to a lovely pair of Christian Louboutin heels. Getting into the Lotus was a bit of a challenge but I tried my best to enter without looking like a fool.

As I got into this very low car I noticed a packet of colourful jellybeans on the dashboard. I took one look at Harry's face and could see that he was a very happy, colourful person. I said the first thing that came into my mind: "I take it you have a sweet tooth!" He said he didn't, but looking at him you'd think he was lying through his teeth, and I smiled like a kid. I wondered what the hell I was doing here on such a gorgeous morning with this overgrown Punjabi lad. As a child, I'd only ever woken up early on a Sunday to watch cartoons, and now a big part of me wished that I'd stayed in bed. His turban (*pagha*) was tied so tight that the excess fat on his face was rolling over and under it, making his face look three times fatter! With his round face, small eyes, slanted eyelids and groomed beard, he looked like he was a mix of Indian and Chinese.

The clean-cut boy was running the runway and the beard invasion began. Harry had the most perfect, thick beard I had ever seen. Also, he weighed somewhere around eighteen or twenty stones, and his excess stomach fat rested on the armrest of the driver's seat. I was lost for words. As he had travelled all the way from Kent to take me out for our Sunday brunch date, I had no option but to be polite for the next couple of hours. Polite and respectful, like the good Punjabi girl I was. I'm not the kind of girl who is vain; however, I did need to find a man that I was attracted to.

Needless to say, there was no starburst running around in my stomach or popping in my heart. Harry was definitely not a *Jalebi*... (*Jalebi* is an Indian sweet made of a coil of batter fried and steeped in syrup.) If anything it looked like he had eaten a box full of them!

Harry and I headed off towards Brindley Place and if I could tell anything about Harry, it was that he was going to enjoy his brunch. We went to the Pitcher and Piano bar and he insisted that we sit outside on the balcony and enjoy the view. I wished I could enjoy the view of him...

As I sat outside enjoying the beautiful, crisp Sunday morning view of good old Birmingham, my home town, we chatted about ourselves, our family and friends. Our food arrived and we were both enjoying the meal as well as getting to know each other. I just couldn't understand one thing about this Harry character: how the hell was he able to afford his car?! He had very casually mentioned that he and a friend were in some sort of business that was doing well. All I could think was here was another Indian in ... let me guess ... the import and export business? He'd chuckled with laughter, every inch of him wobbling away; he looked like an electric sumo in a brightly coloured turban. "No," he replied, "I have a modelling company with a friend who's my business partner." This amazed me even more. He must come across the most beautiful Asian girls every day, so why had he not met his Miss Universe; why was he still single? My thoughts were running wild at this point. I knew Kent was known as 'the garden of England' and, as the saying goes, the garden of England has something for everybody – so what about him?

I asked Harry to tell me more about his business. Were

they Asian women's magazine models? I wondered. He said, "No, not those kinds of models – or girls that I would take home to my mother... No, a bit more glamorous than that, sweetheart."

Every time he called me sweetheart I felt a shiver down my spine. I said: "I'm not your sweetheart. What do you mean – glamour models?"

Casually, he stared straight at me and replied: "No – I own a soft porn company!"

I know the Kama Sutra* was originally an Indian text that was written to help teach men how to have a happy marriage ... but come on, this fat ugly Punjabi was taking the mickey! I didn't like the idea that he worked with girls who weren't good enough to take home to his mother but were good enough to star in his dirty pictures. I hated the thought that these poor girls would think they were getting the opportunity of a lifetime to act or become a Bollywood superstar while this ugly fat Punjabi guy was behind the camera enjoying the view.

By that point, I was on edge. I started to shuffle around; I felt very uncomfortable. In fact, I really didn't want to be sitting there any more so I asked if I may be excused to go to the ladies' room. As soon as I entered the toilet, I called my friend and asked if she was aware of Harry's business. My lovely friend said she knew he had a business but she wasn't aware it was a soft porn company. Well, she knew now. Between us, we came up with a plan. My friend had got me into this situation and she was going to help me get out of it.

Like two little school girls, we giggled and gossiped away on the phone for twenty minutes until I decided that I needed to go back to Harry. I hoped he would be really annoyed I'd been so long and reject me for being rude. But no; to my surprise, he just sat in front of me with a full stomach and the biggest cheesiest grin you could ever imagine. My stomach had had enough of the sweet, savoury, brightly coloured Mr. Singh to last me a lifetime, and watching him sitting there smiling away left a bitter taste in my mouth. It was time to put the plan into action.

My phone started buzzing. As I answered the call, relieved that this could be my one and only chance to escape, my face changed from a lovely welcoming smile to a sad look of frustration and worry. Of course, it was my friend on the phone, pretending to be my younger sister calling about some emergency that needed me to return home as soon as possible. The idea was I would never call Harry again and, with God's will, I would never hear from him again either. I put to good use all those school drama classes and Harry really did believe that I'd had some shocking news and needed to get home – and he insisted on driving me there. If you're Asian, you'll recognise this as one of those awkward moments where someone wants to show you one hundred and ten percent hospitality and offers to do the one thing you really don't want them to do. It was like one of those classic moments when you have a family to visit and your parents keep insisting on feeding them even when they've refused the offer a thousand times, or when the guests have to leave by a certain time but your parents insist on them staying a while longer. I said I was happy to take public transport home, that the fresh air would do me good and the exercise would burn off some of the calories I'd just eaten. But he wasn't taking no for an answer and, once again, I was faced with the challenge of sliding into the lovely low-seated Lotus without him noticing what a muppet I looked.

During the drive back, he seemed to realise this was the final round of the date and he decided to give it his all. He started selling the lifestyle I would be living if I were to marry his fat ass! How lucky I would be to live in Kent, out in the suburbs, with all that greenness around me. How he was a lovely Punjabi boy and how, back home in India, Jatt families were farm owners. How I would lead a glamorous lifestyle married to him, and would never have to worry about cash or affording expensive things. And how lucky I was to be sitting in his lavish car, next to him...

Really? I thought. You've got to be kidding me! By now I couldn't wait to get the hell out of his shiny silver car, the only thing about him that did shine. This time, I definitely didn't find it difficult to walk away in my Christian Louboutins.

*'Kama', which is one of the three goals of Hindu life, means sensual or sexual pleasure, and 'sutra' literally means a thread or line that holds things together, and more metaphorically refers to an aphorism (or line, rule, formula), or a collection of such aphorisms in the form of a manual. Contrary to popular perception, especially in the western world, Kama Sutra is not just an exclusive sex manual; it presents itself as a guide to a virtuous and gracious living that discusses the nature of love, family life and other aspects pertaining to pleasure-oriented faculties of human life. – Wikipedia (en.m.wikipedia.org/wiki/kama_sutra)

REGISTERING ON THE MATRIMONIAL LIST

After the experience I call 'Harry-gate', I decided that I wasn't in any rush to walk down the aisle or, more accurately, to walk into the *gurdwara*. I just wanted to enjoy life.

In August 2006, the same friend that set me up with Harry decided to throw a dinner party. One lovely Saturday evening in London ten professional women who were seeking Mr. Perfect gathered in her flat; it was like 'Sex and the City' but with more Asian spice. As the evening rolled on we shared our life stories – or should I say lessons – with each other, and even though we didn't know each other very well it was counselling gone fashionable.

This evening helped these ten strangers bond like sisters. A girl called Nikki recommended a 'matrimonial list' to us all. Nikki was my college friend Tani's housemate. Tani and I were the only two girls from our college crew who had gone away to uni and we'd had similar life experiences. Nikki had been on a matrimonial list for about four months and she had met some interesting guys. Like me, Nikki was loud and bubbly with a vibrant personality. We got on amazingly well. Most of the evening was spent bouncing chat off each other; it was like friendly banter tennis. I could see that Nikki was taking control of finding her own suitable *dul-ha* (groom) and I thought, why not give it a go? What did I have to lose?

We all woke up the next morning, a serene, sunny Sunday, and some of us girls, inspired by the previous evening's chat, resolved that they would register with the

Matrimonial *Gurdwara* List at Havelock Road, Southall. (Southall is the spiritual centre of Sikhs in the UK, perhaps even the centre outside the Punjab. It doesn't get much more hardcore...)

The Matrimonial List offers a number of services: there are other means to finding your Punjabi prince or princess such as Shaadi.com, Match.com, AsianD8.com and others in *gurdwaras*, not forgetting your local Aunty *Ji* or *Bibi Ji* (Grandma). Registration was only available on Sundays between 12pm and 4pm.

I decided that I was going to join the hunt; I too wanted to snare my own Prince Charming. I registered onto this list. You are required to submit the perfect *ristha* (relationship) photos and write a description of yourself. It reminded me of my primary school, where you had to draw a picture on the top half of the page and write a short story about your weekend underneath. But this time round it was a detailed description of yourself rather than how your weekend had gone. None of the innocence of childhood. It was more strategic, more knowing, more pragmatic.

Here's a written description of the perfect Asian bride; my *Dulhan* (bride) C.V.:

"My lovely matrimonial eyes are searching for fine handsome gentlemen. I am a beautiful and ideal Punjabi girl, with skin that sparkles like pure Indian twenty-four karat gold. I have a degree in fashion and I understand the way fashion works, with hints of eastern and western culture... I am pure at heart, like Sita from the Hindu story of Rama and Sita.

"This story sets an example for Hindu married couples.

I have the world in my left pocket, with dreams and ambitions flying out of my right pocket. I am the one who commits and submits to the man I love. Someone who is Punjabi at heart and born and bred in the UK, who is a search engine of love and can answer every question in the world like Google with the click of a button, while I flutter my beautiful eyelashes, which look like Princess Jasmine's from the Disney film, Aladdin.

"I am the one who listens to music while she is training and running a marathon, the one who knows how to make her man happy, and the one who resides like a prayer in every heart. I'm a modern day girl with a Punjabi soul. I'm the one who is not lazy at work, the one who enjoys cooking and cleaning like a perfect bride, the one who is as fast as 4G networks and yet is tender as a teardrop and can joke and have a laugh. I'm the one who understands relationships and has a spotless heart. I'll definitely be a good luck charm for you and your family. I am taking this search responsibly and with a hint of fun added to my *masala* into this shaadi muffin."

OK. That's what I WANTED to write. But I didn't. That's not the form for such descriptions.

In the world of Indian matrimonials, the last thing they want is confident, self-possessed, marathon-running women with a full working knowledge of Princess Jasmine's make-up regime. It scares most of the men. At the time, I didn't want to scare most of the men. Looking back, I should never have dated a man who couldn't deal with my honesty. And my eyelashes.

ALONG COMES ELIGIBLE BACHELOR NUMBER TWO

2006. October. Bachelor number two arrived on the scene. So many significant moments in my life seem to have happened around the clocks changing, the seasons developing. The moment when autumn slips seamlessly into winter and summer is nothing more than hazy, sun-kissed memories. That lost hour was marked by darker evenings. But the darkness seemed not to matter so much.

I'd been working as a fashion designer in Banbury and had just returned from a busy day in Cambridge, a place I loved to visit for its historic university and wonderful architecture. I'd been visiting a hotel in the city and returned home exhausted, having been questioned about how the uniforms for the hotel were going to be designed.

All I wanted was to switch off, wash away the day's stress and unwind for the rest of the evening. But then my phone rang.

Unknown Caller

Back then, it never occurred to me not to answer an unknown caller. I was on the list. That unknown caller could soon be my well-known Perfect Punjabi Prince. My strategy was to keep my voice neutral until I knew who was calling.

His opening gambit was predictable and confident. "Hello, I'm Sandeep."

Sandeep was a northerner. We chatted for an hour and he seemed lovely; we talked family, friends and general, easy chit chat. He had a Scouse accent, which I liked. But.

There is almost always a 'but'. I couldn't put my finger on it but I felt he had some trust issues. I can't tell you anything he said that made me think that. But I did. A couple of days later he dropped me a text and we arranged for my mother and to meet him the following Saturday at 1pm at the local *gurdwara*. (This was my mother's friend's idea. She thinks she's really clever. "Why bother cooking *samosas* and *pakoras* (onion *bhajis*)?" she says. "Meet in the temple. There's already food there. And if you don't like the look of this boy, you can cover your head and lose yourself in the crowd.") I normally went to a classic Kathak dance class on Saturdays; I loved dancing Kathak. It was the perfect release of life's stresses and tension. But this Saturday I was happy to miss it – for the first time ever – to meet him. Sandeep was going to text me as soon as he got to Birmingham.

***

I received a text at about 12ish stating he was running a little late; he was stuck on the other side of Birmingham with family. He suggested rearranging our meeting for 3pm. I was a bit annoyed. He hadn't explained that he was also coming to meet family in Birmingham. I had originally suggested that we meet at 3pm but he'd turned it down and was adamant that we should meet earlier. I had re-arranged my day to meet him. I missed my Kathak. Rather than releasing the stress and tension, it was added to.

At 2.30pm, I received another text saying he was really sorry but he wasn't going to be able to meet until 6pm. By now I was feeling really frustrated; my mother and I had cancelled our plans for this northern guy with a Scouse accent who had no concept of timekeeping. It was like being at a Punjabi wedding when you're waiting around for the boy's side of the family to arrive, because usually they're running late.

I had been wearing my lovely frost green Punjabi suit; it's not designed to be worn all day. I decided to take it off and relax a bit. I never really wear Indian suits as they make me feel like a Christmas tree, all dressed up. As the day wore on, I received another text saying he would see me at 6pm. So my mother and I got ready and set off back to the *gurdwara*.

This particular *gurdwara* was the one that my Harbans *Bibi Ji* frequented; she used to take us to it when we were young. Every Saturday morning our Harbans *Bibi Ji* would do the *langar seva* (free food service to everybody that attends the *gurdwara*). The *gurdwara* was one mile from the house and the journey would take us past the corner shop that my twin sister and I would race to every morning on our way to school. Attached to the wall outside the sweet shop was one of those novelty vending machines (if you were a kid in the 70s and 80s you'll know what I'm talking about). It was vibrant orange, the same religious orange sported by the Khalsa. Sometimes our Harbans *Bibi Ji* would give us enough change to get a gumball from this vending machine. You would slot your coins into the top and spin the little metal handle 360 degrees until your sweets (in my case gumballs) would pop out into the little metal shaft, where you would then lift the metal flap and retrieve your sweets. It was one of the few times my Harbans *Bibi Ji* let us have sweets. I think she thought the vending machine, since it was orange, was owned and run by the Khalsa.

After the sweet shop came the Red Cow pub, whose sign depicted a cow with a calf under her legs. The cow was painted bright red, the kind of shade that I would like to wear on my wedding day. The cow is holy to Sikhs, sacred; hence the lack of burger-loving Punjabis. Harbans *Bibi Ji* would tell us girls wild stories about how this desperate red cow hid her baby calf from the world, as a reminder of the struggles my mother went through.

It was as if Sikhism had secretly penetrated the consciousness of Birmingham.

Next to the pub was a luxury car showroom full of polished new and exclusive Skoda cars. I realise that Skoda and luxury don't often appear in the same breath. I remember looking at the Skoda logo on the cars. They looked like forged iron, the sort of forged iron that came from the foundries of the Black Country. My relatives all worked in and around those foundries or knew someone who did. That one mile from my house to the *gurdwara* epitomised the Punjabi experience in the Birmingham of my childhood. The Khalsa orange vending machine, the sacred cow above the pub and the iron from the foundries.

Finally, my mother and I arrived at the *gurdwara*. As I took my first steps towards the main doors all of sudden I was bewildered by these most familiar of surroundings. A childhood journey laden with memories now jarred with a potential marital meeting that made me feel anything but a child. Yet I was awash with nostalgia; memories of my first impressions of this *gurdwara* came in the form of the words of my mother's mum, my Amirjit *Nani Ji*:

"The doors to a gurdwara are not just doors but gateways to the Guru Granth Sahib Ji. There are four doors to the Harmandir sahib (Golden temple) and these doors represent the door of peace,

the door to livelihood, the door of learning and the door of grace. These doors must always remain open to everyone."

(http://simple.m.wikipedia.org/wiki/Sikh_temple)

Before entering the hall, I took off my shoes, washed my hands, covered my head with a forest green-coloured *chunni* (scarf) and thought of the *Sri Guru Granth Sahib Ji* which is placed in the main hall of all *gurdwara*s around the world. As I walked into the hall a tall, handsome guy caught my attention. Our eyes met and I just could not tear my gaze away. He was beautiful; he shone. He looked like an Asian version of Jude Law. It's no coincidence that the word 'phwoar' rhymes with 'law'.

Eventually, he looked away and I carefully made note of his style – baby blue crisp cotton shirt, indigo jeans and old-school dark tan brogues. My heart definitely skipped a beat. I was hoping, willing this adonis to be Sandeep, the man I was here to meet; I prayed it was Sandeep. I was in a *gurdwara*. I was meant to pray.

I slowly walked into the main hall. I could hear the *Katha*, the reading of the holy hymns followed by their explanation. Listening to the hymns always relaxed me and allowed me to experience inner peace. I bowed and placed an offering respectfully before the *Guru Ji*. Any sincere expression of gratitude – money, flowers, or words of thanks – is equally acceptable to the *Guru Ji*. After bowing and making an offering, I quietly sat down in the *Sangat* (congregation), trying not to disturb others. Usually in every *gurdwara* men sit on one side and women on the other, in a cross-legged position. As I sat down, my mother, who was following behind, joined me. She spotted Sandeep's parents lingering around the main hall doors and she decided to go over and introduce herself. After ten minutes she returned and asked me to join Sandeep and his parents. Head bowed, I walked up to them nervously and Sandeep introduced himself. My prayers had been answered. Sandeep was the Asian Jude Law. Phwoar. We spent ten minutes with his parents and my mother, and then Sandeep insisted we leave them and find a quiet place in the *gurdwara* to talk.

Quiet spot? Come on, you have got to be joking. There's no such thing as a quiet spot in the *gurdwara*; there's always some *Bibi Ji* or Aunty *Ji* or some other member of the GIA – *gurdwara* Intelligence Agency – who will turn up and ask you what the hell you are doing. Surrounded by noise, traffic and chatter, Sandeep and I couldn't spot a quiet place to sit, so we decided to talk in the car park. There's no romance in a *gurdwara* car park, no poetry. I felt uncomfortable and annoyed; it was evening, typical cold British weather, and I wished I had brought my coat.

Sandeep and I started chatting but it was so cold I couldn't relax and enjoy this moment of the two of us being together for the first time. He repeatedly asked me questions about my lifestyle and my profession. I quickly lost interest and was more focused on the surroundings, like the children running in the cold, than Sandeep's warm willingness to find out more about me. I just wanted this good-looking guy to shut up and stop talking so we could return to the warmth of the *gurdwara*, where I would feel more comfortable

He seemed very insecure. He asked me the same question in three different ways and made it very clear in the first fifteen minutes of us meeting that I would have to leave my chosen profession if I was to choose him as my life partner. I never thought my job would be an issue. I designed uniforms for bars and restaurants around the UK and I had to visit locations regularly to view the interiors and exteriors of the buildings and understand the environment that I would be designing for. It was hardly controversial. But Sandeep was not impressed with my job, or interested in what excited me. He couldn't understand why I had to visit the bars and restaurants just to be able to design a range of clothes.

Whilst I was standing there freezing in my rather apt frost green, trying to be as polite as ever, the conversation went from bad to worse. I told him that I was a vegetarian, that I chose to be one at the age of 15. I had heard all these stories of animals being injected with hormones to make them grow faster and fatter and I didn't want any of those hormones in my body. Being a Punjabi woman, it was hard enough coping with the hormones I already had, let alone ingesting any more – Punjabi women are the hairiest women on the planet!

Sandeep asked me if I was saying things just to impress him. I was confused. Standing there in the cold air, it all seemed like too much of an effort to listen to him. He was clearly deliberating as to whether I had told the truth about not drinking, not smoking and being a vegetarian. And we'd been in each other's company all of twenty minutes.

When he asked me whether I was serious about getting married, I decided it was time to end this. I told him I was cold and I wanted to go back into the *gurdwara*; I had a feeling this insecure control freak would stand there all night firing questions at me. It was like he was Jeremy Paxman and I was Michael Howard: interrogation overdrive. The best Sandeep could give me for a first meeting was a cold car park, six hours late with a full-on, Gestapo type questioning. No thanks, I thought.

As I approached my mother, I could tell from her face that, like me, she was frustrated and furious. She was clearly irritated, her face flushed with anger. All I could think was that I could warm my icicle hands on her cheeks. My mother has always been my best friend and I can talk to her about anything with an open heart. She loves me for the person I am, and she has always pushed me towards my chosen passions regardless of whether or not she agreed with them. My mother knows me, and I know my mother. I knew that this *gurdwara* was the last place she wanted to be.

Sandeep's dad said confidently, "When will we be hearing from you?" Mother and I exchanged a look that said we needed to talk about this before we could answer the question. It was an awkward moment that we had not planned for. If only we could have said "Cheque please!" and made a sharp exit towards the doors.

A LITTLE INSIGHT INTO MY PARENTS RELATIONSHIP

My parents married in 1979. A year later, they were blessed with twin girls. When my mother gave birth to me and my sister, my Harbans *Bibi Ji* was immediately displeased that my mother had given her granddaughters rather than enriching and embellishing the family with grandsons. She would constantly remind my mother and father about this insufferable shock that she had just suffered. She would also verbally abuse my mother and constantly insisted that my father leave my mother, so she could get him re-married to another younger, beautiful Punjabi girl who would have the required hardware to bear him sons. (Sounds a bit like shopping for a new car on Auto Trader rather than dealing with one's feelings…)

My father was over the moon when my mother fell pregnant, as she had previously suffered a miscarriage that broke their hearts. I was not part of the master plan until a week before delivery, when my parents found out they were expecting twins. It was like a typical Punjabi festive offer – buy one, get one free! My father ran out to get another set of everything – it was double trouble! And soon, my father was in love with my mother and his baby girls.

One Sunday afternoon, while Harbans *Bibi Ji* was at the *gurdwara* praying or doing an *Ardaas* (Sikh holy prayers – **https://www.allaboutsikhs.com/introduction/ardaas-the-sikh-prayers**) for a grandson and hunt for inner peace – none of which came – my father decided that he was going to move out of my grandparents' house with his wife and twin daughters and move in with his sister-in-law, her husband and kids until they could afford a home of their own. They lived there for a few months and soon found a good place to stay. My father's sister, Narinderpal, even loaned my parents the deposit for their first house.

After my younger sister was born three years later, no one from our father's side of the family other than Narinderpal *Pua Ji* (Father's sister) ever came to visit us. She was the only one to support my parents when they were in desperate need of some. But when our brother was born, there wasn't even space to get into the maternity ward – it was more packed than a concert hall with Gurdas Mann performing. Everyone from the family wanted to meet Junior Johal. My Harbans *Bibi Ji* was the first person to come running into the hospital wearing the grin of a child. Imagine a romantic scene in a Bollywood film, when the actress runs towards her hero, the outstretched *chunni* fluttering in the air, her arms spread wide. Harbans *Bibi Ji* was followed by the rest of the Johal *tabar* (family). Being the head of the Johal family, what she said was final, and no one could question her authority. My new-born brother was her only worthy candidate to carry on the Johal bloodline, so he became the apple of her eye, while us girls were seen as burdens on her son's shoulders, weighed down to the ground with the liability of paying for three girls' weddings – through in reality my mother was weighed down with the real responsibility for the four of us.

Initially, my father was caring, loving and supporting, an ideal husband and father – until things started to get bitter between my parents after my brother was born. It's a shame that my brother never really got to witness the great man my father was in the early days of my parents' relationship. I'm thankful that we girls got to know his sunny side.

My mother and father separated when I was eleven years old and officially divorced three years later. My mother raised four children on her own, without any support from my father. She had to protect us from my father, who was abusive to us all. Although my mother tried not to show how difficult it was being a single parent, it was hard for her children to see the struggles she faced, as she had no education to fall back on. This made me realise, from a very young age, that I wanted to work hard in my education and become a successful working professional. I dreamt of having a job where I wasn't dependent on anything or anyone. Education has always been very important in my life. I watched my mother struggle to fund me through university; I was the only child in the household at the time to go to university so it meant everything to her. My mother has always been an inspiration to me, even though she wasn't educated. I am so proud of her, of the way she has muddled through the vicissitudes of life and emerged a victor. Deep within, I know I get my strong willpower from my role model – my mother.

When my parents were together my father would drink alcohol like it was tap water, and he only worked when he felt like it. He also had a gambling problem, and if he had a bad run on the cards he would come home and take it out on my mother by beating her black and blue. Each time he beat her, we would escape to the house of my mother's sister, Jaskarjit *Masi Ji*, until she recovered and was well enough to face my father again. Travelling between my *Masi Ji's* house and the home was normal for us; it helped that we lived on the same road. My father never contributed towards the running of the house or supported my mother with the upbringing of his kids. We never really saw him unless he was home drunk, beating Mother or shouting at us. Drunkenly throwing his weight around and abusing us became the norm with my father. He was the king lion of the house. As kids, my twin sister Jasleen and I had to do household chores and work as a team to help my mother take care of our two younger siblings. We would finish school at 3.20pm and one of us would have ten minutes to run to the primary school to pick them up while the other would come home and make us all tea and toast. Then in the evening, we'd share the housework, one of us cleaning the living room and the other cleaning the kitchen. After that, we would start our homework and get the younger two children to start theirs, too. As Mother didn't really write or speak much English we had no one to check that our homework was correct, and even though my father was educated in the UK and could have helped, he dismissed his fatherly duties altogether. Jasleen would check my homework as I was dyslexic. Writing this book has been more challenging than you might imagine.

There were times when Mother would suffer heavy depression and migraines, and be unable to get out of bed. The stress of having to pay the mortgage, run a home and bring up four kids was difficult for a working couple, never mind a single parent; my father never contributed financially or emotionally towards the house while he lived there. He was hardly going to do so after he left, let alone after the divorce. We just got on with it and never really complained about anything.

We all pulled together to prevent outsiders coming into our lives. We lived a double life: no one outside our house – not even our friends and family – knew what was going on within the Johal household. Every time my father was absent from a family function we'd lie and say he was working. Everyone thought he was such a hard-working man, providing for his family, while in reality the man made no time or effort for his family. A double life of lies.

My mother's final, brutal beating was in 1991. Our father came home in a bad mood in the early hours of the morning, knocked the bedroom door down, grabbed Mother by the hair and started using her face and body like a punch bag. Meanwhile, we kids hid in our rooms, petrified. Then, somehow, whilst my younger sister slept through the whole ordeal, my twin sister, brother and I built up the courage to approach our parents. Working together, we started to push him away from Mother, tried to form a barricade between them. He threw us off, one after the other, desperate to finish his futile fight. He pushed Mother down the stairs, from the top step all the way to the bottom. Thirteen steps. Unlike in the western world, thirteen was normally a lucky number for Punjabis, considered to be auspicious amongst the Sikh community as a word that immediately reminds them of God: *"Mere mujh mein kuch nahi, jo kachu hai so Tera"*; "Nothing in me is mine, whatever there is, is yours." **(Solok Kabeer Ji and Guru Arjan Dev Ji, Page 1375 of Sri Guru Granth Sahib**

Ji). *Tera* – lucky thirteen – but not this time. As a child I used to count each step up and down. Thirteen. Mother hit every one of those thirteen steps on the way down. After that, I never counted the steps again.

Mother landed heavily and seriously damaged her back, an injury that still troubles her to this day. When she first landed at the bottom of the stairs she feared she could not walk – until she knew she had no option but to run for the front door while my twin and I held our father back so he couldn't get to her. We held onto his shirt as he tried to run down the stairs to stop Mother leaving the house. Jasleen and I were 11 years old. There was no way we could contain the rage of this man, this stranger, our father. We were left holding the tatters of his sweat-laden shirt, which reeked of Bacardi. It seemed nothing was going to stop him, his madness.

Thankfully, Mother escaped to a neighbour's house and they called the police when they saw how badly beaten she was. My father threatened us kids, told us not to say a word or he'd deal with us the same way. We all sat on the stairs crying before Jasleen and I started to clear away the evidence of the fight. It was normal for us to clear away the crap, but this time was different. This was the first time we had to wipe our mother's blood off the banister, off the rail, and off the wall. The first – and thankfully the last.

My mother's greatest wish was that she wouldn't see any of her children tolerating what she had within marriage. She had always suggested to me that I should take my time in choosing a life partner, and not rush into anything. On the other hand, Mother also said that she wouldn't have the strength to witness any of us going through a divorce.

On that day in the *gurdwara*, when we met Sandeep, Mother mentioned to his parents that having experienced life as a single parent, she knew marriage was a life-changing situation and she would like me to take my time without rushing into anything. The conversation ended when she said we would be in touch as soon as we had made up our minds.

As we walked away from Sandeep and his parents, we chatted as if we were girlfriends. Mother was amazed by how stunning Sandeep was, but she wanted the inside scoop on his personality. When I elaborated on his behaviour, my mother was left stunned!

I knew in my heart that Sandeep and I didn't get on; it was like pairing Tom and Jerry and expecting the best. I started telling Mother he was rude and ignorant but once I witnessed her reaction, I stopped. She looked furious – both her eyebrows had joined together into a monobrow. I didn't have a single positive thing to say about Sandeep, and then my mother told me how his parents had behaved towards her. It turned out Sandeep's darling Mummy *Ji* and Papaa *Ji* had interrogated my mother about why she was not able to work full time and bring up her children; they also felt it was very important to know all the gritty details of my parents' marriage and divorce and why it had failed over 15 years ago.

This was why my mother didn't attend the *gurdwara* on a regular basis; most Asian women love gossiping and networking rather than attending to find inner peace of the soul!

At that point I told my mother that if I was to choose

Sandeep as my life partner I would have to give up my career, my ambitions, and my dreams; sadly, he wasn't the one for me. However much she tried to understand, she looked disappointed. Given that we live in the twenty-first century, she thought that most people would have moved on and had more respect for w

omen wanting to pursue their dreams.

After that evening Mother and I didn't talk about Sandeep again – until seven weeks later, when the phone rang. It was Sandeep's dad pestering my mother about whether or not we were at all interested in his silver spoon son. My mother told him, in a very low voice, that her daughter was focusing on her career rather than thinking of settling down.

A few weeks passed and I overheard my mother telling my twin sister's mother-in-law how good-looking Sandeep was. She seemed full of praise for him as she said what a pity it was that our personalities didn't match. I felt guilty, but I knew it was for the best that we ended our friendship so soon.

ELIGIBLE BACHELOR NUMBER THREE
THREE MONTHS LATER

"Ring ring ring..." My phone rang unrelentingly. I'd had a tiring day at work; the last thing I wanted was to answer a phone call. It was my mother. Apparently, a guy called Ranjit would be calling me from Walsall that evening. The way my mother was talking about him, you'd think she had already made up her mind that he was her future son-in-law.

I was on my way to the gym when my phone rang. I looked at the withheld caller display, deliberating whether to answer or not. I gave it ten rings but they weren't going anywhere. I answered – it was Ranjit's dad! I was confused and more than a little surprised. Ranjit, a grown-up man, had his father calling me. What was all that about? I was going to be marrying the son, not the dad – so why was I made to feel I needed to audition?

Ranjit's dad started the conversation by giving me the guarantee that Ranjit was "one hundred percent a good boy". Experience and life had taught me never to trust an Aunty *Ji* or Uncle *Ji* when they give you that "one hundred percent guarantee" line. They seldom know all the ins and out of the person they are promoting. The dad clearly wasn't backward in coming forward: he then asked me if I had a boyfriend.

"Would I be arranging to meet your son if I was already in a relationship?" I replied.

"Yes, but you women say one thing and do another," came the reply. I didn't really know what to make of this unusual character. But Ranjit's dad would only be an issue if I met Ranjit and decided to take things further.

Clearly I had passed the test because the phone was soon passed to Ranjit. We spoke for about five minutes but I was still in shock about the interview with his dad.

I was meant to call him back. I didn't. But he called me at the weekend, without the introductory interrogation from his dad. Surprisingly, I really liked chatting. We arranged to meet the following weekend. Just him. Without his dad.

At the time, I was working hard on research for a design project. I was on the train to Nottingham when my best friend Jaya called me. I met her in my first week of university and since then we had become like sisters; my relationship with Jaya was actually stronger than with my twin sister. Jaya and I were both working professionals and because of our careers we never had much time to see each other, apart from the odd weekend or two, but we spoke regularly.

As usual, I was excited to hear her voice. We chatted for a while and then I mentioned Ranjit and filled her in on all the juicy details. She asked me where he was from. Walsall, I said. I started blabbering on excitedly. She interrupted: she said that she knew him. Well. Very well. Jaya and Ranjit had been to the same college. Small world. According to Jaya, he was a really good-looking, turban-wearing Sikh lad.

She was really excited. She said she had butterflies in her stomach for me; she couldn't wait for me to meet him. She had a feeling that I would like him. I had yet to see a picture of Ranjit; I had only talked to him on the phone and

I didn't have a clue what he looked like. This was a genuine blind date, Punjabi style. Jaya offered to get me some information on him. I was intrigued and gratefully accepted her offer.

I realised that I really didn't know anything about this Ranjit, other than the weirdness that happened in the beginning with his dad. But that second call seemed to rectify that weirdness. During the build-up to our blind date, I received some sweet texts from him. On the day of the date, I did what I normally do on a Saturday: go to my Kathak class, meet a friend and chill out around the house.

Around 4.45pm, it was time to get ready. I was meeting Ranjit at 6pm at the main entrance to the bold, bright Mailbox in Birmingham, the city of my birth, the city where I had grown up, a city that had seen changes over the years. The Mailbox used to be the Royal Mail Sorting Offices, where my college friend Mariam's mum worked. It was then redeveloped into the UK's largest mixed-use building, a 'lifestyle destination' incorporating premier shopping, exclusive stores, restaurants and café bars. This building with such personal history could now have a hand in my future.

Getting ready I was excited; I felt like a little girl. I arrived at the appointed hour and spotted Ranjit walking towards me. I'd like to say that I was in complete and utter admiration for the effort he had gone to. I'd like to say that. But I can't. Because he hadn't. He looked like Bob the Builder, but wearing a turban rather than a helmet! His jeans were a mess, his t-shirt was almost as old as he was, he was dusty and he couldn't have looked less like someone dressed for a date.

He was also shorter than me, but was strangely handsome; he looked upbeat and had a soft face full of life. As we walked into the Mailbox, he received a phone call. He explained that it was his mum. Apparently, he had met a lot of girls through the family; most of them had been wholly unsuitable, nothing like their pictures had suggested. "They looked as sweet as a sour apple," he said.

I laughed at Ranjit's phrase. He smiled, explaining that he had arranged with his mum that if I was unattractive (like the other girls) he would pretend that he had an emergency he needed to attend to.

"So, have you got an emergency or not?" I asked.

He stepped back, looked me up and down. "You're good enough to keep me here. I bet you're a sweet apple." I couldn't help but laugh. He hadn't made the best first impression, but there was an honest, cheeky charm about him.

As we wandered into the restaurant a fabulous mixed race girl walked past. In my head, I thought WOW! She had the most amazing figure and was impeccably dressed. She looked gorgeous.

Ranjit, who was walking beside me, clearly thought the same. "Check out the bumper on that girl! What a fucking great figure. She looks fit, doesn't she?" My head spun round. I was shocked and disgusted. Here I was, meeting a man for an arranged marriage, but the way Ranjit was talking you'd think he was out beefing with his mates. At that point, I thought I should remain patient and give him a chance – even though I was starting to get the taste of sour apple in my mouth.

Once we'd been seated, I asked if I may be excused to go

to the ladies' room. In the cubicle I checked my phone; I had a missed call from Jaya. I called back and she filled me in on what she'd found out about Ranjit. Apparently, he had been dating the younger sister of Raman, a uni friend of mine. Had been and still was. That was the last straw! I decided I was going to confront him about why he was here on an arranged marriage date with me when he was dating another woman. I really felt for this woman. If she was good enough to date, why was she not good enough to take home to his family? Why date one woman but want to marry someone else to please your parents? From what I had witnessed, his parents had too much involvement in his life.

Back at the table, I tried really hard to disguise my disgust. Ranjit had ordered me a drink. I sat silently, nursing my drink, keeping my eyes averted. Then I asked why he'd not met anyone to marry, why he was single. He sat in front of me and lied to my face. Eloquently, fluently he lied. He certainly wasn't the brightest, spiciest *samosa* in the tiffin box yet he had plenty to say. Plenty.

I interrupted. "Do you know Sharan?"

That threw him. "Who?"

"Sharan. The girl you're dating. She's a friend of mine."

His face reddened with embarrassment, as if he'd just eaten a dozen red chillies. All of a sudden, he had nothing to say. And neither did I.

I got up to walk away; I didn't need to hear about the insecurity issues he had, about how he didn't like himself, about not knowing what he wanted in life. His girlfriend was a beautiful person and he was a lost soul. He didn't deserve her.

I walked over to the Bullring. This was fast becoming a cheesecake moment. I sat with a baked vanilla cheesecake and watched the world, watched people walking by, shopping and enjoying themselves. I felt humiliated and fed up. Maybe there would never be a Mr. Right in my life. You can't have everything in life, right? I could be happy with a simple life, enjoying time with my friends and family and, most importantly, following my career. I got the bus home, wishing for the first time that it would take as long as possible. I knew that as soon as I walked in the front door my lovely mother would be waiting to greet me, wanting to know all about the date, every last detail. The upside was that it wouldn't take long to tell her about the twenty-minute meeting with Bob the two-timing Builder. I'd even brought her a baked vanilla cheesecake to eat while I gave her all the cheesy details about Ranjit.

When I got home I made it very clear to my mother that I was not interested in meeting anybody and that she should respect my decision. The cheesecake left a bitter taste in her mouth. She told me she was upset; she would have loved me to meet someone and settle down.

DEAL OR NO DEAL

Three months later my mother was calling my name across the landing. I was needed on the phone. She was waiting for me on the landing with the phone in her hand. The only person that called my landline was my best friend Jaya.

I took the phone and said hello. It wasn't Jaya. It was a confident-sounding guy who introduced himself as Maninder. For the next few moments, my nose grew as I lied and told him I was busy eating my dinner and would call him back as soon as I finished.

It appeared that my mother hadn't been respecting my wishes. In the last few months, she had secretly been receiving phone calls from potential husbands asking for my hand in marriage. She seemed physically and mentally unable to turn down the possibility of lasting relationships.

Forty-five minutes later and I was still arguing with my mother about the situation. I hadn't even thought to call Maninder back. She decided to use a little bit of emotional blackmail. She told me that she wasn't well and if I was to give it one last try and meet this guy she would leave me alone, she promised. I gave in and said that I would call him back – but if there were signs of any funny business, anything weird, I would walk away from the entire situation.

An hour later I called Maninder. We spoke for a while and this time, the conversation was different. He wanted to know about me as a person; he asked me about things I didn't really like to talk about, like my family and why my father wasn't around. I skipped the conversation when it came to my father, instead talking about the great British weather. Then he said something that made me want to open up, something that made me want to trust him. "It's good to talk about things that we find hard. It makes it easier each time we talk about them."

I realised he was right. I opened up there and then and the conversation between us blossomed. We discovered we had friends in common and I knew people he'd been to school with. We had been on the phone for 30 minutes but the time had flown by. When I finally came off the phone I felt like the page had finally turned to a new chapter in my life.

The next morning, I got a sweet message from Maninder wishing me luck on a project that I was working on. I felt that he had really listened to me and paid attention. He was winning my heart with his warm, happy-hearted personality. For once, I hadn't been interrogated. For once, I could see the relationship progressing.

As the week unfolded we exchanged text messages and emails. Maninder was an easy-going person and what I really liked about him was his personality; he wasn't rushing me on anything. I felt the other guys just wanted to meet as soon as possible. They'd made me feel like I was part of a meal on a production line. But with Maninder it was different. Looking back, I wonder if the difference was down to the fact that for the better part of a week we texted and called and connected, and I didn't even know what he looked like. The time came for the picture exchange. Make. Or break.

When I say exchange, that's not strictly accurate. Maninder had already seen a picture of me; my photo was attached to my matrimonial application at the *gurdwara* in

Southall. He emailed me his photos but typically my PC crashed and I had to wait until I got home to Birmingham to view the images on my brother's computer. It was a tense journey. I had a lot on my mind. Over and above deciding to ditch my PC and switch to the more stable operating system of a Mac, I worried that Maninder might be another Bob the Builder.

Finally, I had the chance to view Maninder's pictures. I didn't want to open them up in front of anyone; I wanted to be alone. I didn't want to know what anyone else thought.

Fortunately, I liked what I saw. He was a proud *Sardar*. He had beautiful eyes, the sweetest smile. Maybe I'd found my Perfect Punjabi Prince. Imagine Gandalf was a Sikh in his mid-twenties. I couldn't wait to run my fingers through Maninder's long, jet black beard. I have to confess, as I sat looking at my PC screen I did a little Beyoncé-style dance in my chair.

He was a Singh – and I liked that.

Singhs, or *Sardar Jis*, are ultimately confident in themselves and respect their faith. With his *pagha* (turban) and his full *dari* (beard), Maninder had the face and strength of a lion. He was a true Khalsa, the hidden warrior that lies beneath yet has the compassion of an angel. That's the beauty of a Singh. That's what I love about *Singhs*.

There were no full-bearded or turban-wearing Singh's in my family. I wish there were... that kind of natural beauty and the confidence and grace of a Singh takes my breath away. A Singh always stands out in a crowd – and then there's the scent in their beards...

My Singh would wear a coloured or printed *pagha* so I could match all my *chunnis* to his *paghas*.

Next step: I had to show the photos to mother. She was taken aback, there was no denying it. He was a full-on Sikh lad. With Maninder there was no beard trimming in the Craig David style, no attempt to tie a slimmer, subtle turban. He was a Sikh; a proud Sikh. And apparently he was exactly the sort of guy that my mother thought I would never find appealing. She held her head in her hands before she burst out laughing. Then she told me about scores of similar-looking Sikhs she had rejected on my behalf. I told her that we had been talking and that I wanted to meet him. Her smile straightened; there was a sombre silence. Then she spoke. Three little words. "Are you sure?"

I said that we got on, we were attracted to each other. He seemed so different to the rest. He didn't own a Lotus, he didn't run a porn website, he wasn't riddled with insecurity and he wasn't dating my old university friend's younger sister. I told my mother that I wanted to arrange the first meeting.

"Are you sure?" she asked again.

I said that I was. But the question "Are you sure?" was one she asked every day until the wedding.

THE FIRST OFFICIAL MEETING

2007. April 28th. Harmony. That's how I felt as I entered Soho Road *gurdwara*. I felt the warmth of safety and none of the nervous nausea I normally suffer from before an arranged marriage meeting. Outside the entrance of the *gurdwara*, I bowed down and touched the three steps outside the door with my hands before slowly moving my hands towards my head and heart.

This is an old Indian tradition, and people can get very baffled when they see children in the Indian culture touching the feet of their elders. Touching elders' feet is the first lesson in manners and etiquette that Indian children are taught. An 'elder' is a senior member of the family or a respected spiritual person. When the elder person's feet are touched he/she, in turn, is supposed to touch the head of the person doing the act and bless him/her for a long life. From a young age, I have followed in my mother's footsteps every time I've entered a *gurdwara* by touching the steps. It makes me feel like my *Guru Ji* is blessing me with his love, and it helps me understand the *Guru Ji* better each time I attend.

I never considered this at the time (why would I?) but retrospection allows you to see things differently. We had arranged to meet Maninder and his parents at the *gurdwara*. It was busy and Mother couldn't find a parking space at the front so she made for the rear car park. We parked there and entered through the back door. Unbeknownst to us, Maninder and his folks were dithering at the front entrance, waiting for us. Maninder and I couldn't have entered the *gurdwara* and that relationship from more opposed directions.

As I walked into the busy human traffic of Saturday midday service at the *gurdwara*, I realised I had walked straight past Maninder, as if I hadn't seen him. This was a rule I was taught by my mother: in Asian arranged marriages, even if you notice the guy, act as if you haven't even seen him. Furthermore, you should never speak to the guy first. Ever. If he is a gentleman, the man will make the first move. It was like the 'What Not to Do' rule book!

Mother and I paid our respects to *Guru Ji* and then turned our attention to Maninder and his parents. My mother got talking to them in the corridor, where there were a lot of people chatting. It's not the widest of spaces, not really designed for idle conversation. I looked over at Maninder, thinking that I had always wanted my life partner to follow the full Sikh tradition yet also embrace modernity.

In my view, he looked as if he had been chiselled by angels. He certainly portrayed the image of one. He wore a soft pink smart shirt with beige chino trousers. His black turban was tight, like *Bhindrawale*, one of the freedom fighters in the 1984 Sikh movement, and he had a full beard like a real Sikh man – which you don't often see these days. It was a good 15 inches long, like a super wizard's. I found him effortlessly simple and beautiful. I had always wanted to marry a guy like Maninder, but never really came across anyone because I had been stereotyped as being very modern in my outlook.

My mother had spoken to an Uncle *Ji* who booked the wedding dates and the *Ghanni Ji* (Sikh priest) guided us into a quiet room where we were able to converse further.

We all sat down to talk, and Maninder's dad and I got on instantly. I had always been nervous of other people's dads, as my own father had not been present through most of my childhood and I was worried I wouldn't know how to deal with the relationship. However, Maninder's dad was the opposite of what I had imagined; he made me feel at ease straight away. He was a funny, over-the-top Punjabi guy who kept chatting away like an Asian version of Alan Carr. I thought I could talk, but his dad took the award from me at that first meeting.

My mother and Maninder's mum were covering the usual topics about the family names, villages in India and any other vital information you need to know from your *rishtaa* CV (relationship CV). Then, after 20 minutes of talking as a group, Maninder's dad recommended that the parents go off together and leave Maninder and me to get to know each other. We started by talking about what we liked, and our friends. We seemed to have a great deal in common and the conversation between us blossomed like a beautiful red rose.

An hour and a half later Maninder's dad came back into the room to ask us how long we would be. I'd felt that comfortable with Maninder that I'd not realised how much time had passed. I had really enjoyed his company and he seemed like a lovely guy who was traditional in his looks but quite modern in his thinking. I'd liked that from the first moment we spoke he had taken the lead. He'd always behaved like a gentleman and his communication was excellent; he never left me hanging on, he always got back to me no matter where the conversation went. As we parted we agreed that we were going to talk to our parents and make a decision about whether or not we would like to move the relationship forward. Maninder told me that he would give me a call on Tuesday to discuss what we had decided.

My mother and I talked about how the first meeting had gone. She felt that Maninder's parents seemed lovely, like a normal Punjabi family. I felt happier knowing that my mother was comfortable with them. If I decided to marry Maninder it was very important that the families got along with one another. In the Asian world, it's not just the two of us joining in matrimony but our families too. I guess you could say we become connected as one.

The following Tuesday I received a text from Maninder saying that his paternal grandma Amritpal *Bee Ji* had fallen ill and been rushed to hospital. He was not going to be able to call me that evening but he said he would call sometime during the week. He rang the following Friday and expressed how much he had enjoyed my company and I told him likewise. It was funny to hear him being honest about how he felt over the phone, as he had been playing it cool like LL Cool J for a while.

MY FIRST EVER SECOND MEETING

We arranged to meet at the Mailbox for our second meeting on 12th May, accompanied by my brother Randhir, and Maninder's sister Gurleen and brother-in-law Loveneet. I was a bit nervous as my brother was only 20 years old at the time but I wanted a man's opinion of Maninder, and my brother's point of view was the closest I could get, even though he was always perceived as the youngest of us four siblings by age. I had always got on very well with him and I knew he would give me his honest opinion. I also wanted to see whether Maninder and my brother would get on.

Up until the second meeting Maninder and I had texted but only spoken once as we had been busy working. On the day, I received a call from Maninder's dad asking to re-arrange the meeting point to Star City rather than the Mailbox as Maninder hadn't been to that side of Birmingham before. Like a car salesman, he was trying to convince me that Star City, a family leisure and entertainment venue in Birmingham, was a better place to meet.

As I'm from Birmingham I know where not to take outsiders, and Star City was one of those places – I think of it as the 'Asian invasion'. Put it this way – I would rather meet at one of the local *gurdwara* than Star City. I started to wonder whether Maninder's parents were the interfering type. I decided to ignore Maninder's dad and texted Maninder to confirm whether we were still meeting at the Mailbox. He confirmed straight away that they had been waiting there for 10 minutes! My brother and I made our way there, Maninder came out to welcome us at the top of the staircase and the three of us walked towards the Mailbox, where we met Maninder's sister Gurleen and brother-in-law Loveneet Gill.

We stood below the BBC building as we discussed which bar or restaurant we would all like to go to. Gurleen and I got along straight away. She was over the moon that I was a fashion designer, as she was really into her fashion. We were like two nursery girls who'd met for the first time; we couldn't get enough of each other all evening to the point that I didn't really speak to Maninder. The three boys got on really well and kept racing one another to the bar to buy snacks and drinks. Eventually, Loveneet recommended that Maninder and I go off to another bar to have some alone time.

We walked along the canal until we found a quiet restaurant where we could sit and talk about past relationships and ask any vital questions. We both used this opportunity to discuss things that needed to be discussed. I know from my heart that I was as honest as an angel and I spoke to him with an open heart. We chilled out in each other's company for about an hour and a half and then decided to return and join the rest of the clique. Maninder set off in front on the way back but then he looked over at me, waited for me to catch up with him, put out his hand and said: "You can take the lead... I'm enjoying the view." I looked at him and couldn't help smirking. "I'm sure you are! It's okay. Enjoy away," I replied.

Before we left he told me he would call me in a week's time to give us time to make a decision before we met again.

A week later Maninder called and asked if I would like

to meet him in Milton Keynes, a town well-known for its rigid grid layout of the roads, much like an American city. I hadn't been to Milton Keynes since university days, when I visited friends there.

Maninder suggested we went for a drive and took some time out to get to know each other better. Third time lucky, hey – and without any family, just the two of us. We arranged to meet after my birthday, when I was going to be doing a skydive parachute jump in Cambridge. I'd decided that I was going to jump out of a plane from 18,500 feet and fly like a butterfly into the air. Maninder couldn't believe how I loved living on the edge... I was certainly not your typical Asian girl.

I loved embracing and experiencing new things; in my view, there was always something new to try out. I knew Maninder would find this part of me strong and probably challenging. I was in no rush to run down the aisle, though I was enjoying his company. So we arranged to meet three weeks after my birthday, on 2nd June 2007.

THIRD MEETING

On the day of my third meeting with Maninder, the weather was lovely. I'd not spoken to him recently, but he had texted me, wishing me a lovely blessed birthday. Arriving at Milton Keynes station brought back a few funny memories. Years before, my university friends had pointed out the row of taxis full of Asian taxi drivers, and they were still here now.

My phone started buzzing away in my pocket. It was Maninder, asking me to meet him past the taxi and bus stand. He said he'd be waiting by the car so I'd know which one to look for. I walked over to meet him and was over the moon to see him – until he explained that his parents and sister had been looking forward to seeing me and they would like to go for a birthday drink with me! I was taken aback; I felt cornered, like I didn't have much of a choice, so I smiled and said that would be lovely. Maninder explained that his sister had come all the way from London to meet me and was really looking forward to seeing me.

Okay, I was excited – but there comes a time when these people needed to give us some space. Still, at this point, I never really thought much about it so I went along with Maninder to enjoy the company of his family for an hour. We talked about my skydiving and how it had made me feel, and they asked how my family was doing. Suddenly I found myself looking at Maninder and wondering why I really liked this special son of *sardar*. What was so special about this colourful Punjabi lad that made him different from all the other sons of *sardars* in the UK?

Maninder's mum was trying to be a modern chick,

speaking her English vinglish with me. She worked at the local Marks and Spencer – only the best for this Punjabi Aunty *Ji,* as she was an officer's daughter. Maninder's dad looked like he'd been in the Indian Army as he was dressed like a soldier. Uncle *Ji,* Maninder's dad, was born in India, came to England and had some schooling here but didn't really study as he was too busy skiving off school with his older sister and brother-in-law to go to the local theatre to watch Hindi films. Maninder's sister Gurleen was a year younger than me, but she was acting like *Bibi Ji* (Grandma).

What was this third meeting all about? I had met them all before and we had all grasped each other's personalities very well. What was going on? I couldn't understand why Maninder and I were in a bar with the three of them. Was he trying to tell me that these three people were very important to him or something? I didn't know; I was confused. What were they trying to show me? What a modern, western family they were, with a touch of eastern culture? REALLY...?!

The weather was warm, bright and fresh that afternoon. After the meeting with his family, Maninder took me to a golf course somewhere in Milton Keynes. I'd never played golf before but I enjoy learning new skills. If only he had told me, we were going to the driving range to practise golf I would have dressed a bit more casually rather than wearing my six-inch heels!

This Punjabi lad really enjoyed playing golf; he even had his own clubs, which he'd bought from America. He started explaining about the various golf clubs and what they're used for during which part of the game, and the position you need to stand in. He'd got into full swing and was in his element explaining the game to me when another guy in the driving range came over and asked Maninder to show him how to play, as it was his first time at the range too. I was in shock. I thought perhaps Maninder had asked a friend to pose as a Dumbo and question him in front of me to impress me.

Maninder loved every moment of it. The smile on his face grew bigger and bigger by the second, and he glanced over at me a few times to see if I was paying attention. He explained to this guy the details of the impact of the club compressing the ball while grooves on the clubface give the ball backspin which would appear as a clockwise spin on the ball when viewed from the standpoint of a right-swinging golfer or as a left back spin clockwise. Or as a counter-clockwise spin when viewed from the standpoint of a left-swinging golfer and blah blah blah... and so on. After he'd finished I made a few jokes about him setting all this up with the lads and asked him how much he was paying the guy to impress me. He was actually quite embarrassed about the situation, and just laughed it off.

It was quite refreshing getting to know Maninder while playing golf rather than sitting chitchatting in a bar. After a while, we were both feeling peckish and we agreed to get a bite to eat at a Chinese restaurant at the other end of Milton Keynes. All I remember was going round and round endless roundabouts. I started to feel car sick after the first five, and all I could think was who the hell designed this town? Did they have a fetish about roundabouts?! Once we arrived, and I finally got some fresh air to stop my head from spinning, I started to feel better. The restaurant looked lovely and was situated next to a lake. The journey had definitely been worth it.

The view was very calming – just what we needed after an interesting game of golf. We'd both relaxed with each other and the conversation was flowing. I felt so relaxed that for once I didn't take the conversation round in circles like I had during previous arranged marriage meetings. The food arrived and was sizzling away, colourful flavours ready to burst in our mouths. The food was amazing, the view was cool and I was enjoying Maninder's company yet again.

After eating so much we couldn't walk, we sat talking and then Maninder suggested we go for a walk around the lake. Why not? I thought. There was an amazing house overlooking the lake; it was a bit like those lakeside properties you see on American TV, with the family fishing, kids on their bikes and couples walking around the lake and enjoying each other's company.

As we walked past the big house on the way back to the restaurant car park, Maninder pointed at it and said it was his family home. I started taking the mick out of him – right, just like he hadn't paid that guy to come up to us and start asking questions. I laughed and told him to relax around me, to stop trying to impress me. I liked him even if he did live in a big home. Maninder offered to drive me back to Birmingham, which was lovely of him – and gave us both more time to enjoy each other's company.

At the time, I was changing jobs, and I knew Maninder had mentioned he would be going to America for a cousin's wedding. He called me on Monday and asked if he could meet me on Friday evening after work, and take me out to dinner. I was a rule girl; I didn't arrange dates on lastminute.com. It was in Maninder's favour that he was the only man I had come across who would arrange dates at least a week in advance, if not more. On Friday evening, Maninder turned up and came into the house to say hello to my mother. I didn't allow him to hang about too much, otherwise my mother's heart would start melting for him to be her son-in-law. We exited the house and went to the Mailbox for a bite to eat.

Maninder and I met several more times over the next two months. While he was out in America he phoned me three times and sent texts every day. By that point, I knew he was into me, and it was lovely to be with someone who really cared about me and communicated it. I liked that he made time for me and didn't mess me around. I had moments when I questioned whether he was too good to be true, but I decided to ignore my gut instinct and enjoy the relationship.

The summer had started and so had my new job as a designer for an amazing company based in the East Midlands. Maninder and I had been dating for about three months. I felt that things were going great in my life and I was happy to have a new job, a partner and a move from Birmingham.

Love was blooming between Maninder and me. He'd been away on holiday and I was also due to have a girly holiday in Greece with my family. Before I went away, Maninder spent the day with me as we were not going to see each other for two weeks. On one of our previous dates, Maninder had mentioned that he didn't like to share food, drinks or any sort of mixing of saliva before marriage. OK, I got that, *Ji*. We both ordered drinks from Costa Coffee and

walked over to a beach, where we sat enjoying the view and talking. Five minutes into the conversation Maninder offered me his drink to taste, and at that moment I knew he was interested in marrying me. He started talking about us getting married and what kind of wedding I would like, and I opened up, as I knew that he was really interested. I never really wanted a big fat Punjabi wedding, having seen how much my mother suffered during my twin sister's wedding. I had visions of a small simple Sikh *Anand Karaj* service with the people I loved. Just the basics, with no reception – but if I had to have a reception I would like it to be simple and private, with only 100-150 people. It was pleasant talking about what we'd like and finding a middle ground that we were happy with. *(Anand Karaj, meaning "blissful union" or "joyful union", is the Sikh marriage ceremony that was introduced by Guru Amar Das Ji. The four Lavan – marriage hymns – that take place during the marriage ceremony were composed by his successor, Guru Ram Das Ji).*
(http://en.m.wikipedia.org/wiki/Anand_Karaj)

Two days before I was due to leave for my holiday Maninder spontaneously turned up outside my workplace to pick me up and take me out for dinner. I was pleasantly surprised, and happy to see him. He took me to a stunning grade two listed Elizabethan inn situated in the beautiful Derbyshire countryside, where they served delicious home cooked food and a variety of non-alcoholic beverages. This place felt cosy and relaxing. We had dinner and then Maninder started talking about how much his feelings for me had grown. We both showered each other with compliments and expressed how much we wanted to be together. He looked me straight in the eye and proposed to me. I was lost for words. I don't know why I was so shocked when my gut instinct had given me signs that he was going to propose sooner or later.

I said "YES!" His face lit up and he smiled the biggest smile I had ever seen. I got into Maninder's car, as he was going to drop me off at my Ranveer *Mama Ji* house, and he pulled out a little blue Tiffany box. My heart beat faster... Every woman dreams of Tiffany! Those little blue boxes contain merchandise that women of all ages dream of. Every girl has pictured the love of her life on one knee, asking for her hand in marriage, offering her a little blue box containing a beautiful Tiffany engagement ring. Maninder held out the blue box, neatly tied with a bow, and looked at me as he waited for me to open it. OK, he wasn't on one knee; however, he was beaming with excitement – and so was I.

"Harleen," he said, "this is a token of my love for you." I was taken aback by how caring and nervous he was at the same time. As I opened the neatly tied bow I was like a kid in a sweet shop – but disappointed find my favourite love heart sweets were missing. It was a Tiffany bracelet. He'd proposed with a bracelet. I'd been so sure there would be a Tiffany ring in the box, and while the bracelet was lovely, I couldn't help feeling disappointed. In fact, I'd actually have been happier if there was an onion ring in that blue box; at least that way I would have had a ring on my finger.

I tried not to show how hurt I was. This was one of those romantic moments that come once in a lifetime, yet it wasn't one I wanted to remember or brag about. Maninder noticed the look of shock and disappointment on my face. He asked me several times if I was okay and I simply said I was fine. He asked if I liked the bracelet; even though I felt disappointed with the proposal I didn't want to come across as rude and I said it was lovely. I was very grateful, but I truly thought that when he proposed he'd do it with a ring...

Anyhow, two days later I was all set to go on my holiday. I sat on the plane thinking about the way Maninder had proposed to me, and I realised I was happy that I was with him. After all, I would rather have the perfect partner than the perfect ring!

Maninder and I called and texted each other every day while I was on holiday. One day he told me that his parents had been round to my mother's house to ask for my hand in marriage and make arrangements for our relationship to go further. I was in shock; I couldn't understand why his parents hadn't waited till I was back from my holiday rather than go whilst I was away. He also told me they had arranged for my family and me to visit them all at their home in Milton Keynes on the day I came back.

I was a little annoyed about this. I love getting a golden brown tan and a healthy glow on my skin when I'm on holiday, but I'd be meeting his grandmother for the first time and I didn't want to come across as a darker coloured bride, as in our culture the darker coloured you are, the uglier you are seen as being. The whole of the holiday resort knew about the situation and I moaned about it until every person understood that I was unhappy; at one point one of the lovely ladies we'd met around our pool laughed to my aunt about the situation and told me to enjoy myself and let my skin go as dark as I liked.

When I got back to Birmingham my mother thought she'd have a good catch up with me before we got ready to leave for Maninder's family home. She told me about his parents popping over while I was away. She was happy they had asked her for my hand in marriage, because in Punjabi culture the girl's family would normally go round to the boy's family home to ask for his hand in marriage. But she had some concerns regarding the wedding. My mother knew I had always wanted a simple, small wedding as I had been very vocal about this from a young age. But Maninder's parents had informed my mother that they would like to have a huge big fat Punjabi-style reception with all the Punjabi-style trimmings, even though they didn't approve of anyone drinking alcohol or eating meat under their roof! They'd used their son-in-law as an excuse, saying that his side of the family would not be impressed if there was no meat or alcohol, and would not turn up to the wedding! Apparently Maninder's parents had provided a grand reception at their daughter's wedding, and they expected to do the same at mine.

I was a bit disheartened. I'd talked to Maninder about what kind of wedding I would like, and I felt that my views had been dismissed and that was why his parents had come to visit my family while I was out of the country. Although I was not impressed with him, I went along to meet him and his parents hoping to have a moment alone with him – but that never happened.

When we arrived I was amazed to discover that Maninder's family home really was the big house he had pointed out on our walk around the lake after the Chinese meal. And there was me thinking he was trying to impress me! It was a lovely four-bed roomed detached house with an oriental theme to the detail of the outside of the building.

Maninder and I had not been together for a fortnight and we were really looking forward to seeing each other! In every good Punjabi household, you always take off your shoes in the hallway of the home; the first thing you ever see is a crisp neat line of shoes running across the hallway. We all entered the living room, which was very warm and typically Punjabi. On the wall were graduation pictures of Maninder and his sister – evidence of a good Punjabi family, with educated kids. It was very clean and tidy – another sign of a good Punjabi family. Maninder, my brother and I sat talking and chilling over our soft drinks until Maninder's Grandma entered the room and was introduced to us all. Like a good Punjabi girl, I walked over and welcomed her in Punjabi by saying "*Sat Sri Akhal Ji.*" (This is a typical greeting in Punjabi, roughly translating as 'God is the Ultimate Truth'.) Shortly after, we all – Maninder and his parents, my mother, brother and I – left the family home to go for dinner at a local Chinese restaurant. Maninder's Amritpal *Bee Ji* was not that mobile so they left her at home for the evening.

The restaurant was interesting: imagine all the foods that you can buy in your usual Chinese restaurant, but done in veggie and vegan style! I was amazed by the menu. But during the meal, Maninder's parents decided to discuss wedding plans. My mother and I were a bit confused about why we were discussing the personal matter of my wedding in a restaurant when the norm was to discuss something like this within the four walls of your home. I felt I was being put under pressure by Maninder's parents, as they wanted us to get married within the next six months. The first things that came into my head were that I had just started a new job that I would like time to enjoy, I had very few savings to get married with within the next six months, and that I wasn't going to put that kind of pressure on my mother.

They went on to explain why they wanted us to get married sooner rather than later: Maninder's dad was playing out family politics with one of his sisters and was desperate for us to get married before her son did. He also used his mother's illness as an excuse, and did the common Asian blackmail trick of saying that she may not live to see us getting married, and of course Maninder would like his Grandma to be present at his wedding. I was a bit confused; if they respected his grandma that much, why were we sitting in a restaurant discussing the wedding plans? Why not in their lovely big home with her? As the head of the house, she should have been present at this important occasion; at least, that's how we respected the elders in my family. All these questions were running through my head like a speedy marathon.

Maninder's dad explained that he didn't have a great relationship with one of his sisters and his mum liked to gossip, so that was why she was not present. As this was the start of her Grandson's wedding preparations I believed she should have been present regardless of family politics. I was a bit disappointed.

Mother and I had not discussed any dates, but I knew this much – I wanted to get married in 2010, and it was only 2007 now. So I told everyone I would prefer not to get married for three years. Maninder and his parents were not impressed with my response! Maninder said he wanted to be with me sooner rather than later. I looked at him blankly, my mind equally blank because I had not thought that far ahead.

Actually, there were all sorts of things going on in my head! Like how the hell were we going to plan a wedding in six months? I wanted to go to India for my wedding shopping – so how was that going to happen? I'd just started a new job and I wasn't even settled in – what was I going to do? Question after question ran through my head and I felt stressed, suffocated and weighed down with all the questions and comments circling round and round. I could see that my mother felt much the same way. I'd always thought I would enjoy the engagement process with my fiancé, but I could feel my blood pressure rising!

We'd all finished our veggie-style Chinese dinner and discussing the gory details of the wedding, so we headed back to Maninder's family home. Now that the family had given me the lowdown on his grandma, I was wary of her – even though I got a warm feeling from her. I can remember looking at her wrinkly face and her big welcoming eyes, silver hair tied back into a bun with her *chunni* over her head. She looked me over from head to toe, scanning every inch of me – and then she gave me a really lovely, friendly warm smile. She'd been sitting slouched on the chair but she suddenly rose up and sat there with her head held high.

We all sat with Amritpal *Bee Ji* for about ten minutes and then Maninder's parents let her know that we had chosen each other as life partners. She looked over at me, called her son over and whispered something into his ear. Maninder's dad ran upstairs and then came straight back to her. He looked like an 80s military Delhi Mr Singh in the Indian Army, or one of those Singh's with rolled-up moustaches you see outside Indian restaurants.

He brought back a red velvet box and handed it over to his mum, who then gave it to me (this felt a bit like Pass the Parcel). In this smooth red velvet box was a gold necklace: her blessing, her acceptance of me as her granddaughter-in-law. And she also blessed me by placing her hand on my head and wishing me all the best in my new beginning with the family. After that, my mother gave Maninder twenty-one pounds of blessing to accept him into our family too. This little blessing between the families is called *shagan* (blessing), and this was a simple, small *shagan* party between two families.

FIXING THE WEDDING DATE

In the Punjabi culture, suitable dates for a marriage can always be negotiated. I found several factors played their part in fixing a date: ensuring the participation of the entire family, avoidance of examination disruption for any children in the family, prevailing weather conditions (well, we were out of luck with that, living in England), location of the two families, a feasible place for the reception of the *barat,* (bridegroom's wedding party) locating a *gurdwara* in the nearby area, making sure the *gurdwara* and the reception of choice were both available for the same day and so on.

The wedding date is planned to allow for a small pre-wedding ritual to be conducted declaring the announcement that the couple have agreed to get married. This function involves the exchange of gifts – dry fruits, sweets, etc. – and both families are given sufficient time to make arrangements. Normally two or three dates are proposed and the most suitable of these is selected after discussions between the bride and groom's families before the date is finally announced.

Maninder's parents and my mother talked regularly on the phone to agree on a suitable date for the marriage, before then setting dates for the second *shagan, chunni* and *kurmai* ceremonies. (The *chunni* ceremony cements the relationship and makes you an official fiancé. The *kurmai* is an engagement ceremony performed in the *gurdwara.* It includes *langar* (a traditional meal) and it is followed by an exchange of gifts between the bride and groom's families.) Throughout this process, Maninder and I still met up on weekends to enjoy each other's company. I felt there was a lot of pressure from Maninder's parents to get us married quickly rather than take time getting to know one another, and the family too. The rush for a date had started!

I was soon receiving phone calls from Maninder's parents asking me how the preparations were going. My mother was upset that they were calling me rather than her and I was also feeling frustrated about it. I was trying to get my head around my new job and I felt that my life had become a never-ending roller coaster ride; there wasn't a pause button in place. This wedding was happening and it was happening NOW! When I wasn't with Maninder, every spare bit of time at the weekend was spent with my mother, trying to arrange a wedding date.

It was proving really difficult to find the right date. One day, Mother and I visited some local *gurdwaras* and reception venues in Birmingham, but finding a date when both were free was a challenge. The *gurdwara* that I had set my heart on getting married in was not available for another 18 months and in my little world I was having fits; I couldn't envision getting married anywhere else. As the day wore on I became silent on the subject, and my mother noticed that I had lost the motivation to find another *gurdwara*.

We popped back home for some lunch. Mother broached the topic with me and asked if I was okay. I tried not to cry as I explained why I was so passionate about getting married in that particular *gurdwara*, but my throat choked up. I wanted to break down and cry. I had grown up attending the Soho Road *Gurdwara* in Handsworth and I had fond memories of going with my siblings when I was a kid. My sister got married there and I had loved the service during her wedding ceremony.

The only *gurdwara* that was available was on High Street, Smethwick where my parents got married. In a sense, I had a feeling it was cursed, as every member of my father's family who had married there went through a divorce shortly after. As I broke down in tears, my mother assured me my marriage would last and that I was overthinking it because I had been scarred by past experiences of how my mother was treated by others after her divorce from my father. My parents and my uncle and aunt had divorced, so that meant I wouldn't? Right! However much sense my mother seemed to make, my worries hung over me.

I decided to call Maninder to ask if we could get married in 18 months' time as I had my heart set on the Soho Road *Gurdwara*. He spoke to his parents about it but the matter just seemed to go round and round like a precise chapatti and eventually they said NO! I should have guessed because sooner was better than later for them.

Many women spend a lot of time fussing over their outfits or choosing a lavish venue. All I wanted was a blessing for my marriage from the *gurdwara* where I had always found inner peace. In our culture, the saying goes that you're not just marrying your husband but his entire family. Though I often laughed at this quote, it was, in fact, true – as the *gurdwara* and reception venue we ended up booking were chosen to please Maninder's parents!

We finally came to a decision and my mother had to put down a deposit for both places. She made a payment of £1,000 to the reception venue, with the balance due the week before the wedding, and likewise with the *gurdwara*. Once the bookings had been made, she called Maninder's parents to let them know the wedding would go ahead in July. The following day they called her back to tell her we couldn't get married on the day we had booked.

They put it in simple terms: we had to move the wedding day forward to March because Maninder's first cousin was getting married on the day we had booked. They hadn't told us about this before, and we were now cutting our plans short by moving the day to March, meaning we only had six months to arrange the wedding – which was stressful, and we were already on a tight schedule. Mother did as she was told and changed the wedding to the new, more appropriate date of 30th March 2007.

One weekend I had an outburst at Maninder when he told me that his mum and he had come up to Birmingham during the week to look at reception venues. Mother and I had gone through so much effort to find and book a venue but it mattered for nothing, as his mum wasn't happy and had decided to find a more 'suitable' venue.

Maninder's mum wanted us to get married at the Botanical Garden, the Burlington Hotel or the Marriot Hotel, as they said they had booked the best for their daughter and they wanted the best for their son. Silver spoon Maninder started making recommendations and he asked me to have a word with my mother about changing the venue. I had had enough at this point, and I lost the will to plan any more of this wedding. It would only be changed again by his mum, I thought to myself. I spoke to my mother and told her their demands were driving me insane.

My mother agreed that they could put a deposit on a venue they liked. In the meantime, she wanted the money back that she was going to lose from the venue that was originally booked. This seemed more than fair to me but Maninder and his parents found my mother rude, and they didn't acknowledge their own behaviour – which concerned me. The process of wedding planning was meant to be enjoyable but instead, I felt drained; the communication between both families was strained, and compromising was even harder.

Maninder and his parents had been inspired by his sister's wedding and the venue where the reception was held. It was a beautiful wedding, judging by the pictures and wedding DVD that I was shown one summer weekend I spent with them. We sat there with several very large overflowing wedding albums, a wedding DVD and his mum with the DVD remote control in her hand, pausing every few seconds to show me every inch and detail of this wedding. I felt like telling Maninder's mum to lay off the TV remote control and get a life! She kept telling me how they had organised this fabulous wedding of the year for their daughter. But this was mine and Maninder's wedding and I was only going to look at places that were within my budget – a budget I didn't really have anyway.

The biggest thing I noticed was that his parents felt it was essential to please the community of Milton Keynes. What you have to understand about the Punjabi community, this nebulous entity so often referred to but impossible to ACTUALLY define, is that they are driven by envy. We envy each other's cars, houses, kids' educational achievements. You name it, we can envy it. Not so much keeping up with the Jones', more a case of destroying the Johals; death by envy. Maninder's dad kept banging on and on about how the community in Milton Keynes still spoke about (envied) the matrimonial magnificence that was his daughter's wedding. He wanted them to be similarly impressed (envious) by the matrimonial magnificence of Maninder's marriage. So it was only the best for his son...

Ironically, I was caught in the crossfire, in a position, no one would envy. Sikhism – my Sikhism – is very clear about these matters. The Guru tells us that *"envy brings terrible pain, and (the envious) one is cursed throughout the three worlds."* **(Page 1091 of Sri Guru Granth Sahib Ji)**

Here's what I wanted:

A venue I could afford

My wedding to be an event where my guests could enjoy themselves honestly.

A memorable day about love, warmth and family

My wedding wasn't a showcase. I had no need nor desire for the community to be impressed. A really good wedding can happen anywhere. You shouldn't be talking about the room or the food or the expense. What was the point of that?

I remember whenever I used to hold girly nights with friends and family I had always said that I wanted my wedding to be very personal, private, and intimate; a simple day that meant something to my partner and me. I didn't want a thousand guests at my wedding. I only ever wanted to please my partner and for him to please me. But all my partner wanted was to please his family with the biggest, fattest Punjabi wedding of the year. None of this was about me. None of it.

As a fashion designer, I had learnt how to sew. I loved sewing my own clothes, realising the ideas in my head into real garments. On one occasion Maninder had asked me to accompany him and his parents to John Lewis in Milton Keynes. His mum wanted a new sewing machine. In the car on the way, Maninder's mum and I sat in the back, his dad and him in the front. A fairly typical arrangement in a patriarchal Punjabi family. I and my stomach were still getting used to the incessant circling around the roundabouts. To distract myself, I mentioned to Maninder that the sewing machine I had used during my degree was from Soho Road in Handsworth. It had belonged to Mother but I ended up pinching it and claiming it as my own.

Maninder and I started reminiscing about our university days, at which point it dawned on me with profound clarity: we were different people. Our upbringings were different; our value systems were different. Diametrically different.

I knew that I had to work hard to succeed in life. Nothing was given to me on a plate and I don't think I would have appreciated things if they were. I grew up watching my mother struggle on her own to pay the bills and put food on the table. My mother had my two younger siblings to support as well as a home to run. I'd been working from the young age of 14, knowing that if I was to realise my dream of getting to university I would have to finance it myself. In my first year at college I opened a savings account. My twin sister decided against university, choosing instead to help my mother run the home. Later, when a job opportunity appeared in a London accountancy firm, she moved out. My twin sister and I always had each other backs. Always. We see eye to eye on just about everything in life. We both know how much our mother did for us. We know that she struggled so that we wouldn't have to. We saw it. Every day. It made me sure about one thing. My life was going to be different.

As a university student, I juggled two jobs to support myself through my degree. I had to take full responsibility for myself. My family dropped me off once. At the end of the year, I had to beg for them to pick me up. I cleaned my bedroom; I washed my dirty laundry; I ironed everything myself. That, study and working two jobs. That was my life.

On the other hand, as a student Maninder had the luxury of his parents driving down south to clean his bedroom and take him out for dinner. They did all his food shopping, took his dirty laundry back, washed it, ironed it and brought it back the following week. His parents bought him his first car, complete with a private registration plate.

I think it is safe to say that Maninder was mollycoddled. Not so much a silver spoon, more a 22 karat ladle in his mouth.

There was a pause in the conversation as I tried to get my head around how different our lives were. His mum broke the silence. "I have spoilt my kids. I know I have. I wanted to. And I expect them to be treated just the same way in the future."

I looked at her and smiled, waiting for her to smile back and acknowledge that she was joking. There was no smile. She meant it.

She went on to talk about how his sister did none of the household chores. I was a bit shocked. I was always expected to help out around our house; that's how a good household is run, everyone chipping in and sharing the work. It's how you learn how to run a home of your own. I was thankful to my mother for instilling those values in me, teaching me these skills.

Maninder and his sister had their parents to fall back on whenever they needed anything and they didn't think it was important to teach their kids the art of hard work. I wasn't even 30 years old and I was starting to think like my mother!

AUGUST, THE EVENING BEFORE THE SHAGAN

A few days before the *shagan,* Maninder rang to ask me how my day was going. He mentioned that his parents wanted to speak to me about something. I was curious to know what this something was, but Maninder said that he didn't have a clue. His dad came on the phone. After asking Maninder to leave the room, he started some general chitchat with me before getting around to the main point, the something. He asked me if I knew if my mother was going to be giving Maninder anything gold during the *shagan* as a blessing. He told me stories of their family *shagan* parties and of the amazing gifts the boys of their lovely well-to-do family had received.

I couldn't believe what Maninder's dad had just said. I felt sick to the stomach. Shocked. I was speechless that he had the nerve to ask me to check with my mother whether she was going to be gifting their twenty-four-karat gold son a white gold ring. I felt flushed, and the walls started to close in around me. It felt like there was no air in the room. I opened the bedroom window to take a deep breath. I couldn't understand what was going on.

Up to this point there had been hints, suggestions, possibilities of the type of people Maninder's parents were. But on this day they showed their true colours. This day I could see who they really were. For the first time, it all became apparent. The blacks and the whites, the occasional greys gave way and, like a technicolour rainbow of terror, they filled my blue sky. I saw the complete spectrum of their self-absorbed selves.

I think about this event a lot. This was the point at which I could have called the engagement off. I could have. But I didn't. I chose to ignore the rudeness displayed by Maninder's parents. Yet I couldn't ignore the very real demand they had made of my mother. How was I going to explain this to her? How? I knew she would be angry when she heard about this; I'd spent all my time trying to manage her stress by living within our means. When my sister got married there had been none of this petty politics, no gauche game-playing. But Maninder's parents were gradually and consistently racking up the level of stress, stretching my mother's budget to breaking point.

If I didn't love Maninder, I should walk away. That much was clear. There was a part of me that had strong feelings for Maninder, feelings that wouldn't just disappear. Was this love?

I was at a crossroads with no streetlights, no road signs, no GPS. Down every road, I saw the same thing: my poor, upset Mother. It was all too much. I broke down. I thought my tears would never stop.

A young cousin saw me crying and told her mum. My Pretti *Mame Ji* (aunt) came into the bedroom to speak to me. Another younger cousin, who had been in the room during the phone call, was not impressed with what had happened, but her mum asked her to keep quiet. Pretti *Mame Ji* listened as I spoke. I told her about my hurt and pain.

She had arranged a few people's marriages over the years and as she had more experience with wedding planning she knew how to handle the situation better than I did. She delicately approached the subject with my mother over the phone and explained what had been said. Gently, carefully she asked if Mother would give Maninder a white gold ring as a blessing during the *shagan*.

My mother was not impressed. As I was working away from home she had to wait until I got back on a Friday evening to discuss the situation. She had already decided she was going to give Maninder £101 in blessing rather than a piece of jewellery.

This whole situation was consuming me. Time to take things into my own hands. I asked Maninder to meet me in Birmingham city centre on the Friday before the *shagan*. At the *shagan*, the groom's family welcome the bride's family into their home. Maninder's folks would be knee deep in the hoopla, preparing the house and the food. Not surprising then that his dad was rather annoyed with Maninder driving across England to meet me. Later I learnt that his parents were also concerned that I would let Maninder know about the white gold ring conversation. Guess who called me? Repeatedly. I didn't answer. I was getting wise to their tactics.

We met at a bar on Hagley Road. I asked him why his parents had been calling me. Had he told them he was coming to meet me? He said he'd told them there was a problem and I was not happy with something and needed to see him before the *shagan*. He told them that I had said it was an emergency.

I told him everything. Everything. Then I sat back. I had thought through the range of possible responses from him. But what he actually said mortified me

"This is not an emergency," he said. "It's just a bit of

gold."

I was without words. Had he not heard me? Then he started showering me with more stories of his cousins receiving gold from their in-laws during their *shagans*! He just wasn't getting it.

I wish I'd had the strength to walk away from Maninder and his family. I wish. But there was a part of me that loved him and I couldn't fight it, even though it was eating me alive.

When I went home my mother gave me a look, a look of disappointment. She didn't want to talk about the situation; she would have been more than happy if I'd returned home that day a single, unattached woman. She'd heard stories about people behaving in this manner and she didn't think she could deal with the situation. She was also feeling the stress of being a single parent for the first time in a long time. This was solely down to Maninder's parents' behaviour.

She asked me if they would expect the same of a girl who had an active, present father. At that moment, I knew she was right. I felt her hurt! My mother had struggled as a SINGLE parent to bring us kids up, and she had done a fine job over the years. Now she was being taunted by disrespectful treatment because she was divorced.

The next morning my mother and I headed off for a special trip to a jeweller. For gold. The sky was big, the sunshine dazzling, giving everything a lustrous veneer. A lustrous golden veneer. I wondered whether Maninder's parents would expect my mother to give them the sun itself, such was their obsession with gold.

The jeweller and his wife had known our family since

my grandparents emigrated from India in the 60s and they welcomed us warmly, asking how they could be of service. My mother enquired about the going rate for gold, what the trend was on rings and how popular white gold was. She explained that I was engaged and it was my *shagan* on Sunday. What would the jeweller recommend we gave Maninder for the blessing? The jeweller walked us through every inch of the sparkly shop, showing us everything from simple items to exquisite jewels. My mother and I were overwhelmed. We decided to take some time to discuss what she would like to give him. I remembered that Maninder's parents specifically asked for a white gold ring, so I asked Mother to get just that – and nothing else.

The hurt I felt was making me sick. I had never asked or expected gold from my mother, not even on a special birthday. We always accepted whatever our mother gave us and we were brought up to expect nothing else. My mother was in tears. The jeweller's wife asked her if everything was okay. My mother said she was just overwhelmed with everything she had to do as a single parent. The jeweller took payment, wrapped up the ring in a lovely red velvet box, handed it over to my mother and wished her all the best for the *shagan*.

The atmosphere was febrile between mother and I as we walked home. We didn't talk; this was the first time in a very long time that we had stopped communicating with each other. I had always felt that I was closest to my mother and I have always spoken to her with an open heart and expressed how I felt. But on this occasion, I was finding it very difficult. We had a great mother and daughter relationship and my mother always seemed to understand me but this was a situation that I didn't really understand myself, never mind trying to get her to see it through my eyes. I never thought we'd have to face anything like this. I felt guilty for making my mother feel weak as a single parent.

We visited my Ranveer *Mama Ji* house to check everything on the 'to do' list had been done. We decided to hide what was going on from the family – and especially from my Ranveer *Mama Ji*, my mother's first cousin, as we knew he'd be deeply upset.

After that hot, humid, stressful Saturday came Sunday, the day of the *shagan*. It was a beautiful sunny morning but I felt a little queasy – not with nerves of excitement, but with feelings of disappointment.

Usually, in the Punjabi tradition, the girl does not attend the *shagan* or *kurmai;* only her immediate family are invited. My family were coming from the north and south of England and my mother had arranged for everyone to meet at a junction near Maninder's home so they would all arrive and welcome Maninder's family together.

I stayed behind with my great *Nani Ji* (maternal grandma) sister in my Ranveer *Mama Ji's* house in Derby. *Bibi Ji* (Grandma) was the oldest member of our family and the most loving person I had ever come across, and my younger cousin too. We all had a lovely chilled out time together and when everybody got back in the evening they filled me in on the fruity details of their day.

Later that night Maninder called me to let me how much he enjoyed the *shagan* and how he couldn't believe that my mother had got him a white gold ring. I felt happy – but not as happy as I thought I would. It probably had something to do with the way Maninder's parents had behaved. I thought I would feel different after a couple of weeks. Despite everything, Maninder and I met up on several occasions over the next month and we continued to enjoy each other's company; our relationship was deepening.

After Maninder had his *shagan* it was my turn. His immediate family had made the road trip to my family home in Birmingham to give me a *shagan* to remember. The difference was that I was not expecting anything from his family. I remember seeing the pictures that my family took at Maninder's *shagan*; a large number of family and friends attended. Naturally my mother was stressed about where all the guests would sit and she called Maninder's parents to discuss who would be attending and how many people to expect. They said it would only be Maninder, his parents, his sister Gurleen, with her husband Loveneet, Loveneet's parents, his Avtar *Nanaa Ji* and Maninder's Amritpal *Bee Ji*.

My mother was surprised. Maninder's parents had pushed for my mother to bring her sister and brother, with their families. Although my mother wanted to keep things simple and intimate between the two families, she couldn't understand why his aunts were not coming. However, we didn't question it. My mother was happy to keep this occasion simple, the way she wanted it from the beginning.

SEPTEMBER, HARLEENS SHAGAN FROM THE PUREWAL FAMILY

My older Jaskarnjit *Masi Ji* and Guruleen *Massar Ji,* and Derby Preeti *Mame Ji* had arrived with her daughter. I was feeling choked up; it felt like my belly was full of Indian sweets. I had no idea what to expect as I had never been to a *shagan* before; my sister had a *chunni* ceremony when she was preparing to get married. I heard Maninder's family pull up in front of the house and I came down from the loft room to greet them and welcome my own relatives. Like a good Punjabi girl, I'd prepared with just a bit of make-up and a simple Punjabi-style suit. My Preeti *Mame Ji* introduced every member of both families to each other; it was a bit like in the film 'Bridget Jones' Diary', with the bride introducing everybody and explaining how everyone was linked to Maninder. I imagined the connections like a link chain that you would wear on your wrist or neck. I was also imagining myself as Anne Robinson in the TV game show 'Weakest Link' and thought to myself, I wonder who the weakest link is!

Before the formal introductions, Maninder gave me a bunch of flowers in front of the two families. It was a nice touch and not expected; I was very pleased and thankful. Then the formalities began. I welcomed each family member with a hug and a "*Sat Sri Akaal Ji.*" When I arrived at my soon-to-be sister-in-law, Gurleen I paused beside her and started a conversation. My young cousin Pee joined us; it was the first time she and Gurleen had met. It was lovely, simple, natural; the three of us just enjoying each other's company.

My sisters and cousin brought in some refreshments and food was served. Maninder's Mummy *Ji* asked me to sit on a chair in the centre of the dining room and to cover my head with the *chunni* of my suit. Maninder's parents gave me an Indian gold necklace with earrings as a blessing. After that, the floodgates opened! Everybody came forward in turn and gave me money as a blessing. For the first time in my life, I had some inkling of what fame must be like! Both families were furiously snapping away, taking pictures of Maninder and me together. It's traditional to sweeten the bride-to-be's mouth and I was force-fed what tasted like a hundred sugary sweet *ladoos* (*Besan ladoo* is a popular Indian sweet dish made of chickpea flour or gram flour, sugar and *ghee* (butter).) I felt more than a little nauseous; nauseous, but with fistfuls of money!

I should have been at my happiest at this point. But I wasn't. Obviously, I had had issues with Maninder's parents refusing to listen to me. But I always felt Maninder listened. He may not have been able to influence his family but when it came to me, I was sure that he was emotionally present. How wrong I was.

There was a rather sensitive situation that I needed to explain to Maninder, which I did well in advance of the *shagan*.

Two years previously I had undergone life-changing surgery. My whole world was turned inside out and I knew things would never be the same again. I had a problem with a left cervical rib in my neck. I underwent major surgery to remove part of the rib and then, to help the blood flow to my left arm and hand, I had both a brachial and a wrist embolectomy. I had never even heard of some of these terms before my operations; now, I'll never forget them. Despite two operations the medical team informed me that my arm and hand would never return to normal. I'd suffered a residual thrombus in the palmar arch, losing movement in my arm and hand. My second angiogram showed a serious blockage and what they euphemistically call an 'anatomical snuff box'. This is a triangular depression on the lateral surface of the wrist on full extension of the thumb. Or in simple terms, I had an extra bone in my neck that affected the circulation to my arm, making it immobile.

My consultant had recommended I go for a vein bypass, which involved moving a seven-inch vein from the upper half of my thigh into my elbow and wrist to improve the movement in my arm. However, there was a high risk of me losing any movement I had in my arm during surgery. I'd already had two operations, with far from perfect results. I opted not to go for a third but in doing so, I knew I may never regain full mobility in my arm.

Instead, I chose to change my circumstances. I joined a gym, started exercising and came off my medication. I regained 90 percent of the movement in my arm and hand. By attending the gym, exercising and eating well, my health improved and I didn't need to undergo this third operation after all!

During that time, all I felt was pain and confusion. I had to change every aspect of my life, from the food that I was allowed to eat to the physical exercise I had to do on a regular basis. Anyone who experiences a life-changing health problem will know that one thing you lose is your inner strength, your belief in who you are. It's so hard to keep a positive mental mindset when everything around you is changing, changing in ways you don't feel you can control.

Unsurprisingly, the operations had left their scars; but there is always good hidden amongst the bad. The experience, the surgery, having to face tough life decisions as a young woman taught me a lot. I learnt that I was to be loved for who I was, not for how I looked. I had hoped that in the months leading up to our wedding Maninder had got to know me better, understanding me as a person. As a result of the operations I couldn't wear jewellery. It was painful to wear necklaces; my nerves couldn't take the weight and I suffered severe pain from the left side of my neck all the way down to my arm and hand. I knew this could be an issue at the wedding so I had explained it to Maninder. I hoped that he would have communicated this very important information to his parents. Somehow, despite their behaviour thus far, I had hoped they would understand my needs, especially when it came to my health. However, once again his parents presented me with something that I didn't want and couldn't use – something that reminded me of an altogether darker time in my life.

After the *shagan*, my mother and I talked. She decided to return the gold jewellery to Maninder's family; that was the respectful thing to do. I agreed. What also played on my mind was that they might ask for more gold now that my mother had given Maninder a ring. To be honest, the word 'gold' seemed to cause nothing but stress during this wedding.

After the *shagan*, my relationship with Maninder

improved and we were getting along just fine. As I was working in the East Midlands, my family home was in Birmingham and Maninder lived in the south, Mother and I only had the weekends together. So we spent them together, planning the wedding.

(ALMOST) LOSING MY ARM AND HEART

While I was at Manchester University pursuing my MA (Marriage Avoidance) degree, I dated the hottest Mr. Singh of the Year 2004. His name was Joshpreet, and I had known him since the first year of my BA (Hons) degree. I found him extremely attractive. However, he had a girlfriend and I had decided I would not cross any line other than being good friends with him, and admiring his handsome physique, his well-groomed *dari* (beard) and *muchi* (moustache) from afar. The summer I received my degree was the summer my twin sister was getting married. Joshpreet somehow got my sister's phone number and called her, asking for my number. After going through the lengthy procedure of getting my number and finally plucking up the courage to call me, he eventually confessed that he was interested in me. We started talking every day on the phone. Then we met up a few times over the summer, and from there we started seeing each other regularly. In no time, we were dating. One day, Joshpreet suggested we should let our parents know about our relationship and he brought up the subject of marriage. However, up until that moment I hadn't even thought about getting married. It had never crossed my mind; I wasn't interested. A few months passed and Joshpreet asked me again if I would let my mother know about our relationship, but I was not ready for that and decided not to tell her anything yet.

Halfway through my degree and with summer arriving, I had planned for a girly vacation with my university friends. While moving out of my Hall of Residence back home for the summer, after picking up my heavy luggage, I started to get pain in the left side of my neck, which shifted through my arm to my fingertips. The pain remained for three months. It interfered with my daily life so much that it was turned into an ongoing joke with all my friends and family. I was in such a great deal of pain that I couldn't even sleep at night. Whenever my Amirjit *Nani Ji*, used to come over from Canada, she'd stop with me, sharing my bed, and I'd picked up some great old-school wisdom from her. For example, before going to bed every night, my Amirjit *Nani Ji* would get me to read a page of *Sukhmani Sahib Paart*.

(https://en.wikipedia.org/wiki/Sukhmani_Sahib)

I would then tell her what I had understood from my reading. One night she explained to me that there are 24 hours in a day, 24 *Ashtpadis*, and 24 *Saloks* in *Sukhmani Sahib Paart*. She said if you read one *Ashtpadi* and one *Saloks* per hour and say *"Ji"* at the end of each one, you will start saying *"Haan Ji* (yes)" at your parents' home and take some welcome virtues into your future in-laws' home.

My Amirjit *Nani Ji* had observed a few of my sleepless nights due to the pain in my left arm, and she brought up the subject with my mother, who asked me to pop into the doctor's to get this looked at. I had several check-ups but nothing unusual was seen.

During the university summer holidays, I got a part time job in Reiss, Birmingham at the Bullring shopping centre. This was where I bumped into a friend, Vik, who was a doctor. I told him about the severe pain in my neck and arm and he suggested I book an appointment with a consultant at the Nuffield Hospital who he knew very well.

I took his advice and booked an appointment, thinking it would be just another regular check-up.

During the appointment, I noticed the neurologist consultant was looking a tad anxious. He called in the orthopaedic consultant, who booked me in for an ultra-sound scan, MRI scan and further treatment. Both consultants looked very confused and were surprised that I still had movement in my arm as the blood flow was not normal past my left elbow. The neurologist consultant called another colleague, a vascular specialist, who then proceeded to examine me. He knew there was a problem with my arm from the moment he saw it. I was booked into the hospital that night for an angiogram the next morning, followed by surgery.

The consultant asked me if I had any health insurance, but I didn't. He recommended that I had some of the treatment privately at the Nuffield and some on the NHS. I would then be transferred to Selly Oak Hospital as an emergency case. Having only come in for a check-up, I was shocked to be facing surgery the next morning, especially when I was told at the time that if I didn't undergo the operation, I would lose my arm.

The next thing I know is that I came around, hearing voices. I was drifting in and out of consciousness, catching a glimpse of the action around me before falling back to sleep. After that, I remember waking up in what seemed to be an intensive care unit with a *Ghanni Ji* (Sikh priest) beside my bed, chanting the *Ardaas* (Sikh holy prayers). The chanting stirred me up, as I thought the *Ardaas* (Sikh holy prayers) was for me. I woke up panicking, all my senses kicked into gear.

A middle-aged man came over to my bed and called the nurse. He was the son of one of the old ladies that the *Ardaas* (Sikh holy prayers) was being chanted for. I recalled meeting him in the reception on the day I came to the hospital for the check-up. As I got up for my appointment he had wished me luck and I had said that I was only there for a check-up and would be home in a couple of hours. You never know what tomorrow holds. I didn't know that I would end up in the same intensive care unit as his mother. The injury had turned out to be lot more serious than I thought and I had lost all movement in the left side of my upper body. The reality hit me hard when I had my first physiotherapy session and realised I had no movement at all in my left arm. Tears ran down my face with the shock. My brain was telling my finger and arm to move but my body wasn't responding. I couldn't understand what was happening to me.

Several weeks later, I left hospital with a hefty bill for the private treatment at the Nuffield. It had literally cost me an arm and a leg. I had been saving up to buy a property with my younger brother, but those funds had to be used to pay the hospital bill. As the saying goes, your wealth is your health, and it was proved that day.

All this time I had not heard once from my so-called boyfriend; he hadn't even been in touch to check if I was okay and this really hurt me. Once I was feeling better, I decided to call him but there was no reply or return call.

Gradually, my health started to improve. One night I was out with friends when I noticed one of Joshpreet's university mates. I approached him and asked how Joshpreet was doing.

"You don't know? He's getting married next month to his long-term girlfriend!" was his ecstatic reply.

My heart fell. I was in shock and disbelief. I was so annoyed at that moment that I decided to call him and ask him to explain everything. The alternative was turning up on his doorstep and demanding answers.

Once again, there was no answer so I left a message. Ten minutes later, I finally heard from the guy who had not been returning my calls or replying to my messages. I asked him to be honest with me about everything, so he decided to tell me everything with an open heart. He said I was his final fling before he got married. He had originally planned just to have a bit of fun with me but then he realised how much we had started to like each other. By this point, he was beginning to have visions of staying with me. However, the whole time he dated me, he was still in a relationship with his girlfriend – he was engaged to her! – and at the back of his mind he knew there was no backing out on that. And all that time he played with my feelings and my emotions and got me thinking there was a possibility we might get married and have a future together.

I was heartbroken, devastated. I couldn't understand how someone could play with someone else's heart, trample on their emotions like they were a football. I cried for days and blamed myself for everything. But one sunny morning I realised I needed to focus on my health. I made up my mind that I wouldn't meet anyone after this situation. I needed time to get over it.

It took me 18 months to get full movement back in my arm. I regained my confidence, and started looking for a job in fashion design. I was lucky enough to get a job with a design company in Banbury as a corporate wear designer. The salary was modest, as I had been out of the design scene for a while. I was living away from home, paying my rent and bills, which left me with little to save.

When Maninder and I first got together I had just left this job to work for another design company. I wanted to wait a while before we got married so I could save up and pay for my own wedding. Maninder's parents just wanted us to get married as soon as possible, to make a point to a number of people on their side of the family as well as to the little community in *mini pind* (small village) Milton Keynes. For me, getting married was about us both wanting to be with each other, rather than making a point to anyone about our status. I liked to live within my means and I had communicated this with an open heart to Maninder, but he chose not to take it on board. Maninder had been brought up having his parents giving him whatever he wanted. Conversely, I was brought up to believe you can achieve any goal, big or small – but you have to work hard towards realizing your dreams.

I also wanted to take time to get to know Maninder after all that I had been through in my last relationship. I needed to be able to trust my partner.

FRIENDSHIP TURNS THE TWO JOHAL FAMILIES INTO ONE

I need to rewind back to the beginning – the very beginning – because this story needs context. Let me share my family history...

What is a family? We all know who our actual family are but occasionally, through time and proximity, firm friendships erode those bloodline boundaries and friends become family. This is exactly what happened in my family.

This is the tale of the two tribes.

This is a fable about friends and family.

This is the story about the joining of the Johals...

Like many immigrants from the sub-continent, my father's family came to England in the swinging 60s. My father and his siblings were British citizens; they held the golden ticket, so to speak. Unlike some, they didn't need to marry a 'passport' in order to obtain a visa. But, as was so often the case with their parents' generation, there was a real fear, a dread that my father's generation would forget their Indian heritage, their Punjabi roots. So my grandparents decided that their kids should marry other Asians, keep the tradition and culture alive. The irony was that my father's generation hadn't been brought up in a traditional manner; they had already started loosening their grip on their heritage. Given how much I love speaking Punjabi, the pride I take in conversing in my mother tongue, it's astonishing to think that, growing up, my father didn't speak a word.

I suppose it was as much about survival as anything else, trying to fit into a very different England of the sixties and seventies.

My older Narinderpal *Pua Ji* had her marriage arranged to an Indian man; she was not far off being a teenage bride. Like a good Punjabi bride, she moved in with her in-laws and soon she gave birth to her first child. Not long after her son, Harminder Singh, was welcomed into the world she found out she was expecting again. Halfway through her pregnancy, she had an appointment for a routine check-up at the hospital. Her husband, my *Fuffar Ji,* was back sorting some family business in India, so he asked his best friend and wife, Mr and Mrs Jandoo, to drive her to the hospital.

As they travelled they made small talk, chitchatted, passed the time. It couldn't have been more normal, more usual. Then the conversation took a turn. Mrs Jandoo started talking about my aunt's marriage; she was asking unusual questions, questions that had my Narinderpal *Pua Ji* on the back foot. She knew something wasn't right. Then the bomb was dropped... Mrs Jandoo said how much she admired my aunt, what a loyal and respectful woman she was. My aunt was perplexed. Why was Mrs Jandoo saying this?

Mrs Jandoo went on...What wife would accept such behaviour, take it in her stride, remain calm and act like nothing was happening? My aunt asked what Mrs Jandoo was talking about. Why shouldn't she be calm?

Mrs Jandoo laughed. "See! This is what I mean. Your husband is in India marrying another woman and you wonder why you shouldn't be calm..."

My Narinderpal *Pau Ji* was acting like nothing was

going on because she had no inkling that anything had been going on. This was news to her. Gut wrenching news. Inexplicable news. His mother, her mother-in-law, had arranged it all. She was in shock. While she was carrying his second child, he was in the Punjab marrying his second bride.

She headed back to her in-laws' house. She packed a small suitcase and, remaining calm, acting like nothing was happening, she told them she was going to visit her parents for a week or so. They had no idea that she would never step foot in that house again. She arrived at my grandparents' house in a state. On the doorstep, she explained everything. You might expect a sympathetic response from her parents. You might. They told her they were not having any of her 'nonsense' and she was to go back immediately. She pleaded with her parents to broach the subject with her husband and in-laws. They had already discussed it with her husband's family. They had known for some time that their son-in-law, their daughter's husband, was going to get married again. They assured her that he had only married her so she could get a visa.

All this, on the doorstep. They tried to close the door in her face but, feisty as she was, she jammed her foot in the doorway, and stepped over the threshold. The threshold is hugely symbolic for a Punjabi bride. The Departure of the *Doli* marks the end of the wedding events. This ritual takes place when the newly married daughter leaves her parental home forever. She stands at the threshold and throws rice backwards over her head, signifying that that is her past life and she is moving on to something new. When she arrives at her in-laws, at the threshold, outside the house, a bowl of rice awaits her. As she takes it over the threshold she marks the beginning of her married life. Gone is the girl. Welcome the wife.

Foot still in the door, my aunt vowed never to return to her in-laws' house. Her parents finally relented. She moved back in with them and her husband never saw his second son, Paul Singh. Life unfolded, as lives do. Harminder and Paul attended the local Smethwick school and were normal Black Country kids. Back in the 70s, mums would walk their kids to school. The kids would play on the street together, lark around and generally have fun. Parents became friends through their children.

When Narinderpal *Pua Ji* had a party to celebrate Harminder's birthday she invited my Jaskiranjit *Masi Ji* and Guruleen *Massar Ji* over with their kids, Mandeep, Pardeep and Sandeep. (Navdeep hadn't yet been born.) The families became firm friends, the relationship deepening around the proposal of my mother to my father. My Guruleen *Massar Ji* suggested to my grandfather that my mother might be the "good Indian girl" that my father's family were looking for.

The two families transformed friendship into official family when my parents got married. What had been two now was one, big family. It was ironic that it was my father's older sister Narinderpal *Pua Ji's* divorce that led to my parents' marriage.

MY PARENTS MARRIAGE

By my age, my mother had been married, blessed with two children and had a third on the way. She always compared her life to mine, my life to hers. Emotional blackmail seems to be some sort of genetically inherited trait, passed down the female line. Indian mums are past masters at blackmailing with emotion. She was always happy to remind me how lucky I had been, uttering the age-old mantra of "When I was your age..."

I was reminded how lucky I was to have had a full education, to follow my dreams.

I was reminded how lucky I had been to have lived away from home.

I was reminded how lucky I had been to have travelled abroad on numerous occasions.

None of this was she allowed to do before her marriage. My mother was 23 when she married my Father, which in those days was regarded as old, left on the shelf; akin to women who marry after 40. As for my Amirjit *Nani Ji,* she was married at the age of 16 in the Punjab. "When I was your age..."

"A different age," I remember thinking. "The world has changed." But it seems the world spins more slowly around its axis if you are a Punjabi woman.

India gained its independence when my Amirjit *Nani Ji* was 16 years old. With independence came Partition, upheaval and a genocide that is rarely spoken about in Punjabi homes. My Amirjit *Nani Ji,* family had to leave everything behind in Pakistan, travel to India and try and start their new lives in a place they didn't know. During

Partition, the creation of Pakistan and India, my Amirjit *Nani Ji's* marriage was arranged by her *Masi Ji* (aunt); she married my Charanpal *Nanaa Ji*.

In those hard times, it was honourable to marry off your daughters as young as possible. Times were tough for the common man, so finding husbands for your daughters – putting a man's shadow over them – was supposed to protect their honour and give them a new purpose in life. It also preserved the family's respect. During the Partition, many women were raped and separated from their families and husbands in either India or Pakistan, whichever they'd taken refuge. These women lost their families, their identities and their innocence. Many women were advised to take poison given by their parents. My grandmother was one of them. But unlike most other women in this predicament, she never emptied the vial inside her.

My Amirjit *Nani Ji* and her family had left their homes and villages to start a new life in India. They stayed in a refugee camp for the first three months before crossing the border with the help of two of their father's friends. One of them was a Muslim and the other a Hindu. They safely crossed the border with their help, as humanity and kindness overcame the frontiers of religion.

During the Partition my Amirjit *Nana Ji* lost her father, her elder sister and her brother-in-law. My great grandmother's only goal was to cross the border safely with the rest of her family, and leave behind the harrowing memories and the trauma that the Partition had caused her. They arrived in India's Punjab having lost their loved ones, but they were hopeful, looking forward to a bright future ahead in a foreign country. This was a land that was very different for the women, especially Pakistani and Punjabi women. My Amirjit *Nani Ji* was educated to a point, but the Punjabi women in India were not. Their outlook and thinking was very different. As soon as the family settled in Punjab, their aunties and uncles were on the lookout for eligible bachelors for them to marry.

My Chananpal *Nanaa Ji* and Amirjit *Nani Ji* married and had three daughters and three sons. My mother's older sister, my aunt Jaskiranjit *Masi Ji*, got married to my Guruleen *Massar Ji* in England, and then visited India with their family. My uncle's good friend was on the lookout for a lovely girl for his son – my father.

My uncle recommended my mother and her younger sister. My father was spoiled for choice as he was a British Asian with a passport to match. He was shown some family pictures and he liked my mother, as she was very simple and beautiful. My mother, on the other hand, didn't like the look of my father at all – she thought he looked like Gabbar Singh from the film '*Sholay*'. For three weeks she did everything she could to avoid the conversation with her family; behaving like the runaway bride, she decided to hang out at her *Masi Ji's* (aunt's) place, as she got on with her the best.

Finally, her parents sat her down and told her that she was going to be marrying my father and she had no option; her flight was booked. When she told me this story she said she cried so much because she didn't want to come to England and get married to our father, but when she arrived she actually enjoyed being here and even liked him. He was a very supportive husband and father – until he started drinking heavily and beating her black and blue on a regular basis. Their marriage failed after 14 years and as you already know, my mother became a single parent in her mid-30s, bringing up four children by herself. It was a difficult time for her, but she did her best to support us and we compromised and worked as a team to get where we are today.

BACK TO MANINDER AND HARLEENS RELATIONSHIP

The date for the wedding was fixed; only the *kurmai* and *chunni* ceremonies had to be carried out. We had just six months to plan our wedding.

I had no idea what I wanted my wedding day to be like. All I knew was that I wanted it to be simple and beautiful. Maninder and I had no idea where to begin! We decided to get some inspiration from a wedding exhibition that was going to be held in Birmingham city centre. Maninder's sister wanted to come along and I didn't mind; she had been married for over a year and had more of an idea than us. Plus, I could do with the support as neither of my sisters seemed particularly bothered. Over time, and partly due to me being away at university, my sisters and I had grown apart and we didn't get along so well now, plus they had their own lives to worry about.

Gurleen *Pehn Ji* and Loveneet *Pah Ji* met us at the Grand Hotel, where the exhibition was being held. As Maninder and I entered the hotel there was an amazing lineup of wedding cars: the very best limousines, stunning Bentleys, modern and traditional wedding cars, sports cars including Ferraris and the Audi R8. The funniest thing was a white Tuk Tuk parked in the middle of them all.

The show brought together the finest wedding suppliers showcasing the whole range of services, from simple invitations to elegant bridal gowns and elaborate decorations. Each supplier spoilt me with choice, the sort of things I could only dream of. And the prices were also the stuff of dreams! I think the reality of how much this wedding was going to cost suddenly dawned on me.

After the exhibition, I needed to talk to Maninder, discuss what we could and couldn't afford. It had been great to have Gurleen's input but I suspected that her parents had sent her with a huge checklist of things that they wanted for my wedding. She had spent the day pointing out things that hadn't even crossed my mind, being pushy and insistent. I made a mental note of everything Maninder and I had liked. It wasn't all the same! We'd have to compromise on some points. After the exhibition, all four of us decided to go to the Mailbox to de-stress and relax. Over coffee, I mentioned some of the things I had seen and liked, things we could imitate at our wedding but without paying exhibition prices. I got the distinct feeling that Maninder and Gurleen didn't want to have this kind of conversation with me in front of Loveneet. I also had the impression from Maninder's parents that Loveneet's family had made a lot of demands during his and Gurleen's wedding. However, my impression of Loveneet himself was that he was quite a chilled out, mellow person who didn't care about cars and other material things as much as Maninder, Gurleen and their parents did. I felt for Purewal family members; it was like they had to keep up appearances in the local area – as would their new daughter-in-law.

What was all that about? I couldn't understand them; I was not one of them. I believed in being me and I wanted to be accepted for who I was, not someone I wasn't. Every time Gurleen spoke about her vision or expectation she sounded like a broken record, as if she had been let down and was not being treated like a little princess. She kept reminding me not to have big expectations. My feet were firmly on the ground and I wasn't expecting anything from anyone. I was happy living each moment as it came to me.

MANINDER'S BIRTHDAY

The following week it was Maninder's birthday. Even though we hadn't been getting on, disagreeing about elements of the wedding arrangements, I decided to put our differences aside and arranged a surprise for him.

Like all children of Indian immigrants, Maninder was a glory hunter when it came to football. Most Indians support either Manchester United or Liverpool – basically the dominant teams in English football during the sixties and seventies. Maninder was a Liverpool fan, despite having been brought up in Milton Keynes.

On the day, I gave Maninder a present and a card. What better way to start your birthday than by receiving an Armani wristwatch from your fiancé, a reflection of the time spent together, the life we would spend together? As he opened his birthday card I watched his face. I wanted to see it when he saw what was tucked inside. I witnessed a mature man become a boy. He couldn't have been more excited. One of my cousin's *Mama Ji* had helped me get hold of a pair of tickets for Anfield. I was told that the seats were really good, in the Kop end, the heart of the hardcore of Liverpool fans. Maninder had never been to a game before.

After the cross words and bickering, it was lovely to be reminded of Maninder's sweet smile, the smile I remembered from that first photo. I'd had the ladies at my local bakery design a Liverpool football cake and Maninder cut the cake with his Amritpal *Bee Ji* while his parents and I looked on. I had a lovely warm feeling thinking that every single person in this room would soon be my family. I was a bit nervous of Amritpal *Bee Ji*, but I felt her love for me that day and I could see that she respected what I had done for Maninder. She told me she couldn't believe how much I had spoiled him, like a big kid. She looked into my eyes and said: "You really like him, don't you, Harleen?" and I replied from my heart: "Yes, I do."

Then the phone started to ring and my father-in-law ran to the kitchen to answer it. It was Maninder's Mohanbir *Nanaa Ji* and Kanchan *Nani Ji* calling from Canada to wish him a happy birthday. When they discovered I was there, his Mohanbir *Nanaa Ji* wanted to speak to me. I was a bit scared as I had not got to know my own Charanpal *Nanaa Ji* as he passed away when I was a kid. Mother had told me lovely stories about how loving he was towards her and her siblings. We had a cupboard in the front room at home that had three drawers to the front with glass panes in each of them. All our family pictures could be found within the wooden walls of the cabinet. The pictures ranged from our baby photos to black and white photographs of my mother's grandparents and great grandparents from the Punjab, who we had never met but knew through the elderly crackling voices we heard on the long distant phone calls we'd get once a month. So this was going to be the first contact I would have with Maninder's Mohanbir *Nanaa Ji* – who was soon to be my *Nanaa Ji* too.

He was very well spoken, as he had been in the British Army in India. In English, he asked me how I was, and how my family were. He said it was lovely speaking to me and he wished me all the luck in the world and said he looked forward to meeting me soon. I'll never forget his sweet warm words and how charming he sounded on the phone. Then I spoke with Maninder's Kanchan *Nani Ji*. She spoke in Punjabi as she hadn't had much education. It was nice to talk to both of them, and I was now looking forward to meeting them on our wedding day.

While I was on the phone Maninder's Amritpal *Bee Ji* said she was not feeling very well so my future father-in-law informed us that they wouldn't be joining us for dinner at the restaurant. I had hoped that all five of us would be attending Maninder's birthday meal but it ended up being Maninder, his mum and me. I was pleased, as it would give me time to get to know Maninder's mum better. I had only ever met his parents together.

Maninder and I chatted and laughed about the first time we came to the restaurant and the walk around the lake, when he had pointed out their family home to me and I hadn't believed him. His mother just sat there observing us. She didn't really say much and I realised that Maninder's dad was the voice and his mum was the thought process behind everything.

At the end of the evening, Maninder dropped me off at home and I tried to explain that I would be grateful if he could just try to understand me more as a person and, in return, I would make the time to understand him and his family. I said that in any relationship both people needed to compromise, not just one person. It seemed his birthday helped clear the air between us. We made a promise to be more open and take the time to understand each other better before shouting and arguing.

After Maninder's birthday, all focus was back on the wedding preparations.

FINDING THE PERFECT LEHENGA

The most crucial aspect of a wedding is the bride's *lehenga* (dress) – the wedding dress or wedding outfit. It has to look a million dollars. I had visited shops on Soho Road in Birmingham, Belgrave Road in Leicester, Southall and Wembley with no luck. The last point of call was Green Street in London. All these places were amongst the most well established bridal shops in the UK, and they all specialised in designer *lehengas*.

It was disheartening not being in India, shopping for my wedding clothes. For a Punjabi girl, the journey 'home' to prepare for a UK wedding is an important part of the process. It grounds you, reminds you of your heritage, re-connects you with your family. Over and above which, the range and quality of shopping is so much better – and cheaper! Time was short, we were being rushed by Maninder's family and I'd just started a new job. Rather than my desired three-week Indian escape, the most I could manage was a week off work, but it wasn't an option to go to India for such a short time.

I hadn't been to India since I was 10. I wanted to spend quality time there with my mother and her family. But more than that, I wanted to tour India and witness its beauty, reflect on the land of my forebears while completing my wedding shopping – central to which was a visit to the *desi* Punjab *bazaar* (shops) where I would find the perfect wedding outfit, the perfect *lehenga*. This Indian adventure would be my last trip abroad as a single woman; I'd been planning it for years. Upon my return, I would marry, and in the words of the Spice Girls, two would become one. It would also have been the last trip I would make with my mother; I had been so looking forward to her showing me her India.

Instead of inspirational India, I had to settle for second best. We travelled around the country, experiencing the Asian invasion areas of England. Anywhere there was a concentration of Indian sub-continental shops, my mother and I shopped.

I was driving her mad because I couldn't find the *lehenga* I had set my mind on, my perfect wedding outfit; not only that, I couldn't express what I wanted. I just knew that every one I saw was wrong. I decided to give up my dream and realised I would just have to settle for something not as special as I had hoped. It felt like I was getting married just for the sake of it.

Instead of the Eastern mysticism of the Ganges, we had the East London mayhem of Green Street. Maninder and I drove down together in November. There was one shop in particular that I was very interested in visiting: Chiffon. I was looking for something unique, as any bride would. It had to be classy and elegant and Chiffon was the place to get it. They once had an outlet in Birmingham but it had closed down; I remember feeling gutted at the time since it was just before my sister's wedding and I needed an outfit. Here I was again, at Chiffon, with a wedding looming, really needing an outfit. But I was a hundred miles from home, and the wedding was mine.

Chiffon is very upmarket, and the owner Bubs Mahil is a fantastic designer. She graduated from the London College of Fashion in the late 80s, and in 2002 she designed outfits for the former British Prime Minister Tony Blair and his wife Cherie. This was my last hope for finding the perfect wedding outfit.

Maninder waited outside. Everyone knows it's bad luck for the groom to see the bride-to-be in her wedding dress before the ceremony. Some wedding traditions and superstitions are so engrained in our culture that we don't even think to question them. This particular one originated during the time when arranged marriages were customary and the betrothed couple were forbidden from seeing each other before the wedding. The wedding itself symbolised a business deal between two families (romantic...). A father would have been pleased for his daughter to marry a man from a rich, land-owning family. But there was the worry that if the groom met the bride before the wedding and didn't like the look of her, he'd call it off, thereby casting shame on the bride and her family. So it became a tradition that the bride and groom were only allowed to meet at the wedding ceremony so that the groom did not have the opportunity to change his mind. Goods and chattel; that's pretty much all women were.

Similarly with the veil the bride wears. Its original purpose was to keep the groom from finding out what the bride looked like until the last possible minute when it was too late to back out of the transaction. Today, although arranged marriages have more of a modern twist to them, most brides still don't want their groom to see them in full bridal mode until the day of the wedding. You have to camouflage the contractual component with a modicum of marital mystique.

Chiffon had hundreds of beautiful outfits. For the first time, I was spoilt for choice. I picked out an outfit and told myself not to look at the price; not till after I'd tried it on. As I held the outfit it slipped off the hanger. The *lehenga* was so heavy that as it fell it actually broke the glass counter below. The owner, Bubs came over to me and said it was nothing to worry about, but I couldn't stop apologising for what I had done. She said, "Would you like to try the outfit on?" After smashing her cabinet, I was shocked she'd still let me!

As she escorted me to the fitting rooms, Bubs explained that the shop was going to be closing for three months to be refurbished. That explained why the cracked shelf was no big deal! It also meant that most of the outfits were on sale. I still refused to check the price of my chosen outfit. As soon as I slipped it on, I was in love. I knew that this was the wedding *lehenga* I wanted; my *lehenga*. This was the one. While in the fitting room, I realised that I should get a second opinion from someone in my family. All of a sudden I got stressed. I called my mother to tell her about the *lehenga*.

She could hear from my voice that I desperately needed a second opinion. But she said that I should get the outfit if I knew it was the one, despite her not seeing it. That wasn't helpful! I felt even more confused. I knew I wouldn't find another outfit that I loved as much but instead of being with my mother I was here with Maninder, the one person who couldn't see the outfit! I decided to call my twin sister, who lived in London, and ask her if she could come to the shop and give me her opinion. She said she was busy doing something important and couldn't make it, so I called my best friend Jaya. I described the outfit in detail and told her how much I loved it. She recommended that I get the outfit;

when she'd got engaged and went dress shopping she had been confused by other people's opinions. In my heart, I knew that this was the outfit I wanted to get married in, so I took it off and looked at the price. I was thrilled to realise it was affordable and within my budget.

Because the store was closing I would have to wait three months to get the completed outfit but it was definitely worth the wait. Bubs had a very calm approach; she immediately put me at ease and took into account my likes, dislikes and, most importantly, my budget. I could not have asked for better service or a superb wedding outfit. My heart felt lighter knowing that I had bought the *lehenga* that I wanted to get married in. Bubs said she would reduce the price further if I paid 80 percent up front on the day, and she'd include all the alterations and an underskirt within the reduced price.

I walked away feeling stress-free. I'd heard so many horrible stories about girls not having a great experience when buying their wedding outfits, and I'd heard both good and bad about shopping for your *lehenga* here in the UK and India, but my experience was great and I was pleased to have used gut instinct for a change.

Bless Maninder, he waited outside the store in the car for ages before coming in and waiting in the groom room downstairs. Not once did he ask me to hurry up or rush me in any way. I really appreciated his support. After buying the wedding outfit we decided to go and get a bite to eat. Maninder had noticed I was feeling much better and as usual, we had a great time together.

I had booked the Sunday off to make more preparations for the wedding but Maninder and I decided to take some time out away from the wedding stress. Maninder booked a hotel for us to spend quality time in during the day. Boys and girls are not meant to be sexually active before marriage but we were, as we were going to get married and we loved one another.

THE RING PROCESS WITH MANINDER'S PARENTS IN BIRMINGHAM AND GETTING HIS WEDDING OUTFIT

Now my wedding outfit was all sorted out, but Maninder needed his, so his parents and he came to Birmingham to look for an outfit.

Badial is one of the oldest stores on the Soho Road and it stocks everything you could think of in terms of Asian fashion, from fabrics to women's ready-made outfits, children's clothes, *sarees*, (a *saree* is a female garment from the Indian subcontinent that consists of a drape varying from five to nine yards) shoes, bags, jewellery, wedding supplies and Asian food. This large store was owned by two brothers who had divided their business into two separate shops. Maninder bought his outfit from the store known as BX Fashion Boutique, where they sold trendy modern bride and groom fashion outfits.

He was getting a *sherwani,* (bridegroom's clothes), which is a long garment that resembles an *ackhan*. It is very popular among men in South Asia, and the traditional dress for Indian men. A *sherwani* signifies elegance and style. It's worn over a *kurta* (a loose shirt falling either just above or somewhere below the knees) and the lower part of the dress consists of a *churidar* (pyjama), or a *salwar* (Punjabi pants). A scarf is also draped over one or both shoulders.

The *sherwani* is now famous as a wedding outfit and it has always been popular as an outfit which can be worn at formal events. A *sherwani* coat is usually knee-length; it fits close to the body and is fastened at the front with buttons. Embroidery enhances the *sherwani's* appearance. A wide range of fabrics, designs and colours can be used and the *sherwani* worn by a groom is ornately decorated.

Having chosen his *sherwani*, Maninder called me to ask for my opinion. Mother and I met the Purewal family at BX Fashion. As I walked into the store Maninder approached me wearing his outfit and asked me what I thought of it.

Maninder looked stylish and amazing. The detail was spot on and the colour was an exact match to the colours of my *lehenga*. I was really impressed with the fit and the detail. However, I was not that impressed with the hem of the scarf he had chosen to be the *palla pharana* (the bride's father or uncle hands her a fabric to tie the bride and groom together for ther vows) that my uncle would hand me during our vows in front of the *Guru Ji*. I advised Maninder that he would need to get a scarf without all the loose threads and tassels, as they would catch on my wedding outfit and accessories. I realised his mum didn't like my advice; she insisted Maninder keep the one he had chosen as she liked it. I was only giving my opinion, which Maninder had asked for – otherwise, I would have kept quiet and minded my own business. This could have been one of those moments where the Mother-in-law kills the daughter-in-law for taking her son from her. It would have hit the local weekly *desh pardesh* newspaper headlines – but I was saved thanks to the lovely store owner's son, who suggested that we go for both.

After Maninder paid and sorted out all the details with his outfit, his parents decided that we would head down the Soho Road to another mini Punjab and check out the jewellery stores for some ideas, as Maninder's dad was going to India to do the rest of the wedding shopping. They needed to get an idea of the kind of jewellery I liked to wear, and my personal fashion style, so they would know what to get for me as gifts from their side of the family. I couldn't understand why Maninder's dad was going to India when Maninder had already bought his wedding outfit here in the mini Punjab of the UK. What was this trip to India really for? Hmm ... all will be revealed in the coming chapters.

Before the trip to the jewellery shop, Maninder's parents decided they needed to have something to eat and they asked my mother if there was a restaurant they could go to. Being a single parent who was used to stretching the budget, my mother didn't really do restaurants. To my mother, going to any sort of restaurant was a waste of money when you could have nice home-cooked Punjabi meals. However, my siblings and I had taken mother to restaurants on special occasions, though we would definitely not take her to any restaurant on the Soho Road, whatever the occasion.

Maninder's parents had come across an advertisement for a restaurant called *Chandni Chowk*. The *Chandni Chowk* was a trading square in India known for its unique set of restaurants and halwais, professional sweet creators. The advert talked about how "you no longer have to travel thousands of miles to enjoy the taste of traditional Indian food as the *Chandni Chowk* restaurant offers you the experience of traditional Indian sweets as well as the finest Punjabi Indian cuisine for all the family to enjoy, all supported by Sukhdev's 30 years in perfecting Indian cuisine, as seen on TV thousands of times through the cheesy advertisement going around the whole of Handsworth. A massive crew cram into this one Punjabi restaurant, so please hurry down with your family for the special offer discount we have on now!!!"

Although I am from Birmingham we didn't often go traipsing up and down the Soho Road, so my mother and I had to ask a few people where this *Chandni Chowk* restaurant was. They seemed a bit shocked that we had no idea. While walking towards the restaurant Maninder's mum suggested we pop into a few of the jewellery shops on the way. As we went into one store she started looking at really heavy, over the top sets. I was amazed at her taste and realised I needed her to understand my more elegant style. Less is more!

I selected some lightweight sets to demonstrate my taste in Indian jewellery. Her face indicated that she wasn't impressed with my choice and she would like me to wear a much heavier 24 karat gold set. I then decided to explain to her face to face about the surgery and why I chose to wear lightweight jewellery. She wouldn't give up! She explained that I was going to be the Purewal family's daughter-in-law and they would like me to be more traditional! What would people think of their status if I wore that kind of lightweight jewellery to weekly *gurdwara* gatherings? At that point, I bit my tongue between my teeth and didn't reply.

Finally, we arrived at the restaurant and all five of us enjoyed the meal. Here and there I kept hearing sneaky comments from Maninder's dad about my mother, about how they were the boy's family side and how the girl's side of the family should always take care of their interests at all times. I felt very uncomfortable around them, and I could see my mother's stress on her face. After the meal my mother paid the bill; Maninder's parents didn't even offer once to pay their share. I was shocked at their attitude. Both of Maninder's parents had talked about their great professions, how loaded they were and how much they owned but they couldn't even offer to go halves on a bill!

After that, we moved on to more jewellery shops. We were all standing outside the Paul jewellery store when my father-in-law decided to make yet another comment, this time about how I didn't have an engagement ring and how they would like me to get a ring and have an engagement party, as that was how Maninder's sister did it! This was about us and what we wanted – and I didn't want an engagement party.

Maninder's parents never failed to show us how much they wanted to show off to their little community. They took me into the jewellery store and asked the guy to start taking out the engagement rings. I was so overwhelmed. I felt like they were forcing me to get something I didn't want. I got so upset with their pushiness that I started crying. I just wanted to leave the jewellery store and go home. I left the store in tears. The in-laws kept asking if everything was okay but I was so hurt by their behaviour that I could no longer cope with them. I felt their pressure now more than ever.

The main bulk of organising a wedding falls on the bride's family's shoulders and my shoulders were getting heavier with this trip. I didn't need to be doing window shopping; I felt my time would be better used on other preparations. But then again, without this trip, I would never have seen this colourful painting of Maninder's parents.

When it comes to engagement rings, the normal tradition in society is that a guy should spend three months' wages on a ring – but this is NOT a tradition at all. This is self-serving advertising perpetuated by that senior founder of the wedding industry. A true tradition would be to use an heirloom ring passed down through your family. In the unhappy event that you didn't already have such a thing, you would traditionally make do with giving the Asian lass the wedding ring itself, to wear on her right hand until you are ready to put it on her left. After all, if you are so bereft of birth right as to have no heirloom to give, then traditionally you would build up your capital to support your bride and not squander it on expensive unnecessary gewgaws.

Of course, the wedding industry does not want you to be aware of any real traditions. They want you to spend. They really don't want you to exercise traditional common sense and independent thinking. By all means, feel free to make the vendor community happy by relying on the opinions of a bunch of internet peers who read wedding magazines.

I didn't have a Cinderella complex and I didn't think that Maninder was my handsome prince, who had to get me a ring. He'd asked me to pick a ring of my choice and I showed him one. The price was out of his reach, so I didn't mind compromising. We both agreed to save up and get an engagement ring after five years of marriage. I didn't believe in fairy tales – or happy endings, for that matter. I knew Maninder loved me and at the time, that's all I took into account.

His dad, however, took matters into his own hands. He believed that his daughter-in-law should have an engagement ring, and he felt relieved once he brought me one from India! Yes, that's right – India! Maninder had shown them the Tiffany ring that I had chosen and his dad thought while he was out in India he would get a copy of the design made – and got matching wedding bands too.

After the shopping trip, my aunt from Derby and Gurleen joined us and we headed back to my family home. We had an appointment with a florist and my aunt, mother and I were attending but Maninder's parents somehow decided to come along too. They were forceful and controlling; they never wanted to miss out on any little thing. Gurleen started taking her parents' side by explaining that it was normal for them to go to the appointment with us, as this was what her in-laws had done with her during her wedding preparations.

The appointment had been made to see if I would like to book this lovely florist that I had met at the wedding exhibition and whether she was in my price range. While I was around Maninder's parents I found it physically tiring to even speak about what I wanted. I didn't even have time to stop and think! The florist showed me her work and there was no denying that I wanted to book her; however, my in-laws once again explained what they would like to have on the wedding day and how grand their daughter's wedding was a couple of years ago. They told the florist what high standards they expected from her.

This lovely lady was from a very educated family, and she lived on a private estate in a house that had electric gates. From what I could see, her standards were very high, even higher than theirs. Her guest living room was the same size as the entire ground floor space of their home.

The only thing that went through my head was to think before I spoke to my in-laws. This lady was lovely, warm, very welcoming and helpful. She could see the pressure they were putting us under and a number of times she advised me to take some time to think things through before I made any plans. This was one of the reasons I liked her; she'd been very honest and helpful at the event too. She had even given me tips on how to save some money and get jobs done myself. We left there without a booking, but wanting to have time to think things over.

Mother and I went home, once again astonished by Maninder's parents' behaviour. I was so distraught that Maninder and I ended up arguing! He believed I wasn't respecting his parents' feelings but all they wanted to do was take over. How about my feelings? I was stressing about the budget of the wedding and now they wanted an engagement party too. What else is going to pop out of the blue? I thought.

I'd had enough of his parents making snarky comments and getting their way, and also taking advantage of my mother. Maninder and I got so deep into the argument that the only thing that seemed realistic was if we ended our relationship. I gave him the option to completely end it over the phone, but his dad heard the tail end of our conversation and grabbed the phone off Maninder. He told me I may have said something that I would regret later so he was going to cut the call off. Maninder explained to his dad that I felt I couldn't continue the relationship with him, and that the only thing stopping me from finishing with Maninder was the fact that we had been intimate with each other before marriage; he said that was the one thing that kept pulling me back to him.

That evening, his dad called me and explained that he was off to India in the morning to complete our wedding shopping and that our fallout had stressed him out. I, however, felt at peace for the first time, for I no longer had them pestering me about the details of the wedding.

BREAKING AWAY FROM THE WEDDING

That moment when I ended things with Maninder made me realise that I could breathe and think for myself without asking if I was allowed to. That's how Maninder and his parents made me feel – but now I could inhale and exhale air without feeling the pressure of breathing or having to gasp. However, I was concerned that Maninder and I had slept with each other – and whether he would use that against me. This is how it happened.

During the wedding planning, Maninder suggested that we take a break and focus on us for a change. I felt as though we were both ready to take our relationship further as we had become a lot more comfortable with one another.

One Sunday afternoon Maninder arrived at my family home to take me out. I got into his car and he seemed very excited as he greeted me. "Hi Maninder," I said nervously. "So what's the plan for today then?"

"I have booked us a hotel room," he said.

"OK. So what are we going to do there then?" I asked.

"Well, we can relax and enjoy each other's company," Maninder replied. There was a naughty atmosphere in the car, like I was an angel and Maninder my devil. We both started telling each other how we were going to help each other relax.

We arrived at the hotel, which was just outside Birmingham. Maninder led the way and I followed him as he checked us in at reception. We flirted all the way into the room. Once we were there, Maninder looked at me and started to redden. I felt very nervous, but I allowed Maninder, my handsome, tall Punjabi fiancé, to take my hand. We sat down on the bed and Maninder leaned forwards towards me and started making love to me for the very first time. It reminded me of that Madonna song. "Like a virgin, touched for the very first time".

This was the reality of why I couldn't just walk out of this relationship. I decided to work at things and stay with him.

I knew that Maninder's dad didn't know we had slept together so I decided to call him and his son. However, I was already starting to feel crushed again through the pressure of the wedding. Whatever I did, I just couldn't shift this deep sick feeling in my stomach. In my gut, I knew that being with Maninder was not a great idea, but I thought it was best to work at things rather than walk away.

Perhaps I was missing the bridal genes. I loved Maninder – that was why I'd said yes when he proposed to me. I felt like a bad person for even suggesting I end the relationship. I questioned whether it would be happy ever after. Of course, it would, I kept telling myself. I felt a sense of freedom once I heard the answer from my own mouth. Was I ever going to feel that great again?

I called Maninder, feeling nervous. When he answered the call, he sounded calm and collected. "Maninder," I started, "I just want to say this to you. When I first met you, I was very fond of you and in true earnest, I found you to be the most delightful human being. My heart melted and I felt I'd found my ideal match. You were everything I wanted in a man, and you made me feel like I was the most beautiful, important woman in the world."

"I love you," Maninder replied. "I care for you a great

deal. We need to remember why we got together, Harleen."

I agreed with him and we ended the phone call. It was the shortest call ever. Normally we would be on the phone for hours.

CHRISTMAS EVE WITH MANINDER AND THE LADIES IN HIS HOUSEHOLD

Maninder's dad had gone to India and Maninder and I had not spoken for over a week. He had decided to have laser eye surgery while his dad was out of the country, as he didn't approve of the operation. It didn't really bother me. I liked Maninder exactly as he was, and he knew how I felt about him. He told me that he had stopped playing some sports as his glasses got in the way, and I said I would support him with his decision.

He later called me to ask if I would attend one of his appointments with him and I agreed, as I wanted to get a better understanding of what was involved in the surgery and aftercare. This surgery was only three months before the wedding and I wondered if there would be any complications in recovery.

Taking the train to Milton Keynes, I couldn't help but feel confused and lost in my own whirlwind of thoughts. I had ended things with Maninder a week ago yet we were back on again. I couldn't explain how I felt – not bad or good, just blank, like a piece of unwritten paper. I felt no joy to see him but no sense of loss either. I was just getting on with things by attending this appointment with him; I wanted somehow to prove to him that I cared about him.

After the appointment, we sat in a bar and reflected on what had happened. I tried to talk open-heartedly but soon gave up, as I felt he would just dismiss what I was going to say. There was no point expressing my feelings to him; I was just made to believe I was a little snobby girl who had, a tantrum. I felt I was bending in every direction for Maninder and his family, but all the bending was going unnoticed and I just couldn't be bothered any more, other than to just get on with things. We were not getting along and at that moment I wondered if that was all I'd ever be doing – getting on with things...

On Christmas Eve, I had a half day at work and Maninder picked me up, even though he was not meant to be driving following his laser surgery. I was looking forward to spending the day with him – and his grandma and mum! This was going to be a bit weird as I had not spent time alone with Maninder's grandma and mum in the same room for more than 10 minutes, yet today I was going to be spending the afternoon and evening with them.

It was strange seeing Maninder without his glasses, and his eyes were bloodshot red because of the surgery. It looked as if he was so angry that the blood had shot into his eyes; it was a scary look! I had put together a box of Christmas goodies, full of surprises to put a smile on his pained face.

Maninder's Amritpal *Bee Ji*, Simranjit Mum, Maninder and I were going to have our first Christmas Eve meal together. This gave me some time to get to know the Purewal women in his household. It was lovely to have a meal with them and chill out. I decided to give Maninder his presents, but his mum stopped him from opening the box and said it would be lovely for us to open our presents together at my mother's place when they dropped me off in Birmingham.

After the meal, Maninder took me home and we all exchanged presents. Maninder had explained earlier that he had not got me anything but I spotted that his mum had noticed I'd brought him a present and decided to give me something from her home – not just anything, but a Marks and Spencer watch that she'd pulled out of the bottom drawer in her bedroom! My face was a picture when I opened the little black box, and all I could think of was the Marks and Spencer adverts, especially the Christmas ones.

Then I waved them goodbye as Maninder and his mum travelled back to their house. I didn't see Maninder much over the festive season as we were both busy doing other things – plus he was also recovering from his laser eye treatment.

NEW YEAR'S DAY: THREE MONTHS UNTIL THE WEDDING

New Year: the beginning of a fresh new year of our lives together. I had an appointment at the wedding register office in Sandwell on 3rd January at 4.30pm. I visited a beautiful grade 2 listed building in West Bromwich, which was absolutely stunning. Maninder and I had decided we would have our civil ceremony there on the same day as our *Laava* (**https://en.wikipedia.org/wiki/Laavaan**) in the *gurdwara*. This appointment was for me to give notice of marriage, a legal necessity before you get married or form a civil partnership.

Notices are displayed on the public notice boards at Sandwell Register Office for 15 days. After 15 days, the paperwork you need to get married or form a civil partnership is issued. A Notice of Marriage is valid for 12 months. Couples must collect this paperwork from the Register Office before their ceremony.

Once this process was complete I went back to collect the paperwork and dropped it off at the *gurdwara* with my mother.

THE STORY OF THE WEDDING BANDS

I got a phone call from Maninder. His voice was full of excitement mixed with nerves. I wasn't sure what was going on. He asked me if he could drive over to Birmingham on Saturday afternoon to meet me. Maninder hated driving to Birmingham, even more so on a busy Saturday; whatever it was, it had to be very important. I felt a little nervous, and curious. I was sorting out other bits and bobs for the wedding but agreed to meet him and asked if he would pick me up from my family home.

I noticed him park up and I walked towards his car and got into the passenger seat. Curious now, I asked what was up. He looked at me happily and presented me with my engagement ring and our matching wedding bands! I was in even more shock than when I received the Tiffany box. I could do nothing more than break down and start crying my heart out.

His sister had warned him not to show me the rings as she thought it would upset me – and I could understand why. She had told him that I would be hurt because the ring was small and tacky, but it was by far the ugliest monster rock I had ever seen. The wedding bands were not understated either.

I just couldn't believe the joke that had been made of the situation; I was exhausting myself just thinking about it. I wanted to walk away every time a 'wonderful' event like this happened and Maninder and his parents showed me their ugly side.

Why couldn't this family just accept that I didn't want to have an engagement ring at all? I had already found the one I wanted; why couldn't they just accept that I had compromised with Maninder that I'd wait five years to get the one I liked. Why did I have to have an engagement ring right now to show off to the Asian society? Did they think the size of the rock on my finger would make people think I was happy in my relationship?

Maninder could see I was hurt and he let me leave the car. I couldn't even talk to him. Yet again Maninder's parents had caused another upsetting situation between Maninder and me.

The following weekend we were going to a friend's birthday party and we had time during the day to pop into the Jewellery Quarter to look for some lovely simple plain wedding bands. We looked around together but a part of me had really closed down on Maninder. It seemed like whenever I spoke to him there was an odd silence, as if he didn't want to listen to me; he made out like he was being forced to shop for wedding bands. We started arguing yet again, as he felt I was being ungrateful for the rings that his parents had bought.

I didn't ask his parents to get my engagement ring and our wedding bands from India and do an Indian Del Boy job on them! Being a designer, I had taken the design of the rings into account rather than whether they were platinum, gold or silver. We both had to wear something we agreed on, and as I didn't wear jewellery generally I wanted my wedding band to be simple, not complicated – the relationship itself was doing all of that aspect for me.

After looking and arguing for a few hours, we had both had enough of each other. We walked back to the car still arguing, blissfully unaware of the silent watchers-on. When we got into the car Maninder decided to teach me a lesson by threatening to drive the car into a wall. Yes – into the wall! I was frightened at this point. I had to get out of the car. I couldn't imagine this was normal behaviour. I was crying and gasping as I ran away from him.

Maninder then drove the car beside me as I walked, begging me to get back in. A part of me didn't want to get into the car but the other half of me knew that I had family waiting for us back at my mother's house. If it wasn't for the family I would have given him a lesson to remember, to teach him not to pull a stunt like that again. I got into the car and he apologised. Back at my home we both put on our happy faces and behaved like nothing had happened. We set off for the party in Nottingham and again I behaved like everything was normal – though we didn't talk.

On the drive back from Nottingham Maninder realised what he had done earlier in the day. He apologised again and I explained that if he was ever to do anything like that again I would not tolerate it. Having cleared the air between us, we both moved forward.

The following weekend we went to Lincoln. We popped into the cathedral, one of the symbols of the city. We loved it! It was a stunning piece of history, and the beautiful architecture dominated the skyline and shone through the city. Lincoln Castle was next door. There were many quaint independent shops, pubs and restaurants within easy walking distance. However, I'll never forget the steep hill into the heart of Lincoln – or the pain that went through each and every muscle in my legs while walking up the hill.

It was in one of the little shops on the steep hill that we found our wedding bands – titanium rings from a unique jewellery designer, and they only cost £90 for the pair. I was happy, and Maninder loved titanium jewellery too.

Maninder went back to the flat concrete roundabouts of Milton Keynes feeling as high as that steep hill in Lincoln, and showed his parents his wedding ring. They were shocked at our choice and couldn't believe how little the ring had cost us. I felt that Maninder's parents needed to take a leaf from my book. It might help their account balance.

A lot of things had been checked off the wedding list. Maninder's parents had gone into Birmingham to pick up his *sherwani* and they asked if they might pop over to go through some more details with my mother before the big day. We were only two months away from the wedding.

THE PUREWALS JOIN THE JOHAL FAMILY FOR A PEACEFUL MEAL

My mother invited Maninder's parents to have a Punjabi dinner with our family. After the meal, Maninder and I were standing on the landing talking when his dad asked if he may use the loo. When Maninder spotted his dad he asked him to take a look at my loft bedroom, as he had recommended a loft conversion to his parents. Every person's bedroom reflects parts of their personality, though my room at this time was in limbo between my present life and what lay ahead in my future, and some of my things were already packed in boxes. The first thing that came into Maninder's dad's view was a table with a picture of *Guru Nanak Dev Ji,* the *Guru Ji* who was the founder of Sikhism. I loved all the stories my Amirjit *Nani Ji* would tell me of *Guru Nanak Dev Ji*, who spent his entire adult life roaming the world.

His travels included the entirety of the Punjab and South East Asia, Mecca and Rome. By the time he left his *Ghadi* in 1539 he had launched a powerful movement with a radical rejection of castes, dogma, ritualism, gender inequality, and superstition. The Sikh religion's stories linked into his vision of life. In Indian society, women were usually subject to various caste rules and severe restrictions. They remained illiterate and were ill-treated. Female infanticide was often practised. *Guru Nanak Dev Ji* challenged the idea of inferiority and evil associated with women and freed them from slavery and taboos of society. In one of *Guru Nanak Dev Ji's* hymns, it quotes:

From woman, man is born; within woman, man is conceived; to a woman, he is engaged and married. Woman becomes his friend; through woman, the future generations come. When his woman dies, he seeks another woman; to woman he is bound. So why call her bad? From her, kings are born. From woman, woman is born; without woman, there would be no one at all. O Nanak, only the True Lord is without a woman. That mouth which praises the Lord continually is blessed and beautiful. O Nanak, those faces shall be radiant in the Court of the True Lord. || 2 || **(Guru Nanak Dev Ji Raag Aasaa Mehal 1, Page 473 of Sri Guru Granth Sahib Ji)**

Guru Nanak Dev Ji and his successors gave women an equal status to that of men. They regarded women as man's companion in every walk of life. The gurus thought this equality worked to their mutual benefit. For example, a woman is the first teacher of man as his mother. Her function is to mould children and discipline them.

She has to be educated so that her children may develop their potential to the fullest. She was allowed to join holy congregations, participate and conduct them. They were appointed missionaries. They were called 'the conscience of man'. The practice of Sati (the custom of burning a woman with the dead husband on the funeral pyre) was prohibited and widow remarriage was encouraged. Women soldiers fought side by side with male soldiers in one of the battles which the tenth *Guru Ji (Guru Gobind Singh Ji)* fought.

In the Sikh way of life, women have equal rights with men. There is absolutely no discrimination against women. Women are entitled to the *Khalsa* baptism. (In Sikhism, the *Khalsa* is considered to be the brotherhood of the pure and is an order of spiritual warriors or saint soldiers. **Sikhism.about.com/od/glossary/g/khalsa-pure.htm).**

They have equal rights to participate in social, political and religious activities. Women are allowed to lead religious congregations, to take part in the recitation of the Holy Scriptures, to fight as soldiers in the war, to elect representatives to the *gurdwara* committees, Indian Parliament and Provincial Assembly.

Sikh women have played a glorious part in history, and examples of their moral dignity, service and upholding of Sikh values are a great source of inspiration. Sikh women never flinch from their duty, never allow their faith and ardour to be dampened, and have always upheld the honour and glory of the *Khalsa*.

Ganesha Ji is considered the master of intellect and wisdom. I first fell in love with *Ganesha Ji* while at college, when someone told me a beautiful story that highlights the spiritual insight that is so typical of *Ganesha Ji*.

Ganesha Ji and *Kartikeya Ji*, both sons of Lord Shiva and Parvati, entered a contest to see who could go around the universe the fastest and was thus the most befitting to temporarily replace *Shiva* and *Shakti*. While *Kartikeya Ji* rushed off on his peacock, *Ganesha Ji* walked around his parents at leisure, declaring the universe to be nothing more or less than *Shiva* and *Parvati*. All deities applauded him and *Ganesha Ji* wins for me; my mother was my universe.

This is why I grew to love *Ganesha Ji* and had a picture of *Maharaja* Charan Singh *Ji*, which was given to me by my Jaskiranjit *Masi Ji*. *Maharaja* Charan Singh *Ji* teaches *Sant Mat* (the science of the soul) and *surat shabd yoga* in *Dera*, India. It teaches transcendental meditation focusing on the 'third eye' in the forehead region.

I found that *Maharaja* Charan Singh *Ji's* teaching in *sant mat* was the essence of the *Sri Guru Granth Sahib Ji* – there is one god of all creations, though people worship the lord by different names and through different practices; while *Sant Mat* repeats all faiths, it stresses that religion has two dimensions, outer and inner. **(www.sos.org/page/sant-mat.html)**. 'The Science of the Soul', a book I had read during my first summer of university holidays, helped direct me towards meditation. This was a book given to my mother by my Jaskarnjit *Masi Ji* and I ended up reading it and loving what it gave me. I am a Sikh, but not a baptised Sikh. I believe if I find something beautiful and I understand it, I will adapt that beauty into my life. I am not at all religious, but I find peace in Sikhism and other beautiful faiths too.

I also remember meeting the *Maharaja* Charan Singh *Ji*, when we went to *Dera Beas* in India. Every morning *Maharaja* Charan Singh *Ji* would drive through the *dera* (a place in India) in his car and welcome everybody who had been standing on the edge of the streets waiting to catch a glimpse of him and feel his beautiful soul, which you could see in his eyes. I remember attending one of his morning *Satsang* (prayer sessions) while there with my Mother on holiday.

When Maninder's dad saw my bedroom, his mood changed dramatically. It was a bit like those Punjabi dramas on Asian TV when the cameraman captures someone's reaction from several different angles and some drums play in the background. Both Maninder and I couldn't help but notice it, but I was clueless as to what was going on. His dad left my bedroom, went straight downstairs into the dining room and sat on the sofa like he had lost his voice; his head bowed down to his body as if he was upset.

Everybody started noticing his aura and couldn't understand what was going on. As Maninder's parents had come to talk with my mother, I thought it had something to do with that. I cracked a few jokes about him losing his voice but it did not help to shift his mood at all. Then everybody sat at the dining table to have a home cooked Punjabi meal, and he asked if I would sit next to him with Maninder on the opposite side.

Maninder's dad turned to me and asked what faith I was.

"What's that meant to mean?" I asked.

He replied: "Why do you have so many images in your room that belong to other faiths? I want my grandkids to belong to the Sikh faith."

The shock on the faces of my mother and me was a picture.

I couldn't believe that viewing my room had turned into a conversation about my faith. I felt that I didn't need to prove anything to anybody, and I asked him what he would like it to be. Sikhism, he said. I replied: "Well that's what it is if that's what makes you happy." He gave me a disgruntled look and then started going on about how if Maninder and my views on faith were not the same there would be complications when we had kids.

He tried to stress how important it was to him. Then he turned to my mother and explained that they hadn't been aware that my *Masi Ji* was RS *(Radha Soami)*. I couldn't believe the nerve of it – yet the best was still to come.

The problem Maninder's dad had after seeing my bedroom was he was left feeling confused about my acceptance of multiple religious faiths; he had a moment of doubt that I may choose not to bring their grandkids up into Sikhism. What threw him was *Ganesha Ji's* statue and my picture of *Maharaja* Charan Singh *Ji*. However, if I was to marry a non-Sikh I would allow my child to have my heritage and understanding of my background, so why was there a problem here?

However, he started talking about the wedding details. The number of guests had gone from 350 to 500 thanks to Maninder's parents inviting a few more muppets from Sesame Street that they probably didn't even know or get on with – but wanted to show off to about our wedding. They were making it into an exhibition for all to view. This was turning into something I had never wished for and was a far cry from the simple wedding I so wanted.

WHO PAYS FOR THE WEDDING THESE DAYS?

As you probably know, tradition has it that the girl's family pays for the majority of the wedding costs. The girl's side also needs to offer a dowry in the form of property, jewellery and money. Historically, the dowry in India was not what we think it to be today. Some historians question its very existence. Others thought it to be security for the bride, effectively the taking of her inheritance as she left her Father's house. Although the dowry was legally prohibited in 1961, it continues to be highly institutionalised. The groom often demands a dowry consisting of a large sum of money, furniture, gold jewellery and electronics.

The daughter is seen as a burden, therefore there needs to be an incentive offered to a prospective groom to take the girl. And the grooms' families were only too happy to be incentivised. Romantic, huh? The financial stress can be overwhelming for the parents of the bride. I know some parents, with adult grandchildren, who are still paying for the dowry. That's two parents. Can you imagine how it was for mymMother; my single mother?

Tradition dictates that this bride's family covers the cost of the following goods and services:

- Four different events prior to the wedding, catering for between 70 and 120 people
- Cash and gifts to maternal uncles – nine, in my case
- The bridal dress, make-up, hair and nails
- Wedding day jewellery – mine was to be a twenty-four karat gold jewellery set

- All the *milni* (introductions) gifts for the groom's family
- The *gurdwara* ceremony and the preceding breakfast for between 500/600 attendees
- The entire cost of the reception:
- venue hire
- video and photography
- a three course meal
- all beverages – from soft drinks to whisky, beer, Bacardi etc.
- decorations for the room and on every table
- flowers
- a chocolate fountain with staff
- security at the venue
- A tropical fruit display bar
- the wedding cake …and (not to forget)
- the red carpet for a grand entrance

All this for 550 people.

The groom's family, on the other hand, are traditionally responsible for the following:

- Entertainment, hiring the DJ and *dhol* players
- Photography and videography
- Honeymoon
- Wedding gift for bride and groom

Tradition has not been financially kind to the bride's family. Thankfully times have changed. Tradition has developed. The modern way is for families (and sometimes the bride and groom) to share the expense rather than burden one family with practically the entire cost of a wedding.

But Maninder's parents weren't about the modern way.

No. They had no desire to share the wedding costs. They were quite content taking the traditional boy's side and ripping off the girl's family. Yet they were the ones with highly paid jobs, the big house by the lake and the love affair with all things Marks and Spencer. They had never missed an opportunity to remind my mother how successful they were, how they were living the middle-class immigrant dream, rising above a lot of the common or garden Punjabi. So successful yet more mean-spirited than the humblest Punjabi families of Smethwick, families who would give you food off their plate. Yet the Purewals, pompous and puffed up as they were, didn't even offer to share any of the weddings costs. Well, why would they? It's the girl's side's duty to give to the boy's side in the Punjabi culture. They had done the same for their daughter's wedding and had given so much to their son-in- law Loveneet's family.

MODERN DAY DOWRY LOVERS

We had agreed on a wedding list of 350 guests. But the Purewals decided that wasn't enough. They wanted 550 people. With the increased numbers came increased costs, none of which the groom's side were footing. So more stress for my mother and me. To cap it all, Maninder's dad then had the audacity to ask my mother for twenty-four karat gold jewellery to be given to the main members of the Purewal family. I bit my lip but my blood pressure had risen to its highest point ever. I was ready to explode. I gave my mother a look across the table. I had taken so much from Maninder's parents, so much – but no more. I had to intervene.

As I started to speak Maninder cut me off. "Harleen, the parents are talking. I think it's best if we don't disturb them."

This was the man who I was going to be marrying. He just sat there watching his parents hang my mother out to dry; the two Purewal parents bullying my single parent mother, trying to get as much out of her as they could. I thought the tradition of dowry had gone out of the window, but not in this family's case. They wanted to squeeze as much as they could out of my mother. And having almost doubled the size of the wedding they had the nerve to ask for gold. That was the most hurtful thing they could have done. My groom was now worth twenty-four karat gold. His parents should have entered with a goldsmith's catalogue and selected the jewellery themselves. And all the while my groom sat and listened while his parents prompted, prodded and pushed my mother. I was powerless, an onlooker allowing that behaviour to carry on.

They had crossed every line that I could ever imagine; I had seen every colour of the rainbow of this relationship. But right now the sky overhead was slate grey and a storm was coming. I knew I had to stand up to them. They could not be allowed to get away with this. After the Purewals left, my mother was defined by disappointment. She looked bowed and broken. They had turned her strength into submission. I decided it was my turn to talk…

I called my future father-in-law to be and made him understand that my mother was giving them an educated daughter. My mother had supported me through university. Not only did I have a degree but I had a good job, a well-paid job that would add to the value of their household. And while these things might be perceived as 'modern' qualities, I had a strong traditional skill set. I could cook all kinds of Punjabi food, a wide variety from vegetarian to meat dishes. I was a great mix of both eastern and western cultures. I felt they needed to be reminded of my qualities; I had to sell my skills and qualities to prove my worth. Painful though it was, I had to present myself to them in the rather crass terms they understood. I was on a roll. I kept going. I mentioned to my future father-in-law that the number of guests had increased at their insistence, therefore they should contribute towards the wedding costs. He said he would need to discuss it with my future mother-in-law. Before coming off the phone my future mother-in-law, through her husband, decided to gently remind me that I was going to be upgrading to a better area code. I had to bear that in mind. I wasn't aware that grooms were measured by their area codes… What a way to define the perfect *ristha* (relationship). According to my future mother-in-law, I was clearly out of my depth; Maninder was my upgrade. Mr Purewal hung up. I felt as though I was closing the biggest business deal of my life. I was nothing but nerves.

As promised, my future father-in-law phoned back. He informed me that they would like to contribute £5,000 towards the wedding reception. I was pleased to tell my mother the news. I also decided to talk to my mother and Amirjit *Nanaa Ji* about the gold jewellery that Maninder's parents had asked for. I explained very respectfully that they should give nothing to Maninder's family. I warned them that if they went against my will I would simply walk away from this marriage. To put it nicely, it was either my way or the highway.

Bless my Amirjit *Nanaa Ji,* she told me horror stories she'd heard over the years about girls being mistreated by their in-laws if they didn't give the dowry gifts that were demanded. I couldn't care less – I knew I had to find the strength to deal with this. I wasn't going to hide or run away from the problem.

OUR FIRST VALENTINE'S DAY TOGETHER

The week of our first Valentine's Day I was working. I knew that Maninder and I had different views on planning this wedding, but finally we were getting on better. We were just six weeks away from our big day so I thought he would have made an effort. Not for the first time, I was wrong.

He claimed to have forgotten that it was Valentine's Day. In this day and age, it's impossible to miss Valentine's Day. Even those who abhor the global consumerism that defines this age can't plead ignorance about the plethora of pink, the ubiquity of over-priced roses and the general free market representation of romance. But he had forgotten about it; either that or he didn't want to spend any money, being the miserly Punjabi he was. He didn't seem to think it was necessary to make an impression any more. The prize had been won. The game was over. I'd already agreed to marry him.

At the start of the relationship, Maninder would go out of his way to surprise me with little treats. I didn't hear from him all day; I wondered what was going on.

During the day, I had three calls come through to my desk phone asking me to come down to reception to collect some beautiful red roses full of love. Each time I got the phone call I thought a bouquet of flowers had arrived for me. Each time I arrived to collect the flowers I discovered they were for my colleagues. None for me. I decided to call him on the way home to ask if everything was okay. He seemed off with me – and there was no 'on' button. I was making so much effort to please him and all he could do was question why I was getting so upset over wanting attention from my future husband.

I called him later that evening and explained that I was not going to have him treat me like a doormat, that he needed to start respecting me. I knew I was beginning to sound like a broken record, craving to be fixed by him. Disappointment and hurt seemed to cloud my love for him.

COLLECTING MY WEDDING LEHENGA

The special morning had arrived: the morning that I was to collect my wedding *lehenga*, the outfit that perfectly brought out my feminine grace. I pushed all my problems and stress below the surface – today was all about the *lehenga*. It was heavily embellished with Swarovski stones and intricate embroidery in elegant, coloured threads. This *lehenga* was all about grace and nobility. I loved it! Upon arriving at the shop I was told I would have to wait for my *lehenga* to be completed. I sat patiently and waited.

That evening Maninder had booked us tickets for a play about a newly-wed couple living with their in-laws. The play was called 'Rafta, Rafta' and was based on actual British Asian marriages. I was running late from collecting my outfit and the final fitting, so Maninder came to Green Street to pick me up and take me to the theatre. We had decided that for one evening we would chill out and not mention the wedding and so not have to argue.

However, our plans changed as soon as I got in Maninder's car with my lovely outfit in its white covered bag. He had cancelled the tickets for that evening and re-arranged for us to attend the show in the Milton Keynes Theatre at the end of February. We decided to walk down Green Street, which was another mini India, a livelier, bigger version of Soho Road in Birmingham.

We walked and talked. Maninder wanted to know why it had taken so long to pick up my *lehenga*. I told him I had to have it altered. He Mumbled something about them not being able to measure me properly the first time. I explained that since my initial fitting three months earlier,

I'd dropped almost two inches around my waist. The stress was clearly having an effect.

MOTHER AND NANI JI SEE MY WEDDING LEHENGA FOR THE FIRST TIME

When I got home I went upstairs immediately and put my *lehenga* on. I knew that my Amirjit *Nani Ji* and Mother would want to see it. I was so excited to share the feeling of happiness and satisfaction with my family. As I walked into my mother's bedroom where they both sat, my Amirjit *Nani Ji's* eyes filled up with tears. They couldn't believe how breathtakingly beautiful my outfit was.

Of course, my Amirjit *Nani Ji* started crying. This set my mother off. And predictably I joined in, creating an ocean of tears with them. It was sink or swim. Realisation dawned. I would be getting married in a few weeks; I would be leaving my family. Planning the wedding had been so stressful that I hadn't had time to think about leaving my loved ones until this moment in my mother's bedroom.

I stood in my wedding *lehenga* in front of my Amirjit *Nani Ji* and Mother, who sat on the edge of the bed like Britain's Got Talent judges. There were no red crosses here! I knew that I'd won this panel's hearts.

MY NANI JI AND MOTHERS WEDDING DAYS

We all sat on my mother's bed, talking. Three different women, three different generations. My Amirjit *Nani Ji* told me the story of her wedding day and my Mother talked about hers. Emotions were mixed. We discussed how times have changed and with them the nature of weddings. For the Indian diaspora, everything seems to be measured by weddings getting bigger and bolder. They have definitely become a place to show off! In my Amirjit *Nani Ji's* time, weddings were very different.

Amirjit *Nani Ji* was married shortly after the Partition, when India and Pakistan became independent. Her family had left behind everything they owned in Pakistan, and her wedding was hurriedly arranged when she was just 16 years old. When she married my Charanpal *Nanaa Ji*, it was a very small, private, intimate wedding; only 20 guests attended the *Anand Karaj Laava*. The Sikh marriage took place in the middle of a *vihare* (courtyard). My Amirjit *Nani Ji* had not met my Charanpal *Nanaa Ji* until the day of their wedding.

My youngest Raspal *Masi Ji* got married to my Veer *Massar Ji* in the same way 35 years later in India in their home *vilhare* (courtyard). Their wedding had something of the simplicity of my Charanpal *Nanaa Ji's*.

Prior to marriage, my mother had only ever seen a picture of my father. They were married in the UK in the late 70s. There was the simple yet beautiful *Anand Karaj* ceremony at the Smethwick High Street *Gurdwara,* followed by a small party for the men in the local school hall. The British Punjabi Bhangra band Bhujhangy Group and the godfathers of Bhangra Balbir and Dhalbir Singh Khanpur performed live. This group was based in Smethwick, my hometown in Birmingham, and they sang a few songs while guests were served home-made chicken *tikka masalas* as a starter followed by basic home-made Punjabi meals. To drink, there was a choice of Coca-Cola, Famous Grouse Whisky, Bacardi – or any combination thereof. While the men had their party, women from both sides would be doing non-stop *gidda*, a Punjabi folk dance, at the bride and groom's house.

The neighbours knew there was a wedding going on because they could hear the *gidda* noise and the floorboards moving in the house as we *chuck de phatey* (pick the floor boards up). Such was the energetic dancing, there was every chance the ladies would end up falling through to the basement of the house. Luckily, the floorboards remained intact.

During the seventies and early eighties, wedding receptions were held at home rather than in expensive venues. They made do with what space they had – everything was accommodated for and provided by guests, from the music to the food. After the wedding, the family would distribute any leftover food to the neighbours. That's how a great deal of local Brits started appreciating our *desi* home-made cooking. Through the food, we become friends with neighbours on our roads. Punjabi women soon became known for their cooking skills rather than just for being the wife of Mr Singh.

That was the tradition back in the day. Rather than booking every little fine detail or finding wedding planners to organise it all for you, it was all organic and natural. The whole family pulled together. It's a spirit I love so I decided to get my family members to help out with some aspects of my wedding. It felt like a nice touch. It reminded me of how, back then, the people of our community really wanted to go out of their way to help and support each other. Today, everyone worries more about their expensive outfits, how good their car will look in the *gurdwara* car park and whether this wedding will put pressure on them when they have to marry their daughter off. No one thinks to help anymore.

Traditionally the groom's sisters and sister-in-law would go with the groom to collect the bride from her family home. The wedding party would be a maximum of six people and the wedding itself would have only 50 to 80 guests in total, all of whom were close family members. Nowadays the guest list can be anywhere between 350–1200 guests. Unfortunately, I was having 550 guests at my wedding.

If I was only having the *Anand Karaj* ceremony, I bet you most people wouldn't attend. Most people don't even bother with the main morning service and go straight to the reception, as that's where all the fun, laughter and partying goes on. Meat, beer and frenetic partying. And a fight. There's almost always a fight at a Punjabi wedding.

With five weeks to go until the big day, I decided to enjoy every moment I had with my family, especially with family from abroad. I only had a handful of relatives that I really got on with; I saw them rarely but adored them.

THE KURMAI CEREMONY

The *kurmai* is usually an immediate family affair. My family went to Maninder's family home and *gurdwara* carrying gifts that included sweets, clothes and money. The bride's Father or guardian – my Guruleen *Massar Ji* – gave Maninder a twenty-four karat gold *kara* (bangle). The *kare* is part of the five K's.

(https://en.wikipedia.org/wiki/The_Five_Ks) The bride-to-be is not allowed to attend the *kurmai* ceremony; it's just the family of the bride.

Before the *kurmai* ceremony, Maninder's parents called. It wasn't unexpected; there was probably a new demand in the offing. But this was a shock to us all. They asked if Maninder's *kara* could be in white gold. White gold was the latest fad and fashion; it was also a great deal more expensive. It afforded the Purewals better bragging rights. They could show off to all and sundry what their new in-laws have given their son. They'd be so jealous down at the local *gurdwara*…

I put my foot down and told my mother that Maninder was no one special. Why would she be getting him a white gold *kara?* He was no white tiger.

I heard from the family that Maninder's younger Punit *Pua Ji* and Inderjit *Fuffar Ji* weren't there. There were more friends than family there and we started to question this – especially as Maninder's parents had increased their half of the guest list, bring the total to 550 people. I thought this was because they had a big family, but all my family could see were friends of the Purewals. I didn't come from a big family; I only had my mother's relatives. Apart from a few friends, everybody on my side of the guest list were family. It all seemed rather curious…

THE CHUNNI CEREMONY

Four weeks before the big day was my *chunni* and my family were busy getting things prepared for this ceremony.

I was seriously stressed; my hair had started falling out in clumps and my skin seemed to be scarred with a stress rash. I seemed really run down all the time and felt like bursting into tears at any given moment. I didn't know what was wrong with me. Why did I feel physically and mentally drained? My mother had spoken to me about the wedding; she had questions. My head started to pound and I could feel myself getting angry. It was weird, but I just kept hoping things would somehow get better as the day approached.

I kept arguing with Maninder – I wasn't sure if he was ready to be with me the way I wanted and expected. I'll be honest – I hadn't known what to expect from a husband but now it was all fixed up, I'd realised that I wanted it all. No half measures. I wanted my husband to love me wholeheartedly, to live and breathe me, to make me a priority in his life. I didn't want a *chamacha* (spoon); I could never respect a man who didn't have his own identity, ambitions and independence. Like any other girl, I wanted my husband to cherish me and form a beautiful commitment. Maninder seemed to accept the fun bit of being a good future husband and left all the responsibilities on my head or his parents'. He didn't seem to appreciate me and sometimes he treated me like I was just there to fulfil his dreams and make him happy. Although I loved him and wanted to make him happy, I felt like my happiness had taken a back seat, moved to the back of his heart. Resentment started colouring my every mood.

I just didn't know how to be any more. He was so laid back about everything; he was carrying on like normal, enjoying himself like he was still a lad. Then he'd have a go at me for being too uptight and stressed. I wished I could be more like him and leave everything to everybody else, take no responsibility for the wedding. But I had to be the responsible one otherwise we would have no wedding day at all. I just felt like everything was getting on top of me and I wished I could press the pause button on my life and escape for a while until my head was straight. It seemed that, just when I'd got over one obstacle, another was waiting for me. Was it going to get better?

On the evening before the *chunni* ceremony, I got a call from Maninder to tell me that his Amritpal *Bee Ji* had a heart attack and he was on his way to the hospital to see her.

My mother called his parents to see how the Amritpal *Bee Ji* was getting on. She told them Maninder's grandmother's health was more important than the *chunni* ceremony, and she understood if they wanted to cancel the ceremony. However, they decided to go ahead. They informed my mother that because of Amritpal *Bee Ji's* condition, neither of Maninder's *Pau Jis* or their families would be attending the *chunni* ceremony. Overall, there would be fewer people – about the same number as attended the *shagan*. There were more new faces, faces that I had never before seen. Jaspreet, Loveneet's sister, came along. It was a lovely private event and I felt very comfortable with the ceremony.

The *chunni* ceremony cements Maninder as my official fiancé. This ceremony involved Maninder's family visiting my family's home and bringing gifts. It's the usual Punjabi stuff: fruit, Indian sweets, *meva* (dry fruit) and a complete outfit for me. Some families opt to bring many more gifts, although this is neither expected nor necessary.

Maninder's sister Gurleen and her sister-in-law Jaspreet presented me with a lovely red Punjabi-style suit. Gurleen then helped me get dressed in the new clothes, matching cosmetics and nail varnish. I was head to toe in red... full of deep love from the Purewal family.

Once dressed, I was brought back to the main room where all the guests had congregated. Maninder and I were seated together, which is when the crucial ritual of the *chunni charauna* ceremony takes place. Maninder's mum placed on my head a red *chunni*, matching my outfit. Then she and other significant women from Maninder's family adorned me with other gifts. I was showered with glass bangles in red, green and gold. I was also given another traditional gold jewellery set; again, this was something I would not be able to wear. It would weigh me down and hurt my neck and my arm. Gurleen and Jaspreet put *mendhi* (henna) on my hands. Maninder's Father put a handful of *meva* (dry fruit) into my *jholi* (lap). Maninder's parents fed me a whole dry date.

Maninder put *sindoor* (vermillion) on my head; on some occasions the groom would put the engagement ring on the girl's finger, hence this being the official engagement. This was a very sensitive topic for both of us and thankfully there was no engagement ring! Thank God they didn't pop out with the one that he had presented me with earlier in the year.

The parents gave *shagan* to both of us. Then we were fed a *ladoo*, the king of kings when it comes to Punjabi sweet things. The rest of the family imitated paparazzi as they flashed away, capturing forever on smartphones this age-old moment of intimacy!

I knew that I would get extremely emotional when I left with my *doli*. I pictured myself sobbing away uncontrollably on my wedding day. I'd need to make sure my mascara was waterproof.

I was close to my mother and I had a few moments where I filled up and wanted to cry, but I managed to control myself.

RETURN OF THE GOLD TO THE MOTHER-IN-LAW AND ANOTHER LIST COMPLETED

After the *chunni* ceremony, Maninder and his mum were in Birmingham to pick up his wedding outfit and they came to visit us at my family home. My future Mother-in-law had given me some of her Punjabi suits to take to the local dry cleaner and they were ready for collection.

Once tea was served my mother asked Maninder's mum which of her family members were to receive Punjabi suits at the *shagan*. Our family were to gift them to the Purewals. She sat down with my mother and Amirjit *Nani Ji* and gave them a list of everyone that should be given a suit. This wasn't the first list she or her husband had given us; it was one of many lists. It had become normal for them to ask for things or give my mother lists – and not once had she politely declined! We were the girl's side; we were compelled to respect the boy's side and fulfil their needs.

Then something quite unexpected happened. For all my mother's polite acceptance of events, she pulled a master stroke. My mother briefly left the room, returning with an old battered briefcase. She opened it. It was full of all the jewellery I had been given during the build up to my wedding. She handed it over to Maninder's mum.

"Here is the jewellery you have given Harleen for the wedding, *Pehn Ji*. We would be grateful if you would take it back. It belongs to you; it's your responsibility, *Pehn Ji*."

This was news to me! Technically the jewellery had been given to me but I had no issue with it being handed back. Neither my Amirjit *Nani Ji* nor my mother had to ask my permission as far as I was concerned. I had been brought up to respect the decisions that my mother and Amirjit *Nani Ji* made, so I firmly stood by them.

My future mother-in-law smiled as she placed all the heavy twenty-four karat gold jewellery into her bag. Her skin glowed with all that gold ... She was the queen bee (although more like a wasp with a sting in its tail). Ten minutes later they left. This was the shortest visit Maninder and his mum had ever made to my house. The jewellery and gifts didn't matter to us. However, my mother said it was important to keep their respect by accepting the jewellery at each ceremony and then returning it. I saw her point of view.

TRY TO TREAT OTHERS AS YOU WOULD WANT THEM TO TREAT YOU

A week later Maninder and I were talking on the phone. He mentioned the return of the gold jewellery and made some flippant remark about how he hoped it wasn't because they didn't want to gift his family with the gold his dad had, had the nerve to ask for earlier in the year.

I was more than a little annoyed. "If you want to make demands of my mother and me," I said, "I too can make demands."

"What do you mean, demands?" he said, sounding agitated.

"I thought that the boy's side was meant to give the girl a gold teka?" A *teka* is a piece of ornate head jewellery that a bride wears on her wedding day. Why had his parents not gifted me with one?

Maninder got upset.

He hung up on me.

He ran and told his mum.

Guess who called soon after? I couldn't be patient any more. If they were going to throw their weight around, I would too. I was worth more than twenty-four karat gold. I could make them feel the weight that they had been heaping on my mother's shoulders.

I asked Maninder's mum when they were going to give me my twenty-four karat gold *teka*. My future mother-in-law was outwardly shocked. I imagined her on the other end of the phone, like one of those women in Asian drama series. The bombshell drops; the camera zooms in from every angle. The music heightens. She screams an aggressive *"Naaaahhhhhhiiiii!"* I hoped she would now understand how she made my mother feel when they had the nerve to ask her for gold jewellery.

She couldn't believe I had the courage to ask such a question, and she asked to speak with my mother. Luckily, Mother was out. I heard that she came off the call with a face that resembled the night sky over Chernobyl. Apparently she had a long conversation with her own mum, Kanchan *Nani Ji*, who was over from Canada, and Maninder before calling my mother on her mobile. When Mother returned from shopping she asked me what I had said to my lovely future mother-in-law. I told her about the conversation with Maninder and that I had decided to ask for a *teka*.

My mother was deeply upset by my behaviour. She took me to the local Asian jewellery store to pick out a *teka*. I broke down in the store and told her how I felt about Maninder's parents asking for jewellery all the time, about how they had hurt my feelings. My Amirjit *Nani Ji* and my mother both told me that I should have expressed my feelings to them first before saying anything to Maninder or his mum.

I realised I had made the situation worse, operating at their level. My mother said that if I didn't choose a *teka* now they would think she couldn't afford to get me one, which was why I so desperately asked them for one. She begged me to select one, otherwise she was going to pick one for me. She didn't see that I'd asked for the *teka* hoping they would understand the pressure they were putting my mother and me under, not because I wanted a piece of jewellery from them.

Later that evening my future mother-in-law called and informed my mother that they would pay for the *teka* at a cost of £400. Till this day they've never mentioned the money again, nor paid back my mother. Once again it was all for show – and my mother allowed our entire family to think that Maninder's parents bought my *teka*. Why do us old school Punjabis readily elevate the boy's side and place them on a pedestal? It's all "Yes sir, no sir, three bags full sir." Why do we do that in our culture?

During the call, Maninder's mum also made another demand for the jewellery they would like my mother to give their family members. I gently reminded my mother and Amirjit *Nani Ji* what I had said would happen if any gold jewellery was gifted to them. I had never before met people like them. I couldn't understand their broad daylight hypocrisy. They were upset about my behaviour but never took their own into account. Up to the day of the wedding, they carried on asking my mother for more things lastminute.com.

PUNJABI WEDDINGS: A BRIGHT AND COLOURFUL EVENT IN ONE'S LIFE

I had booked three and a half weeks off work for the wedding and honeymoon, starting on the Wednesday before the big weekend.

The Indian wedding is spread over many days and marked by rituals and celebrations. It is not just a matter of one day but a grand affair. There are many customs to be followed before, during and even after the wedding. These customs differ according to the different states, religions, castes and cultures. In the Punjabi culture, marriage is an event full of merriment, fun, music, songs, colours and sweets. A lot of sweets.

The first ceremony took place the weekend before with the *khorai* (outside catering for traditional Indian wedding). Back in the day at our family weddings, all the ladies would get together to cook Indian sweets and savoury nibbles for the wedding guests. However, we are in the 21st century now; all the women have full-time jobs. No one has time to travel or take time off work to make *Jalebi's*. My mother booked the *gurdwara* kitchen and hired a group of lovely older *Bibi Jis* from the *gurdwara* to help, joined by my Jaskarnjit *Masi Ji* and two of my mother's friends. They did most of the cooking. I had to be there to help out as it was for my wedding. Another group of ladies from the Kent branch of the family got together and did the rest of the cooking. Those Kentish Punjabans make the best home-made *ladoo* sweets. Yum!

On the first day of my holiday, I booked myself into a

spa to get pampered like an Indian princess. It was lovely to take time out and relax. On my way back to the house I finally felt like it was my wedding. You know there's a wedding when the fairy lights come out and you get served your *dhal sabzi* (vegetable curry) on a plastic *thal* (plate). Let the good times roll...

I had an average of four hours of sleep a day for the entire weekend... Needless to say, the guests and I would feel a bit drained once this festive occasion was over.

It was an all-nighter for my cousins from Canada and me. All the girls were sleeping in my bedroom and we had a great deal of catching up to do. Thanks to Raman, Raj and Dips and my two other cousins Pee and Jas, we had a lot of fun. Friday morning rolled on and it was my first *Vatna/Maiya ceremony. Halad* (turmeric paste) is applied to your body before you bathe in preparation for your wedding day. This ceremony is carried out by family friends and relatives. A flashback of the 80s advertisement of the vicco turmeric *ayurvedic* cream played in my head as I looked around at everyone singing along.

This ubtan cream is meant to bring lustre to the skin, thus preparing you for the most memorable day of your life. Basically, I looked like a brown person with yellow foundation; one of those girls who spent too long under a sunbed.

The *Sangeet* ceremony is performed immediately before the wedding. *Sangeet* is where all the family and friends dance and sing traditional Punjabi folk songs. *Mehndi* (henna paste) was applied to my hands and feet a day before my marriage. This adds to the beauty of the bride. It certainly made me look more like a bride.

In the evening, another *mehndi* artist came to the house and pasted henna on everybody else's hands and feet. This requires each sitter to be still; the designs are very intricate and can take time to apply. It slows the whole pace of the partying down. It was lovely to watch members of my family having the *mehndi* applied, and we laughed and joked amongst ourselves.

The next day before the wedding, as always, there were too many people in the house – and everyone was an expert. Not so much a case of too many chiefs and not enough Indians; just too many Indians. There was always someone telling me to do this or that and then when I did it there was someone else to tell me that I was doing it wrong. Eventually, I went up to my bedroom with my cousins and locked the door so I could have some peace and quiet. Jas, Raman, Raj, Dips and I all had a nap and then talked about girly stuff and chilled until the guests started arriving. The house became even more overcrowded and busier than ever.

We had to do the turmeric paste thing again; there was a professional movie man filming the whole wedding as a lasting memory for Maninder and me to show our kids.

Then there was the *Chura*. This is when all my *Mama Jis* (mother's brothers and first cousins' brothers) gift me with '*chura*', red and cream ivory bangles. I was quite lucky to have all my uncles at the ceremony. Derby, Kent and even Canada were represented.

I counted my blessings that all the lads from my family were there. We chose not to book a hall, deciding instead to have the party at my family home. My cousin and maternal aunts *Mame Jis* adorned my wrist with the bangles. Then they placed on me the twenty-four karat gold jewellery set that my mother's side of the family had given me. Finally, a red *chunni* was draped over my head and shoulders. With my red *chunni* and jewellery, I felt like I was finally ready for marriage.

The cycle continued with seemingly never-ending ceremonies leading to the *Jagoo*. This happens the night before the wedding and is usually led by the eldest *Mame Ji* and the rest of my mother's side of the family (Mother's sister-in-law, my aunt). I don't have just one aunt – I'm from an Asian family so I have about eight *Mame Jis*. Back in the day, they would have carried pitchers full of water on their heads, but nowadays the pitcher has lamps made of flour *diyas* (candles) placed on it. These *diyas* are filled with mustard oil and cotton wicks dipped in oil, and then lit. My Parmjit *Mame Ji* and Preeti *Mame Ji* (Mother's brothers' wives) led my sisters, cousins and family friends too, as well as other members of the family. They all danced and sang classic folk songs, and generally teased and entertained people in the neighbourhood. All of us walked around a few houses near us and into the narrow alleyways that led between the four conjoined houses.

Ceremonies are also performed at the groom's house the night before the wedding. Maninder would have to go through the turmeric paste and other traditions too. One thing is clear. Turmeric merchants make a small fortune thanks to Punjabi weddings.

The morning of the wedding arrived and I was up very early. I had lost an hour as the clocks had gone forward. I sat on a sofa in my mother's dining room posing like one of those *desi* Asian brides, pulling cheesy faces; all a bit filmy and romantic. I felt totally awkward doing these strange yoga moves. I laugh out loud at dodgy Asian wedding films whenever I see a bride posing in this way. Why was I getting the feeling that everybody would be laughing at my cheesy yoga moves when the wedding DVD came through? Apparently, it was the trend because Asian supermodels and Bollywood stars did the cheesy poses on the morning of their weddings too.

After the cheesy photos were wrapped up, then came the *desi* portrait with the family to put on a special wall in the house, so my mother could bang on and on about her daughter being married. This was going to be the picture of the year, and the wedding was going to be talked about for ages; well, certainly until the next family wedding.

We left home at precisely 7.30am to ensure an 8am arrival, an hour before the groom, his family and friends arrived. For the first (and only) occasion in my life, I was on time at the *gurdwara*. At 9am the *Bharat* arrived – the groom's relatives and friends who have travelled for the wedding. The *gurdwara* was on High Street, Smethwick – my hometown. It was also the *gurdwara* where my parents got married over twenty-nine years ago. Here I was taking the biggest step of my life in the same *gurdwara*.

Maninder had decided that he wanted to arrive the traditional way – on a white horse – with the *Bharat* dancing up to the *gurdwara* flanked by two lovely *dhool* players. It was an entrance befitting a perfect Punjabi Prince – although I was not convinced that the locals appreciated the noise first thing in the morning. But it was my big day and the atmosphere was beautiful.

Maninder, his friends and family danced all the way up

to the entrance of the *gurdwara*, where my family welcomed them in and the *milni* (introductions) took place. I spotted Maninder's dad on his phone, standing at the entrance. He was calling his sisters to check if they were going to make the wedding or not. That's right – his sisters! They didn't make it so the *milni* continued without them. I couldn't understand what Maninder's parents had done that meant his sisters were not there for their only brother's son's wedding.

As soon as the two families are assembled the *milni* ceremony is performed. This involves the meeting of parents and close relatives of the bride and groom and (predictably) the exchanging of presents. A priest or any Sikh (man or woman) may conduct the ceremony, and usually a respected and knowledgeable person is chosen. Appropriate hymns for the occasion are sung while family, friends, guests and the groom arrives.

There were several *milnis* between the two families. Because of the situation with my father, and his lack of involvement in my life, there were no members from my father's side of the family at my wedding. But Maninder's father spoke to his side of the family regularly yet neither of his sisters was there.

When there was to be a *milni* with a *Pua Ji* and *Fuffar Ji* they replaced the family with friends. It was ironic and sad at the same time. The Purewals had more friends than family at the wedding, though Maninder's cousins from Canada and America and his mother's side of the family came along. From what they had told me, Maninder hadn't had much interaction with his mother's side of the family until a couple of years ago when they attended his sister's wedding.

I was seated in a room and told I could enjoy the view of the *milni* taking place from one of the side rooms. I couldn't help but feel tired and sick to my stomach with nerves.

My Canadian *Mama Jis* welcomed Maninder's side of the family while my older cousin *Mama Ji* from Derby fed Maninder from the Punjabi Quality Street box – the king of all kings, the sweet *ladoo*. Maninder and I would be fed this throughout the day during any *muh mittha* (mouth full of sweets) moments. Every now and then that diabetes in a box would occasionally pop up until we were all high on the E-numbers, just like the colourful box of *mithai* (sweet dessert).

OUR CIVIL CEREMONY

Traditionally, the bride and groom enter the room separately – the groom first, with the best man and family, followed by the bride. I walked into the service on the arm of my brother. It was a beautiful moment between two loving siblings.

Balbir Singh, the minister, then welcomed the congregation. Families have an important role to play as witnesses and supporters of a marriage. The minister read an introduction explaining what Sikhism believes about marriage. He asked, as the law requires, for anyone who knew of any reason why the marriage may not lawfully take place to step forward. It is similar to the vows of marriage in Christianity.

Wedding vows are promises a couple makes to each other during a wedding ceremony. In this country, all legal registration is a requirement.

"You are asked to promise before God, your friends and your families that you will love, comfort, honour and protect your partner and be faithful to them as long as you both shall live."

After making the declaration to Maninder and me, the minister also asked the congregation to declare that they would support and uphold our marriage.

Then Balbir Singh faced both of us and said: "I need to ask you both one question before I proceed. Are you guys happy to marry each other?"

"Yes!" both Maninder and I happily replied.

Balbir Singh continued. "I am going to read two declaratory words."

Maninder went first. "I do solemnly declare that I know not of any lawful impediment why I, Maninder Singh Purewal, may not be joined in matrimony to Harleen Kaur Johal."

Then it was my turn. "I do solemnly declare that I know not of any lawful impediment why I, Harleen Kaur Johal, may not be joined in matrimony to Maninder Singh Purewal."

Then followed the wedding vows. "I call upon these persons here present to witness that I, Maninder Singh Purewal, do take thee, Harleen Kaur Johal, to be my lawful wife."

"I call upon these persons here present to witness that I, Harleen Kaur Johal, do take thee ..." I paused. Yes, there was a pause at the most crucial moment. I went blank. I could see everyone staring at me. I quickly said: "Sorry, say that last bit again."

Everyone started laughing. Balbir Singh, repeated Maninder's name again, and I continued. "Take thee, Maninder Singh Purewal, to be my lawful husband."

During the civil ceremony, my Derby Pretti *Mame Ji* was the witness from my family's side and Loveneet *Pah Ji* was the witness from Maninder's side of the family. I knew if there was ever an issue between Maninder and me, these two people would encourage and help us to work towards our marriage. They were people who loved us both and had our best interests at heart and I was content knowing that they were our witnesses.

Then came the posing as a couple for the wedding photographer – more memories created for the wedding album. The more pictures we had, the more we could show off how grand our wedding was.

STARTING A RELATIONSHIP WITH YOUR BEST FOOT FORWARD

When my twin sister got married five years earlier at a different *gurdwara* it cost £501. Ours only cost £250. Mother had discussed with me that she would like to contribute the same amount of money to this *gurdwara*.

There were a few new *Ghanni Ji* who had taken over the committee after we booked our date. They had increased the cost of a wedding to £500. A week before the wedding we had gone to clear the outstanding balance to the *gurdwara*; we had only paid £100 as a deposit. I didn't think the price increase would apply to us as we had a receipt to confirm our deposit and all the details. However, this one guy started demanding that my mother should pay £500. It wasn't a very edifying advert for Sikhism.

We understood that the prices had changed but we said it didn't apply to us as we had booked the wedding before the change came into place. Everything was stated on a piece of paper, which we had in our hands. We should have been informed of this change by letter or, at the very least, a phone call. My mother was going to be donating that money on my wedding day anyway. Why was she being made to feel guilty, forced to pay more? I told my mother not to pay a penny over the amount that had been agreed on the receipt – more so out of principle, because this man was talking to my mother very disrespectfully.

At the end of this fiasco, we paid the *gurdwara* the £250 that was agreed. I had words with my mother that she was not to pay any more as they were rude to her and she explained that on the wedding day she would donate more money. I agreed that she may offer another £51 but no more. Because of the way my mother had been spoken to, I was unhappy to be taking any *laava* in that place. Mother and I had discussed donating the rest of the money to the Soho Road *Gurdwara* after the marriage.

While everybody was leaving the civil ceremony, Maninder's mum and my mother gave the *gurdwara* donations as a blessing. My mother put forward £51, as we'd agreed. However, Maninder's mother donated £101 and gave my mother a snarly look, as if she was disgusted with my mother's contribution. She turned to Mother and said, "I think, *Pehn Ji*, you should match my blessing."

But my mother left it at what we had discussed. Maninder's mum then decided to take matters into her own hands: she pulled out another £50 and put it on the table. I stood right next to my mother-in-law, watching what she had done moments after our civil ceremony. I didn't think this was how you started a fresh relationship with your only daughter-in-law's mother. Maninder's mum was not aware of what had happened a week before and now she had made a tactless pronouncement, been rude to my only parent in front of me and pressured my mother into contributing more money. My mother picked up the £50 off the table, gave it back to her, pulled another £50 out of her own purse and put it down. I couldn't believe what Maninder's mother had done. I stood there next to her in shock. But I couldn't say a word as it was my big day, after all.

THE LAAVA DE RASAM

In India, weddings are not only about tying a couple in a sacred knot, but about two families being tied to one another.

Families and friends of both Maninder and I gathered in the main wedding hall of the *gurdwara* for the *Anand Karaj* ceremony. We were going to be assembling together in the presence of the *Sri Guru Granth Sahib Ji* – the eternal *Guru Ji* of the Sikhs, who may never be replaced by a human being. The scriptures are formally referred to as '*Sri Guru Granth Sahib Ji*', meaning 'respected scripture of the supreme enlightened'. Hymns were being sung as men and boys sat on one side of a central aisle, with the women and girls on the other side. Everyone sat on the floor reverently with their arms crossed and legs folded.

Maninder walked into the main hall with close family members behind him. Then I followed into the *Darbar* (main hall) with my brothers and sisters. We bowed before *Sri Guru Granth Sahib Ji*, and then everyone sat side by side at the front of the *Darbar*. Maninder and I and our parents stood up to signify that we had given consent for the wedding to take place. Everyone else remained seated while a *Ghanni Ji* (Sikh Priest) offered *Ardaas*, a prayer for the blessing of a successful marriage.

Maninder's sister removed his *Kalgi* (headdress worn by the groom) before the start of the *Anand Karaj* (vows). This was given to the oldest member of Maninder's family.

Here's a bit of history for you.

The Sikh marriage ceremony is called *Anand Karaj*, meaning 'ceremony of bliss'. The most important part of the ceremony is the reading of the Laava, a hymn written for weddings by the *Guru Ram Das Ji*. It has four verses which are spoken one at a time and then sung, whereupon the couple encircles the holy *Sri Guru Granth Sahib Ji*.

Guru Ram Das Ji, the faith *Guru Ji*, originally composed *Laava*, the wedding song, to celebrate a holy union between the human soul (*Atma*) and God (*Waheguru*). He wrote it for his own wedding vows, a formula for a successful marriage. The guru wishes that our married life should also be moulded on the ideal laid down for our union with *Waheguru*. The Sikh marriage is monogamous. In the case of broken marriage, divorce is not possible according to the Sikh religious tradition. The couple can, however, obtain a divorce under the civil law of the land. In Sikhism, marriage is regarded as a sacred bond in attaining worldly and spiritual joy. About the ideal marriage, the Guru says: "They are not husband and wife who only have merely a physical and legal contract but there is a fusion of the souls; rather they are husband and wife who have one spirit in two bodies." The bride and groom then share their life, happiness and sorrow; from two individuals they become *Ek Jot Doye Murti,* meaning one spirit in two bodies.

The musicians, who are called *ragis*, sit on a low stage and sing the hymn *'Keeta Loree-ai Kaam'*, to seek God's blessing and to convey a message that a successful marriage union is achieved through grace. While a Sikh offers an *Ardaas*, a prayer is then conducted invoking God's blessings for the proposed marriage and asking His Grace for the union of the couple. Maninder and I and our parents stand up to signify that we give our consent for the wedding to take place. A short hymn is sung. Upon translation, the hymn would read as follows:

Call upon God for task thou wouldst have accomplished,
He will bring the tasks to rights, so witnesseth the Guru.
In the company of the holy thou shalt rejoice and taste only
nectar,
Thou art the demolisher of fear, thou art compassionate, O' Lord,
Nanak singeth the praises of the Incomputable Lord.

This is followed by a brief speech by the *Ghanni Ji* addressed particularly to the couple, explaining the significance and obligation of the marriage. The couple is then asked to honour their vows by bowing together before *Sri Guru Granth Sahib Ji*. Before the Sikh vows, the groom's sister drapes a long scarf, shawl, or length of turban cloth called a *palla* around the groom's shoulders and places the right end in his hand. Then the bride's father takes the left end of the *palla* and arranges it over the bride's shoulders, giving her the left end to hold.

In my case, my Guruleen *Massar Ji* had acted in my father's stead, giving me away and doing the *palla di rasam*. This signified the start of my new life with Maninder. Guruleen *Massar Ji* had been like a father figure for me throughout my teenage years. He was the oldest member of our family from my mother's side. My Guruleen *Massar Ji* had the blessing to do four *kanyadaan* of his two daughters and my sister and myself. He was a strong man; strong like the steel core at the centre of my family. He held everyone together.

After the *palla di rasam,* the *ragis* (priests) sing the hymn *'Palai tendai lagee',* which symbolises joining the couple with a *palla* to each other and God. Thus joined, the two take the vows. This is followed by a short hymn.

Praise and slander have I all ceased to relish, O Nanak. False,

I count all other relationships; to the fold of Thy fabric am I now affianced. **(Sri Guru Granth Sahib Ji, Page 963)**

Sri Guru Granth Sahib Ji is now opened and the first verse of *Laava* is read from it. The same verse is then sung by the *ragis* while the couple slowly encircle *Sri Guru Granth Sahib Ji*. The groom leads in a clockwise direction and the bride, holding the scarf, follows as gracefully as possible. When the couple reaches the front of *Sri Guru Granth Sahib Ji*, both of them bow together and take their respective seats. The same protocol is repeated for the remaining three verses.

The four verses of *Laava* explain the four stages of love and married life – the journey of the souls towards the almighty. After translation into English, the *Laava* quartet or the Sikh epithalamium would read as follows:

First Laava (Emphasises the performance of duty to the family and the community)

By the first nuptial circuiting The Lord sheweth ye His Ordinance for the daily duties of wedded life. The Scriptures are the Word of the Lord. Learn righteousness through them, And the Lord will free yet from sin. Hold fast to righteousness. Contemplate the Name of the Lord, fixing it in your memory as the scriptures have prescribed. Devote yourselves to the Perfect and True Guru. And all your sins shall depart. Fortunate are those whose minds are imbued with the sweetness of His Name, to them happiness comes without effort; the slave Nanak proclaimeth that in the first circling the marriage rite hath begun.

Second Laava (Signifies the stage of yearning and love for each other)

By the second circumambulation, Ye are to understand that the Lord hath caused ye to meet the True Guru, the fear in your hearts has departed; The filth of selfless in your minds is washed away, by having the fear of God and by singing His praises I stand before Him with reverence, The Lord God is the soul of the universe! There is nought that He doth not pervade. Within us and without, there is One God only; in the company of saints then are heard the songs of rejoicing. The slave Nanak proclaimeth that in the second circling Divine Music is heard.

Third Laava (Signifies the stage of detachment, or Virag)

In the third roundabout, there is a longing for the Lord and detachment from the world. In the company of the saints, by our great good fortune, we encounter the Lord. The Lord is found in His purity, through His exaltation, through the singing of His hymns. By great good fortune, we have risen. In the company of the saints wherein is told the story of the Ineffable Lord. The Holy Name echoes in the heart: Echoes and absorbs us. We repeat the Name of the Lord, being blessed by a fortunate destiny written from of old on our foreheads. The slave Nanak proclaimeth that in the third circling the love of God has been awakened in the heart.

Fourth Laava (Signifies the final stage of harmony and union in married life during which human love blends into the love for God)

In the fourth walk-around, the mind reaches to knowledge of the Divine and God is innerly grasped: Through the Grace of the Guru we have attained with ease to the Lord; the sweetness of the Beloved pervades us, body and soul. Dear and pleasing is the Lord to us: Night and day our minds are fixed on Him. By exalting the Lord we have attained the Lord: the fruit our hearts desired; the Beloved has finished His work. The soul, the spouse, delighteth in the Beloved's Name. Felicitations fill our minds; the Name rings in our hearts: the Lord God is united with His Holy Bride. The heart of the Bride flowers with His Name. The slave Nanak proclaimeth that in the fourth circling we have found the Eternal Lord. **(Page 773 -74 of Sri Guru Granth Sahib Ji)**

The ceremony is concluded with the customary singing of the six stanzas of the *Anand Sahib* (Song of Bliss), followed by *Ardaas* (Sikh holy prayers), and *Hukamnama* (a random reading of a verse from *Sri Guru Granth Sahib Ji*). The ceremony, which takes about an hour, ends with the serving of *Karah Parshad* to the congregation.

(https://en.wikipedia.org/wiki/Karah_Parshad)

Then the entire congregation sings '*Anand Sahib*', the 'Song of Bliss'. The hymn emphasises the fusing of two souls into one as they merge with the divine.

Concluding the ceremony, the *ragis* sing two hymns. '*Veeahu hoa mere babula*' celebrates the marriage of the couple and their union with God. This hymn also symbolises the soul bride's spiritual union with her groom. It is a reminder to the newly wedded pair that the material world is temporary, and places emphasis on the spiritual nature of marriage by likening it to being wed with God. '*Pooree asa jee mansa mere raam*' describes the happiness of having found the perfect partner.

Everyone stands to show their respect for the final *Ardaas* prayer. After it has been said, everyone bows and takes their seats. The *Ghanni Ji* reads a verse called a *hukam,* which concludes the ceremony. Lastly, a *ragi* serves everyone a handful of *Prashad*. When we receive *Prashad*, it is not just flour, *ghee*, sugar and water mixed together, but *Gurbani (Sri Guru Granth Sahib Ji) Prashad* blessed by *Guru Ji*, a sacred sweet blessed during the prayer. The wedding party guests congratulate the newly married couple, and everybody gathers to give them their blessing.

At this point, I spotted Maninder's elder Prabhjot *Pau Ji* (Auntie) and Satnam *Fuffar Ji* had come to give us blessing.

His younger Punit *Pau Ji* (aunt) didn't come to the wedding – nor her family. I had not met them before but one of his cousin's sisters came over to introduce herself. She seemed warm and loving. It was lovely to see so many familiar faces among our families and friends.

I was very nervous throughout the *laava* though I was happy we had been joined in union in the presence of *Guru Ji*. I have to say the hardest thing was sitting there being blessed by the entire guest list. My legs went to sleep and I was praying for that moment to be over with as soon as possible. I have to add my thanks to everybody who gave me *pyar* (love) with their hand on my head – for every time somebody did this, my hair pins dug into me. I could hear my head pounding and couldn't help but feel flustered with it all. The sugar intake was reaching a high point by now; I was gasping for something savoury in my mouth. I just wanted comfort food – *masala*-baked beans and toast, you can't go wrong.

Whilst taking our *laava* the bride's brother, cousins and close family friends hold the bride's shoulders, move her around and pass her over to the next person like a game of pass the parcel. During the first *laava* Maninder was walking very quickly, as if he was about to run a marathon! I wondered what the hell he was doing and decided to ask my brother to tell him to slow down in the second *laava*. My brother's mate Bhupi eventually asked him to slow down as I couldn't keep up with him, so for the third and fourth *laava* we both walked together at a normal pace.

After the *laava,* I asked him what the hell happened and he explained that his trousers had come undone and he was afraid they were going to drop at any time! He was really nervous when I asked him to slow down. All he could think was what would happen if his pants fell down! He just wanted to get the *laava* over and done with as soon as possible. I thought: here's a funny story about the groom, for a change.

All our friends and family attended the wedding party at the Samson Banqueting Suite in Oldbury, Birmingham. While everybody made themselves comfortable at the reception, Maninder and I had some more pictures taken outside the *gurdwara*. Then we joined our immediate family outside the reception, along with the *dhool* player that Maninder's family had booked. This was the first time I got to see all the guests. It was nerve-wracking but, as with the wedding ceremony, I had someone directing me on what to do next. All I remember of the reception was that I had people coming from everywhere wanting to dance with us and celebrate our day with us. Some people I didn't know personally came up and asked us if they could have pictures taken with us. That was strange! I remember asking Maninder if they were from his side of the family. He didn't answer. He just told me to smile for the camera. I would have loved to know who the hell I was being photographed with! We hadn't yet eaten and I told Maninder that I needed to sit and rest for a bit as I had started getting pain in my arm and needed to take some hot water and strong painkillers.

Finally, we were seated on a special stage for the bride and groom and served our starter. Some of Maninder's friends came up to congratulate us and decided to start busting some moves. I could feel the stage moving and I had visions of it collapsing so I whispered in Maninder's ear to ask them to get off the stage. Instead, he waved his arm in the air and invited a few more boys up! I couldn't believe it – I did not appreciate having all these guys dancing behind me; it was very uncomfortable.

The reception continued and everybody was enjoying themselves before the main meal was served. The first plate – or plastic *thal* (plate) – comes out to the married couple. The male members of my family took the *thal* (plate) to the groom's side of the family and they blessed the meal and offered money on top of it, and then men from both sides started playing a bit of *desi Kabaddi* (an Indian sport of wrestling) over the money given to the bride as a blessing. The bride's side didn't want to take the money and the groom's side kept insisting and offering until they decided to take one Scottish pound, in my case. Then the meal was brought over to us and we were fed by immediate family members from both sides of the family – first my side, then Maninder's. This represented that I was part of Maninder's family by virtue of sharing the meal together. I got quite emotional during this moment when my mother, brother and two *Mama Jis* fed me. I was so close to my mother; I just wanted to break down – but I held it together and avoided crying on camera, as the lovely movie man was literally in my face.

All I remember was leaving the reception when the famous old school Punjabi rail *gaddi* (car) song came on and my Pretti *Mame Ji* suggested we leave while Maninder was leading the rail *gaddi* (car) with our entire family behind him.

The party was almost over. All that remained was the *doli turni* (palanquin walking) - this is where the bride returns to her family home and the groom and his *Bharat* guests come to collect her. Before being allowed to enter, they pay the bride's sisters and cousin money and play games and have fun at the door. The entrance to the bride's home is blocked by the girls with a ribbon, which the groom has to cut before he and the *Bharat* guests are allowed into the house. Maninder's *Bharat* guests paid £101, which was returned by my mother to Maninder's dad. We took the money to keep face but felt it was respectful to return it.

Once the groom and *Bharat* guests were allowed in they had to wait for me to be escorted by my Brother and cousins to the main room where, once again, my Parmjit *Mama Ji* put the *palla* in my hand. Before leaving, my Pretti *Mame Ji* advised me to throw rice over my head into each corner of the house to wish for prosperity for the parental home I was leaving behind. This also symbolised that my wheat and water had finished in my parents' home and may my wheat and water be blessed in my new family home. Then all the male members escorted me to my *doli*. In the olden days a girl would leave her parental home in a palanquin but today generally it's a car decorated with ribbons. Each member of the family came to the car to say farewell and wish me all the best in my new beginning. This was an emotionally charged moment. I got on well with many of my family and breaking away from them was going to be very hard.

Then my brother, cousins and older members of my family pushed the car before it left and Maninder's dad threw coins over it as a symbol of the prosperity this alliance would bring to the family. All the kids ran towards the money on the floor, and the driver had to be careful not to run any of them over! I had early memories of collecting the money at my cousin Mandeep's wedding. Back in those days, all the kids would line up in front of the car and as soon as the dude with the bag threw a handful of loose coins – on your marks, get set, go! – the kids raced to collect the change and then compare how many bronze and silver coins they had collected and who had picked up the most.

I was taken to Milton Keynes *Gurdwara* for *matha tekna* before arriving at my new home. Upon arriving at Maninder's family home, Gurleen greeted us and fed me some more *ladoo*; I would turn into a *ladoo* if I wasn't careful! I had help out of the car and then my new mother-in-law welcomed us, the newlywed couple, outside the house. Then she walked us through the door and into the family home while she moved a bowl filled with water and milk over our heads seven times, drinking a small quantity of the liquid each time. Every time Maninder stopped her, but the seventh time is the most important one as everybody tries to stop her. This symbolises the willingness of the boy's mum to take upon her all future troubles of the couple. Then everybody welcomes the newly wedded bride into the house. This ritual is called *pani vaarna*. Once this ceremony was completed we both hugged Simranjit Mum. She then poured some oil at the *choukhat* (opposite end of the door); this ceremony is called *tela chauna,* and this mischievousness symbolises the happiness in the wedding house at the arrival of a new family member. I was then allowed to enter the family home and I was taken into the main living room by my new Simranjit Mum, who gave Maninder and me a glass of milk to share. Then Kabir Dad and Simranjit Mum presented me with four twenty-four karat gold bangles and another twenty-four karat gold jewellery set, and all the relatives of the boys offered cash and gifts to me too. This ceremony is called the *mooh dikhai Ki Rasam* (show your face to all the new family and friends).

Normally the family would show me around their home for the first time, but as I had hung out with them before getting married I knew where I was going downstairs. However, I had never been allowed upstairs. Gurleen took me into one of the bedrooms and all the cousins followed. We all sat talking before someone decided to order some pizza. Thank God! I was sick of eating Indian food – and my arteries were too.

Finally, my new sister-in-law dropped Maninder and me off at a hotel. This was the first time in God knows how long that we were both alone without being pulled and pushed in different directions and told what to do.

I have to tell you there is no such thing as a romantic moment on the first night of marriage. Normal weddings are two days, three functions and a honeymoon, but Punjabi weddings are seven days, twelve functions, two fights, eight hangovers and unlimited fun. Thank God this wedding was over. I had no energy to do anything romantic. I just wanted to take out the thousand pins in my hair and the hairpiece, which was giving me a headache, take off my heavy *lehenga*, shower off the wedding and sleep for a lifetime like Sleeping Beauty – and that was exactly what we both did.

THE DAY AFTER THE BIG FAT PUNJABI WEDDING

Next morning, I woke up at 10am and lay in bed talking to my husband about the wedding. My husband. Weirdly, I had very few memories; I was so tired of the whole process that everything was a blur. I felt overwhelmed by the day and couldn't believe how quickly it had gone, after all those months of preparation. Now I needed to look forward to the reality of our marriage.

In the evening, Maninder, his family and I visited my mother's home, in a tradition called *fera pauna rasam* where the two families have an evening meal together. Games are played with the groom vs bride's sisters and family. My husband and I were dressed in matching outfits like we were in a Punjabi music video – but without the irony.

I wasn't used to wearing much makeup and I wanted my skin to breathe, as I'd had makeup plastered all over my face the day before. I tried to keep it simple but Simranjit Mum came into my bedroom while I was getting ready and insisted that I apply more. The family could tell by looking at me that I was a newlywed but they felt that the amount of makeup I had on wasn't enough. As I was married now, I couldn't care less about looking like an Asian Barbie doll.

We arrived at my family home and my close family from the UK and abroad were all there to welcome us back. During the *fera pauna rasam* all my sisters and cousins played games with Maninder. The reward for winning the game was he gave them each a silver ring and some cash.

Before I left my Mother's house I decided to give her my house keys back, but she asked me to hold onto them until I was settled into my in-laws' home. But my mother-in-law intervened, saying it was great that I was giving my mother the keys back, and that she should accept them as my new home's keys were a blessing for my future. In Punjabi culture, a girl is seen as a temporary guest at her parents' home as her future in-laws' house will be her permanent family home after marriage. Well, that's what I was brought up to believe and I'm sure most other Punjabi women are, too.

When we got back to Maninder's parents' house I discovered that Maninder hadn't packed his suitcase for the honeymoon. I was up all night helping him pack. Finally, we slept for an hour and woke up at the crack of dawn to go to the airport.

THE HONEYMOON

Thank God we were off on our honeymoon! I was really ready for this time out. I couldn't wait to get back to some sanity and normality and enjoy married life – it was the only bit I'd been looking forward to! Seven days of pure relaxation, which I was in desperate need of. I'm going to have a massage every day and just relax, I thought. I just wanted to chill out and have fun.

Maninder's father drove Maninder, Gurleen, Maninder's cousin Rav, who was from Canada, and me to Luton airport to catch our flights. See ya laters, Punjabi alligators!

I had always wanted to go to Rome. I had been to other parts of Italy but never the capital and I had heard that the eternal city was steeped in history, with many things to do and see. Rome was perfect for a romantic getaway, a weekend break or a honeymoon. Historic, modern, traditional; Rome is like visiting several cities in one. There were several church museums to explore so I certainly wouldn't be bored. It also had a vibrant nightlife with a huge number of shows, events, gigs and amazing restaurants and pubs. I'd heard that Rome deserved to be seen at least once in a lifetime, so when Maninder asked where I would like to go on our honeymoon, I knew straight away. He was taken aback as he thought I would want to go somewhere like Dubai, Mexico or Thailand. I should have known then...

I had grown up fascinated by people like Leonardo da Vinci, the Italian artist, scientist and engineer. He was an all-round genius whose paintings and inventions changed the world. I was also a fan of Michelangelo, more for his painting on the ceiling of the Sistine Chapel than for his theological impact on the Catholic Church. And then there was Raphael, who was commissioned by Pope Julius II to create the large-scale fresco at the School of Athens, as well as other decorative work at the Vatican. Raphael also took over as the architect of St. Peter's after the death of Bramante (1514), contributed ten tapestries to the Sistine Chapel and painted some of the most prized and reproduced holy pictures of the era, including the Sistine Madonna and transfiguration. His work was often cited for its harmony and balance of the composition. Raphael, Michelangelo and Leonardo da Vinci were all famous artists of Italy's high renaissance and some of the greatest influences in the history of western art – and I had taken an interactive journey through their work to discover what made them all true renaissance men. I was desperate to see their work and discover the passion and history behind each piece. I was also reading the book 'Angels and Demons' and I wanted to visit most of the places that were mentioned!

Maninder booked a driver to collect us from the airport and take us to the amazing Aleph – a Boscolo luxury hotel which was chic, modern and fashionable. I was really impressed. We entered our room and the manager of the hotel welcomed us with flowers and strawberries. As he told me about all the surprises he had in store for our seven-day honeymoon, Maninder seemed full of energy, like a little kid who can't wait to show his parents the painting he did at school that he needs a pat on the back for. This boy had been busy planning every last detail, making sure we'd get the most out of our time here. He had booked a tour of the heart of Rome, a 'Fact, Legend and Mystery' tour, a tour to the locations in the 'Angel and Demons' film, which was being produced while we were out there. We also had a tour of the underside of Rome – the crypts and catacombs, a private tour of the Vatican museums, Sistine chapel and Raphael rooms, a small walking group trip to St Peter's Basilica and finally, a tour of Rome by Segway. I was in shock. I couldn't believe he had planned so much, that we were going to all these wonderful places. I was happy with the hotel but now, with all of that in store, I was so excited! We had an early start for some of the tours; one of them was late at night and another very early in the morning. I was excited – but I didn't really care about the details. I wanted to do it all but first, I wanted to do nothing more than catch up on my sleep.

I can say this much: my room saw no serious action as it was that time of the month and I was feeling exhausted and drained from the wedding. After sleeping for most of the first day, Maninder and I got ready to go out. Our hotel was only a five-minute walk from the Trevi Fountain, and I was already realising what a beautiful city Rome was. I had always loved Italy and I couldn't wait to explore Rome and discover the history hidden away under each layer.

We found a place to eat where we could enjoy the view of the Trevi Fountain. We had just decided to head back to the hotel when some guy walked straight up to Maninder and called him Bin Laden! I was shocked. I couldn't believe it. Within seconds, Maninder had lost his temper and stood his ground against this guy. I tried to pull him away but then another five guys turned up. I could see a police officer, so I went up to him and told him about the situation. The officer then intervened and asked whether there was a problem. Maninder explained that the guy had made a racist comment towards him. The guy was drunk, and the officer took him to one side.

We decided to leave. I was a little shocked at Maninder's aggressive behaviour. The guy was visibly drunk and the best thing to have done was walk away, I thought. I told Maninder that something serious could have happened to him. What a great start to our honeymoon! I'd been scared and had broken down crying. Maninder apologised as we walked back to the hotel, but I could feel the tension between us. I didn't want him to get hurt, but he thought I was overreacting. That night we slept on separate sides of the bed, worlds apart, like a lion and lioness looking into different directions of the jungle of life, the gap between us like the Rify Valley in East Africa. We were far away from behaving like a romantic couple in the heart of this beautiful city.

The next morning, we got up at about 10am and went down for breakfast. There was another couple in our hotel who'd just got married too. One of the waiters mixed up her drink with mine as we were both wearing bright red and cream *chura*. We exchanged drinks and started talking. We didn't see the other couple again as this was the only morning when we got up so late. Little to my knowledge, this honeymoon was going to be like being in the army.

The first early morning tour was called Crypts and Catacombs; this was all about discovering imperial and early Christian Roma by peeling back layers and millenniums of history as you descended into the eternal city's underground burial chambers, long winding catacombs and crypts. We loved every minute of the tour, which was very interesting and informative; it really took you back to ancient Rome and the way things were then. After the tour, we went to find a place to eat. I was a bit quiet and Maninder kept asking me if I was ok. He thought I might be disappointed by the honeymoon, as his sister had felt her honeymoon wasn't organised to her standards. I explained that he needed to stop worrying and stop comparing me with his sister. We were two different people with completely different upbringings.

Maninder's parents may have set Gurleen expectations high before she got married but I had none; I just wanted to enjoy everything as it came. I wasn't expecting the world or any fancy laa di daa things from Maninder, other than for him to consider my feelings and be caring towards me. I wanted my husband to love me and respect me as his life partner and I wanted this honeymoon to be more chilled out and not itinerary-based because I was always a 'go with the flow' kind of person.

Once again we discussed our different backgrounds. I was brought up to believe material things don't make you happy, but Maninder believed having a bigger house and better things made you more successful – especially in his parents' view – and pleasing the local community was everything for him and his family. But for me, I had always followed my passion and done what I loved doing, not what wowed other people. Maninder wanted me to see his point of view, but we got into an argument. This was only the second night of our honeymoon and I was already tired of the bickering.

We'd spent so much time being told by our families what they wanted and how they wanted our wedding day to be, but now the two of us needed to get to know each other away from everybody else – and this was hard. I felt a part of me didn't know Maninder at all. I had to start again, from the beginning. We had not lived together or even been on holiday together before, and I realised lots of things remain hidden when you first get to know someone.

We got on okay for two days but by the time of the Heart of Rome tour I was so exhausted I just wanted to sleep. I really wanted a day at the hotel to chill, to lie in bed, watch TV, not do anything else and order room service meals. Maninder wanted to tour the whole of Rome during our honeymoon. We spent more time visiting places than connecting with each other. In fact, I felt I connected more with the buildings, art and culture of Rome than I did with my husband.

I didn't want to go on the Heart of Rome tour as it took place at night, when the weather was chilly, and my arm was in pain from the cold weather. It was stopping me from enjoying things that I wanted to do, but I had to learn to understand when my body was telling me that it couldn't continue any more – I needed to rest up. I explained to Maninder that I didn't want to go and he was a little disappointed. All I really wanted was to be wrapped up in his arms, warm and safe. All I really wanted was to enjoy his company and spend some quality time together to help us connect our souls. But he made me feel guilty, so I decided I'd better go after all.

We had a giggle on the tour – until the pain in my arm

got too much for me and I started whinging like a child. I wanted to go back to the hotel but Maninder just wanted to enjoy the evening and the city. The pain in my arm was unbearable, to the point where lack of blood supply had made my fingers numb and my hand turn blue, but Maninder wasn't willing to understand that I was not feeling well.

I lost my patience with him and ordered a taxi back to the hotel. I needed some painkillers and a hot water bottle to ease the pain. We argued while we were waiting for the taxi and I told him that he didn't know me or my health needs. I didn't care about the tour; I cared more about my health. I had already changed my lifestyle once when I had a health scare and I didn't want anything going wrong again health-wise, especially not over a tour of Rome. Once we arrived back at our hotel room I had some painkillers, took a hot bath and got into bed. Maninder's face looked like it had been slapped and he decided to give me the silent treatment, like a child who has just thrown all his toys out of the pram.

In the early hours of the morning, I felt that I was in the wrong on this occasion – I was a lioness who had no ego – so I rolled over to his side of the bed and cuddled up with my lion husband. I wanted us to enjoy the rest of our honeymoon, so I thought I should explain what was happening to my arm and how the cold weather affected it. I just wanted to get on with things. I knew neither of us would be able to understand the other person and I wanted to find a middle ground we could agree on. I was the more patient of the two of us, and I was the one who would give in and apologise. I never really cared who said sorry first, as long as we could get past the arguing and occasional bickering.

Once Maninder knew that I would give in quickly he started to take the mickey with my feelings; he knew that he could start playing up to things. I started to notice him doing this but I kept telling myself that I was the better of the two of us and I had to be more understanding.

Maninder knew I loved Dan Brown's novels and he had booked us on the 'Angels and Demons' tour. This tour introduces Rome's most famous landmarks as you follow in the footsteps of Robert Langdon, a character in the book, as he sets out to rescue the Cardinal and save the Vatican from impending doom. The book was a fun-filled adventure through the eternal city.

On the morning of the tour, we met our guide Marco at Piazza Del Popole on the eastern side of the Tiber River. The tour began at the church of Santa Maria Del Popolo. Marco was a history student who had also travelled the world. This lovely gentleman had been to India. He took one look at me and came straight over to congratulate me on my marriage. I couldn't work out how he could tell that I was a newly-wed, but he had been to a few friends' weddings while travelling in India and Pakistan and he said it was the *mendhi* and *chura* that gave it away.

There was an older couple with us on the tour who had just got married for the second time round, and they had a great outlook on life. They were the most positive couple that I had ever met and we all got on well; we even played a few jokes on Marco. Marco was getting married the following month and he was doing this job to bring in extra income to help pay for his wedding. You could see his passion for the tour compared to other tour guides. He shared so much knowledge while we toured the Pantheon, the remaining altars of science: air, fire and water or, respectively, St. Peter's Basilica, Santa Maria Della Vittoria and St. Agnes in Agony (across from the fountain of the four rivers in Piazza Navona), and finally, Castel Sant' Angelo, where Robert Langdon saves Vittoria and lives happily ever after – and where the tour concluded.

Maninder and I had been getting on really well throughout this tour, almost as if we were the water, fire, wind and earth. For the first time, everybody outside looking in could really see a happy couple.

On our last but one day in Rome Maninder had booked a tour of the city on Segways. We had visited most of the places in the time that we had been there, but it was lovely to sightsee on a Segway and have a private tour guide take us through the city. It was great fun; we were on these Segways and people were coming up to us to take pictures of us! We were like two serious *pindoos* on scooters. I was on a scooter outside the Coliseum wearing my helmet, body warmer, Posh Spice sunglasses and a bright red and cream *chura*.

This was a Kodak moment. It reminded me of the black and white pictures that I had seen while I was a young girl, looking back at photos of some member of my family who had got married back in the 70s or 80s. They would have had their pictures taken in a professional photography studio but ours was taken in the heart of Rome.

To the outside world, everything on the surface of our relationship appeared to be perfect, the ideal match made in heaven. If only they knew the truth… We had not connected on this honeymoon – in fact, we had more misunderstanding between us and we both felt more disconnected than we had ever been.

RETURNING TO THE UK AND STARTING MY MARRIED LIFE AS MRS PUREWAL

I was now looking forward to getting back to the UK and settling into my new home and new bedroom.

When we arrived back at Luton airport both of Maninder's parents had come to pick us up. They were looking forward to hearing all about our honeymoon. However, I just wanted a home cooked Punjabi meal and to chill out. As I stepped foot into my new home I thought to myself: it's official. Our married life has finally begun.

Maninder's parents, Kanchan *Nani Ji* and Amirtpal *Bee Ji* were at home and we hung out with them for a while before going up to our bedroom. Before leaving for Rome I had given my mother-in-law all my twenty-four karat gold jewellery as I didn't want to take anything that expensive with me. While we were away she had put some of my personal things in the wardrobe in the bedroom and she let me know where they were.

The next morning, I woke up in my new home and decided that, as I still had a week off work, I wanted to arrange all my things in my new bedroom and start to feel at home. After having breakfast with the entire Purewal household I started unpacking my things, and I got Maninder to help too.

As we were unpacking I shared some ideas about how I would like to decorate the bedroom and change some things around. Maninder got annoyed and agitated with my input. He left our bedroom and went back into his old room.

After a while, I went looking for him. He was lying silently on his old bed. I asked if he was okay and if he would prefer for us to move into the old bedroom. He said there was not enough space for both of us. I was happy to make do; I just wanted to enjoy the company of my husband and I'd rather keep things simple.

I explained that this was going to be hard for me too, moving in with him and sharing my private space. As singletons entering into new married life as a couple, we had to share a great deal – even the wardrobe space – and compromise on the interior of the bedroom. I suggested that we add some of our personality to the room but my lovely Simranjit Mum got involved, saying she had a family picture on the wall and she would prefer for us not to change or move anything as it had previously been her room. It spoke (or rather shouted) volumes about her personality. This was never going to be a newly married couple's bedroom. She had chosen the new bed sheet – not my kind of colour – and the hand embroidered cover that she had created a very long time ago, which was lying on a chest of drawers. I also couldn't ignore the matching flower photo frames that went with the bed sheets. The family photo, which was of Gurleen wedding day portrait, hung opposite the bed.

I told Maninder again that I would like to inject some of our personality into our new bedroom, maybe change the colour of the walls and some other details so we felt settled in our new room. He said Simranjit Mum had decorated the bedroom before my arrival and I should just put my things away and not think of changing the room; rather, I could add to it through my possessions. From that moment I realised this was going to be hard.

We went to Ikea, bought some accessories and got some ideas about styles and designs we liked. I just wanted to get settled into my place without having Simranjit Mum interfering or throwing another family portrait on top of my head.

We headed back home and Maninder decided to relax whilst I got on with unpacking my things. My mother-in-law came in to help. The walk-in wardrobe was full of her things so I kindly asked if she would be able to give me more space. She replied that she would need a few weeks to move her possessions, slowly and surely.

I felt upset. Many years ago she had been a newly married woman in this family. Did she not want me to settle in and feel at home? Why hadn't she moved her things before we arrived back? It would have made it much easier for me to unpack, rather than be made to feel as if I was a burden on her for asking her to move her things so there would be space for me in the wardrobe – and between her son and her.

One morning Simranjit Mum knocked on our door and walked straight into the bedroom. Maninder and I were getting down to having some fun; yeah, we were fucking. But that didn't stop her. After a quick glance at our coitus, she placed her hands over her eyes, saying "Sorry, sorry…" She claimed she couldn't see anything but she needed to get something important from the walk-in wardrobe. I know this much: no other girl would have tolerated this kind of behaviour. I was annoyed, and Maninder was too. I asked him to remove himself from me. I then explained this was exactly why I had kindly asked Simranjit Mum to remove her things from our bedroom. Maninder got dressed and told her that she needed to remove her things as we would not like a repeat of the embarrassing episode.

Eventually, she came into our room, sulking and annoyed, and pointed out that she would take some things, but would leave anything that wasn't important. I felt that I had spent most of the week getting the mother-in-law to adapt to the changes in her home. She was making it very difficult for me to settle in. It was as if she was fighting the change and a part of her couldn't cope with seeing her son all grown up and supporting his wife.

Like any other person I often enjoy some alone time, but now, walking into my own private space was like a dream; I didn't have any at the moment. I used to enjoy reading, drawing or just sitting and allowing my thoughts to go where they wanted but now there would be none of that.

MAKING BEST FRIENDS WITH ONE ROOM IN THE HOUSE: THE KITCHEN

One particular tradition was doing my head in following the wedding: a ritual called *chauke charna* (entering the kitchen), where the bride is not allowed to cook anything for the first six weeks in her new home. I have always been a hands-on kind of person and I didn't expect others to do things for me. My mother had brought us up to take care of ourselves and to do things for ourselves too. I knew how to clean the house and cook every single Punjabi dish. I'd been married for two and a half weeks and every time I went into the kitchen to put away my own cups and plates, Simranjit Mum told me off.

However, eventually, she decided with Maninder's Kanchan *Nani Ji* that she would let me prepare my first meal for the family in my new home. I was looking forward to showing off my *rasoi ke raaz* (kitchen secrets) to my new family. Simranjit Mum explained that I would need to make a full *desi* Punjabi meal accompanied by a sweet dessert. There was no starter, so I headed straight for the main meal, which was an Indian vegetarian recipe, as we were all vegetarians. I could also cook meat dishes too; my Mother had taught me, just in case I met a partner who was a non-vegan.

For this first meal, which was a *desi shagun* to celebrate my first cooking session, I cooked brown lentil *dhal*, cauliflower *sabzi* (vegetable curry) and salad, which was decorated in a stylish Indian way making it a colourful event. I also made round *rotis*, which I had learnt to cook at the age of eleven, and for dessert, I did *zarda* rice, a sweet rice dish which is an easy version of *metha chawal*. I loved cooking in the Purewals' *rasoi ghar* for the first time, showing off the skills my mother taught me and being a mini Masterchef in my new home and kitchen.

The funny thing was that my Punjabi suit was a *zarda* rice colour too. I had put my *chunni* across my side and decided to get stuck into the real hard work of cooking. Mother-in-law was watching over me and checking that I was cooking everything to the Purewal family standards.

Once I had finished preparing the meal, the family – Maninder's Amritpal *Bee Ji* and Kanchan *Nani Ji* from Canada, Kabir Dad, Simranjit Mum, Maninder and I – got together in the conservatory and I served the food and waited for everyone to give me their judgement on how good my cooking skills were. Before I sat down Kabir Dad did *Ardaas* (Sikh holy prayers) and I knew I had to cover my head. Then I took off my *chunni* and started serving food onto the plates. My father-in-law laughed and asked me to put my *chunni* back on my head. I thought he was teasing me and I laughed too – until he asked me, in a serious voice, to put it back on. He explained that it was a tradition within the Purewal household that any girl who married into the family would have to cover her head while eating her first meal. Then Maninder decided to make it a Canon moment by pulling out his camera and taking a few pictures. I was really confused. I couldn't understand if this was a tradition as no one had mentioned anything about it. Was this a rule in their household or were they making it up? I wanted to know if my sister-in-law Gurleen had to do this – and why she had not warned me beforehand.

Glancing around the table I saw that every plate was crystal clean and Kabir Dad was licking his fingers clean too. I knew that I had passed the first test with my *desi* cooking skills. Simranjit Mum and I cleaned away the plates and everybody decided to give me *shagan*. First, Amritpal *Bee Ji* came over and gave me the family heirloom necklace as a blessing for cooking my first meal; it made our relationship much more personal. She wanted me to understand that she would like me to hand this family heirloom down to my daughter-in-law and explain that I had received it from Amritpal *Bee Ji*. She told me Maninder's Iqbal *Babba Ji* had given her this necklace – which was in an old-school design and heavier than twenty-four karat gold – when she married him.

Simranjit Mum ran out of the room in shock as she realised the necklace had just skipped a generation and missed her out! Kabir Dad felt he needed to point out how lucky I was to receive the necklace; he said his sisters would be very unhappy that I had been given this particular piece of jewellery. Amritpal *Bee Ji* must have cared about me to bestow me with her necklace, which she had worn her whole life, until this moment when she handed it over to me. I was touched that she hadn't handed it to my father-in-law's wife but rather to me; that's how special I felt.

Then Kanchan *Nani Ji* gave me £50 and both Kabir Dad and Simranjit Mum gave me another £50 as blessings.

After that evening, I handed the necklace to Simranjit Mum and never saw it again. I put the money in one of the glasses in the glass cupboard and that disappeared too. I never knew who took it.

The next morning Simranjit Mum introduced me to every element of the kitchen as well as her dos and don'ts (almost the rules of the road). For instance, they had a broken kettle you had to handle with care and switch on in its own special way. As she was talking me through this intricate procedure I was just thinking to myself, wouldn't it be easier just to buy a new kettle? If they were that hard up I would have brought one in my dowry!

My eyes were drawn to the view of the garden in front of me so everything she said fell on deaf ears. This became apparent when I then made the mistake of switching the kettle on and blowing the house fuse. Simranjit Mum shouted at me (whilst pointing her finger, which *desi* parents love to do) in an aggressive manner and asked me if I had been listening to her and why had I not done it right? I was feeling the steam from her for not switching the kettle on correctly as opposed to the steam of the *ghram* (hot) water. I had never seen this side of her before and I didn't know if she was feeling stressed after the wedding or stressed that a new girl had entered her kitchen – a new girl with contemporary cooking skills

The weekend before returning to work we all went out bowling. It was a lovely evening spent with Maninder, Kabir Dad, Simranjit Mum, Kanchan *Nani Ji* and Amritpal *Bee Ji*. I was really looking forward to spending time with Amritpal *Bee Ji* as I had not done so before getting married. Because she was housebound and not as mobile as she was a few years ago, she wasn't able to join in much and it was lovely to get her out of the house.

My job was based in Derby and I knew it was going to be tiring for me to travel there every day from Milton

Keynes. However, as the bride is meant to visit her parental home anyway, my mother, my Pretti *Mame Ji* from Derby and a younger cousin came on Sunday evening to take me back to Birmingham. I was looking forward to visiting my mother's house and having some space, enjoying some me time and getting back some normality in my life.

After two days I was missing Maninder. I called him every day for at least 30 minutes and we would talk about this and that. I was happy to be back at work; it had been a stressful year and I just wanted to get my head into my job. At times, I found that I was struggling as I had a great deal going on outside of work, which was stressful and didn't allow me to settle into my job. I felt that in previous jobs I had settled in quicker but then I'd only had to focus on the job and nothing else. This time I'd had ten months of ups and down with this relationship on top of spending the previous six months preparing for the wedding. Now that it was over I was hoping to focus on my career and to feel more settled, to put my feet in the right direction.

That week I stayed at my mother's place to help me focus on my work, and then I stayed over with Ranveer *Mama Ji* in Derby while there was a big project on board that needed to be completed. The support I had from my own family was amazing; they were positive and pushed me towards my chosen career. After three weeks I started travelling from Milton Keynes to the East Midlands every day. I would leave home at 6.30am and arrive back at 9pm. I didn't have time to get to know my in-laws that much; I'd only have an hour in the evening so we only really spent weekends together.

I remember one Saturday in particular, Kabir Dad

commented that I didn't really know the family well and I laughed in surprise. I asked him what else there was that I needed to know, given that I was married to the family and living with them. Was I missing out on something? He smiled and said: "You'll be surprised." I never really understood what he was getting at and I didn't want to question him any further. Looking back, though, I wish I had. All will be revealed in the coming chapters!

One evening Maninder suffered a headache in the middle of the night. As I was travelling with my job my sleep was important, and he had woken me up. I got some painkillers for him and asked if there was anything I could do to help. He asked me if I would massage his head. It was 3.30am in the morning but I gave him a massage for the best part of 10 minutes. He kept telling me that I wasn't doing it right. I tried a few different techniques and I couldn't understand what I was doing wrong, or how he wanted me to massage him. I felt a bit fed up and in the end I gave up and asked if I could just stop. I got back into bed and fell asleep.

I woke up at 6am to find my husband wasn't beside me in the bed. I thought maybe he was in Amritpal *Bee Ji's* old room, the spare room, but he wasn't. Perhaps he was downstairs – but he wasn't there either. I went back to our bedroom to check the en-suite bathroom, thinking he may be there. He heard me walking up and down the stairs and came out of his mother's bedroom. I asked him what he was doing in there. "Harleen," he said, "I was in pain and my mother knows what to do to soothe the pain away." I was shocked that he left our bed to go to his Simranjit Mum's bed in the middle of the night. I was actually speechless; all I could feel was hurt. I couldn't understand why Simranjit Mum allowed him to sleep in her bed knowing that he was married. After massaging his head, she should have encouraged him to go back to our bedroom. He was no longer a child; he didn't need to sleep in his mum's bed. What the hell was going on here? Why was his mum not treating him like the grown man he was?

The situation completely baffled me. Maninder's dad's words "You'll be surprised" rang through my head. I was. It played on my mind throughout the day. That evening I brought it up with Maninder. He ended up arguing with me, saying that I should have got up and massaged his head just as his mum did. Then I asked Simranjit Mum what she did that I couldn't do. She replied: "It's just I massage him whilst singing a song. I used to sing to the kids when they were young!" That was exactly my point. He was no longer a child; he was a grown man and he shouldn't need to be going through that process at all. She might as well have joined us in bed that night, I thought. Why was she rocking him to sleep? But when I voiced my opinion she just looked at me blankly. Maninder and I talked about the situation and I expressed how it made me feel. He said I was 'overreacting' which ultimately led to further arguments.

I went to bed with a heavy head. I wasn't going mad; this was not normal behaviour. Why was Maninder still holding on to his mummy's *Ji palla* rather than mine? I wouldn't have cared if he had gone to his mum's room for the head massage and got into our bed after. However, it was the fact that he slept in her bed that bothered me. Amazing to think that he was once a helpless little baby, but now he was a giant helpless man.

I didn't really know the family as much as I thought I did – as Kabir Dad had previously suggested. I wish now I'd had a crystal ball to pre-warn me about what they were really like.

Travelling to the East Midlands every day for work was a bit too much. I loved being a designer but until I could find time to apply for a job further south I just got on with it.

The weekends were spent with the family and Maninder. One weekend he wanted me to get to know his close friend Ali. We met at the V&A Museum and chilled out. I could understand why Maninder wanted me to meet Ali as he was the only one of Maninder's friends who was creative and he had the most respect for women. Ali was also into design as much as I was and Maninder wanted two like-minded creative people to get along and feel that they could both enjoy each other's our company. Through this, I became friends with Ali's whole family.

I felt warm towards Ali and I respected him from the moment we met, and likewise he did too. He made me laugh as he had a very dry but witty sense of humour. It was a great day out in the company of my husband and his friend.

A few weeks went past. Weekends were the only time I had with the family – and some of those weekends I brought home work as I had fallen behind on my deadlines.

We were getting along with both our marriage and our careers. Life was a lot more hectic than I had imagined. My work life seemed to rule everything at times.

SOMEONE I LOVE WAS NEVER BORN

There's a simple expectation of Asian marriages.

Family.

We were a few months into married life and although I had not missed a period something definitely seemed different. It wasn't that I had put on a little weight; that was expected for Punjabi women after marriage; the stress prior to the big day had seen me lose a stone in weight. While outwardly everything seemed fine, inside I knew something wasn't right. I felt nauseous and sick. My birthday was a few days away and I wanted to make sure all was okay so I could celebrate with a clear head.

On the way to my GP, I bought a pregnancy test from a local chemist. I explained how I felt to my GP, told her about the nausea and sickness. I also told her that I hadn't missed a period so it couldn't be pregnancy. She gave me a blood test to check if everything was okay. I had to wait for the result.

When I got home I hide the pregnancy test in our bathroom; I put it in the medicine cabinet, secreted under cotton pads and sanitary towels. Ironic. I sort of forgot about the test kit. I was working long hours and was a new bride.

For some reason, I decided to take the test on my birthday. I wholly expected the result to be negative. I despatched the necessary fluid onto the wand, for want of a better word! You're meant to wait a minute before checking but I was so convinced that I wasn't with child that I left the wand and wandered downstairs. Twenty minutes later I found myself looking down at my future. Looking down in disbelief.

There was a clear blue cross. There must be some mistake. I almost fainted. I read the directions on the box. I had clearly left it too long. That's why the test was positive. I waited the stipulated three minutes after the second test. A second blue cross.

I was torn.

I was lost.

I was pregnant.

Much as I was scared, I was also so excited. I couldn't wait to tell Maninder that I was pregnant with our baby. I knew he would be very happy to become a Father. Although we had only been married for two months, we'd discussed the notion of having kids. For Maninder the ideal would be to start a family after a couple of years of marriage. His parents had him in the first year of their marriage but he wanted to enjoy this time alone first. I knew this was sooner than we had planned but I thought he would be over the moon to hear the news. We were husband and wife. We were in a happy place in our relationship.

While we were courting we had even talked about how I would tell him that I was pregnant: it would be in a *gurdwara*, in the presence of the *Guru Ji*. The *Guru Ji* was at the centre of our joint, married lives; we were the centre of each other's lives; our children would be the centre of our family life. This is what our vows had meant to me.

I was going to become a mother. And I found out on my twenty-eighth birthday. Could a woman have hoped for a better birthday present?

***

It was my first birthday as a Purewal. Maninder and his family surprised me, showering me with gifts. There was, of course, more twenty-four karat gold jewellery, very much the Purewal way, and a beautiful Punjabi suit. As I held it up to admire it my mother-in-law noticed the look on my face. "Do you like it?"

"It's beautiful," I said, knowing that within weeks I'd not be able to wear it. Little did they know that the best gift was yet to come.

On our way to the restaurant for my birthday dinner, we stopped by the *gurdwara*. I walked into the *gurdwara* and up to my *Guru Ji*. I bowed before *Guru Ji* and asked for his support and blessing. Maninder sat on one side of the *Darbar Sahib* and I sat on the opposite side, shoulder to shoulder. I walked over to my husband, sat down and looked him in the face. "Maninder..."

"Harleen... I know you're pregnant." Without another word he got up and left the *gurdwara*.

I was shocked. What had just happened?

I was devastated.

I flashed back to when my father left.

I closed my eyes and asked *Guru Ji* to support me through this process, a process I had hoped was going to be joyful. He needed to give me the strength to face the situation. I didn't shed a tear, despite what had happened; in this one instance, I can truly say that God was my witness.

Alone, physically and emotionally, I left the *gurdwara* and joined Maninder in the car. The atmosphere was like nothing I had ever experienced. It was as if I was swimming, struggling in a sea of silence.

I wanted to speak, to share a tsunami of sentiments, but my thoughts were all at sea.

His mood was as dark and deep and despondent. He was sailing a different sea from me, another ocean altogether.

But why? We were married. What was the problem? We had been sexually active for months before our marriage – that's why I hadn't walked away from him. What would he have done if I had become pregnant then?

Frankly, he was behaving as if that was the case – as if this was something to be ashamed of. It was as if I had committed a crime.

I couldn't make any sense of this. The rest of the evening was singularly silent.

Silently we drove to the restaurant for my birthday dinner.

Silently we both ordered our food.

Silently we both ate our food.

Silently I was screaming inside.

***

On the way home Maninder pulled the car over and finally broke the silence. "We can't have the baby. The timing's just not right."

He then went on to list a series of materialistic reasons for not having a baby. While I wanted to focus on my career, buy our own house, enjoy lavish holidays – how does any of that come close to the joy of having a child? Those are lifestyle choices; a child is your life.

He hadn't even asked me how I felt, whether I wanted to keep the baby. This was the guy I had chosen to marry. I should have known he didn't have a backbone, that he couldn't take responsibility for anything; he had shown me this throughout the planning of our wedding.

I don't know why I hoped he'd change. I wanted this to all go away. I didn't want to face it. I was changing. I hadn't cried at all; I just sat there, feeling completely numb. We got home and I slept on my side of the bed; he slept on his. A great end to a new beginning.

***

The next morning, Simranjit Mum was throwing me a small birthday party, inviting all my family from Birmingham and my sister-in-law Gurleen's family from London. I was stressed and could do without facing the family. I lay in bed late. I hoped Simranjit Mum would question why I got up so late and ask if I was feeling okay, maybe offer to cancel the party. I had told her that I was not feeling well but she just ignored me and carried on cooking the food.

Gurleen wanted to chill with me but I just wanted to be left alone. But I had to play along. She helped me pick an outfit for the evening, but nothing seemed to fit. I hadn't told anyone about what had happened though it had crossed my mind to confide in Gurleen. Just as I was about to tell her everything, Maninder stormed into the room.

"Gurleen, get out of the room and leave Harleen alone. She's a grown woman, she can dress herself." Looking sheepish, Gurleen left.

I thought Maninder was also turning to leave but he closed the door. He walked straight back to me. We're face to face. His words came like swords. "Don't want you to tell anyone about… this. No one."

I didn't break his stare. "This?" I knew he was alluding to our child, the child I was carrying in my womb.

"You know what I mean. No one." He turned and left. All I wanted was someone to hug me, to comfort me, to tell me that everything was going to be okay. I was yearning for my mother's loving embrace – her embrace that, without words, lets you know everything is alright.

But she wasn't here.

It wasn't going to be alright.

I couldn't tell anyone.

I had to get used to the silence.

But even the silence was deafening.

I got up, got ready and forced my face into a smile. It was the sort of smile that told the world that I was loving life and in a happy place. Inside I felt nothing. I wanted to crumple up in a corner and just fade into forgetting. For years, I watched my mother lying to her family and friends. As a child, I heard her talk about what a great marriage she had. If she had done it, this should be easy for me, right... how hard could this be?

I stood in the doorway welcoming every member of my family into my new home. My face was aching with the effort to keep smiling. My Amirjit *Nani Ji* scanned me from head to toe, her loving eyes brimming with pride. If only she knew...

"Are you happy, Harleen?"

I couldn't bear to lie to my Amirjit *Nani Ji*. But I had to. "Of course I am."

She smiled, happy that her granddaughter had found love. They all loved Maninder. They thought I was the luckiest of all the girls in our family having chosen a lovely guy who treated me well. He wasn't like some of the old school Punjabi men who abused their old school Punjabi wives, the sort that spoke with fists and fury.

It was the first time my family had visited me at my in-laws' home. My traditional mother could never visit her newly married daughter and arrive empty-handed. She arrived at the front door, laden with Indian sweets and fresh fruit. Knowing how much Maninder loved mango *lassi* (a yogurt- based drink from the Indian subcontinent), she brought a box of mangoes especially. At the end of the evening, Simranjit Mum took a look at the box of mangos in the kitchen and asked my mother, in front of the entire family, to take them back to Birmingham. The ensuing awkward silence was broken by my mother. "Why, *Pehn Ji*?"

"I won't support Pakistan or give them any funding. Not in this house."

Maninder backed his mum up. I wondered what the hell was going on here. I couldn't believe what was being said to my mother. I intervened. "What do you both mean?"

The mangoes were Pakistani, apparently. I'd never heard of fruit having a nationality.

My mother wasn't going to be bested.

"I bought these mangoes from relatives of yours. They own that supermarket in Smethwick, don't they? You'd better speak to them…"

They were clearly Black Country mangos.

This was surreal. Had I made the biggest mistake of my life in choosing this family as my family, and their golden son as my husband? I couldn't believe the way they spoke to my mother in front of both our families.

Before my family left, Kabir Dad and Simranjit Mum

wanted to show off how proud they were of their home and showcase it to my Amirjit *Nani Ji,* who was over from Canada. I was concerned; I didn't want everybody just walking into my room and I had left the pregnancy test in the bathroom – and there were my in-laws, showing off how amazing it was for me to be living in their amazing home, married to their amazing son. I just hoped they wouldn't start opening wardrobe doors and bathroom cupboards. If they did they would soon discover more than they needed to about my not so perfect life…

When the Indian immigrants first arrived, back in the 60s, 70s and 80s, it was common for a single Punjabi family of as many as 15 members to live under one roof. This was not dissimilar to life in the Punjab, where the extended family all lived together. The difference was that there was much more space in the Punjab! I remember my father once telling us a story of his childhood; there were 11 people living in a three-bedroom house with one bathroom. My grandparents, my father and his six siblings and two kids; eleven. It was mayhem, as well as great fun. 'Compromise' became their middle name. Of course, there were tough times but they were all in it together; homes were full of love. That's how Punjabi families started off in the UK. As they began to save money and buy their own homes they soon moved on, moved away. Families fractured as folk chased the western dream of having bigger and better homes.

Simranjit Mum told everyone about her lovely big house; she would continually compare it to my mother's humble home in Birmingham. Simranjit Mum shouted about all the space they enjoyed; unlike my mother's house.

My new family had empty hearts and big mouths. They loved showing off: their house, their careers and all their cars – each with a private registration plate.

It was all for the community. Nothing was done from the heart.

In the *Sri Guru Granth Sahib Ji,* it says *"true wealth does not burn; it cannot be stolen by a thief."* **(Page 991-13, of Sri Guru Granth Sahib Ji)**.

They had no wealth when compared to my mother. The Purewals couldn't understand why my mother had such close links with her cousins and brothers. That was probably because Maninder's folks didn't talk to their extended family. While I might have grown up in a smaller house, it was a home: full of love and full of life.

The evening ended. Maninder and I went to our bedroom and readied ourselves for bed. He wanted to know what I was going to do in the morning. I might have shared a bed with him but I really didn't want to share my thoughts. "I'm going to work tomorrow," I said. What else did he think I would be doing?

He looked me in the eye and said: "Don't you think that you should see a doctor?" I had no more room for negativity in my life. I decided to ignore him and try to get some sleep.

***

It was 2nd June 2008. I had known about my pregnancy for a little over 48 hours. It was a normal day. I got up, as usual. I left the house, as usual. I went to the station with my husband in the car, as usual. Three days ago, we were getting on brilliantly, loving life. Now?

Maninder dropped me off at Milton Keynes station.

Instead of going to work I decided to go to Birmingham and call my doctors for an emergency appointment.

My doctor had received my test results back and could happily confirm that I was pregnant.

I suspect he was hoping for a different reaction. Mine was matter of fact. I told him that I already knew and I explained how Maninder had reacted. I needed an abortion: there was no other option. I hated myself for saying that; I hated the guilt.

My doctor looked at me with a a smile as pure as the life that was growing inside me. "Please accept my heartfelt wishes, Mrs. Purewal, on the beginning of a new journey in your life!" He smiled wide. "It'll be an awesome experience, trust me."

I felt a jolt inside me. I knew his feelings were as real as the heartache I harboured inside me. I was about to break his heart. I was about to break mine. Literally, I was also about to break my child's. So I mustered the strength to say, "I came here for an abortion."

His face fell. "What did you say?"

I was quiet for a few moments, before I whispered, "Yes, I'm here for termination."

"Have you gone bonkers?" he snapped. "You two are happily married, you have well-paying jobs, you've got a fine place to stay. What in the world is stopping you from having a child?" I stayed quiet. He glanced at the closed door and said, "Look, I don't care how many people are out there waiting, but I'll see this through." He looked straight into my eyes. "Do you know how lucky you are to have a healthy child growing inside you?" He pointed at the door. "They all come here because they can't conceive! Because they can't have a healthy child! And here you are, blessed with a robust and blooming foetus, and you come to me for an abortion! What's your problem, Mrs Purewal?"

"My husband…" I said gloomily, "he doesn't want me to have a child right now."

"Is he serious? Why?"

"I'm not so sure. He says he's not ready."

"I don't see why he is not ready," the doctor said. "You have everything ready to start a family. It's not like you're going to kill the foetus on a whim just because your husband says he is not ready." He took time to explain to me how it feels to be a father. "When my first one was born, I felt like I was drowning in love. The feeling is out of this world. That's when I realised nothing material can replace that pristine form of love and the joy it heralds."

I noticed an innocent smile surfacing on his lips as he carried on talking to me as if he were my father. But I was too stubborn. I stuck to my guns.

"Okay, then hear this out!" he said. He threw his pen. It rolled across the table and hit the floor. "I have taken the oath to give life, not take it away. For silly reasons like yours, I am not going to have blood on my hands! With your basic rights, you can always visit another clinic where they'd oblige, but your abortion is not going to happen here under my supervision." He pulled out a letterhead. "I can refer you to them if you want." He gave me some details and contact numbers I would need to call to book an appointment.

I sat outside the doctor's surgery, pondering that I never thought I would ever be faced with having to end the life of my child before it was born. I hadn't yet shed a tear about my pregnancy but there and then I broke down. Tears. So many tears. I felt nothing less than hatred for Maninder. He left me to walk this path alone. He hadn't even begun to comprehend the mental and emotional impact this would have on me, let alone the physical procedure.

I needed to get into work and face the music. I knew if I broke the news to my colleagues they would be over the moon. But that couldn't happen. This baby was not going to be a part of my life. I had to explain to work why I was late; I needed to tell them what was going on with my life. I needed to tell someone about the innocent life that I was carrying around with me.

My design director and manager took me into the board room. I broke the news. They were both surprised. Then I told them that Maninder and I were not going to keep the baby. They gave me paid time off work to sort myself out.

You have no idea what goes on in the mind of a woman who goes through an abortion. I'd been sent home from work to have time to think everything over but I felt there was nothing to think about. I had been told by the one person I relied on that he didn't want the baby and I just had to follow through with the process, regardless of my own feelings.

Maninder's parents were surprised that I was home so early and asked if everything was okay. I smiled and told them that I was fine and that my manager had just given me some time back that was owed to me. Maninder came in from work and, like his parents, was shocked to see me and asked why I was home so early. I explained that I had told work and visited the GP during the day. I needed to call the clinic to book an appointment for the abortion. My GP had given me the details of a clinic local to me in Milton Keynes.

Maninder was more bothered about what I had told the GP – and why the hell I accepted details for a Milton Keynes clinic. He was furious. There was no way I could go to any local clinic, he told me. Someone from the Asian community might see me and find out why I was there. He made everything feel so sinful and wrong. It was a baby – why was he acting like I was trying to treat a sexually transmitted disease? His reputation was at stake.

He told me to book an appointment to terminate the pregnancy in Birmingham. My reputation or feelings weren't his concern; he didn't care that I may be seen by my family members and friends. Why was this all about him and his high standards? He hadn't even asked me how I felt or how the appointment with the GP had gone. Selfish was an understatement. So now I needed to call the surgery in the morning and arrange to get the phone numbers for the Birmingham clinic. Great… This just got better and better.

***

A few days later Simranjit Mum and Maninder were in the kitchen making mango *lassi* with my mother's Pakistan-funded mangos. What bloody hypocrites! I just couldn't understand them. I called my mother and told her. She just laughed in amazement and disbelief.

Why would you behave so badly towards your daughter-in-law's family? Life wasn't a *desi* drama series! My mother-in-law didn't get on with the majority of her husband's family, and now she was doing the same with mine. I simply couldn't see it from her point of view. Where had it come from? Who did she think she was? Her true colours had finally come through after the wedding.

On 5th June 2008, after an assessment at the Birmingham clinic, I told my best friend Jaya that I was pregnant. She was over the moon. I would have loved my so-called husband to respond the same way. She came crashing back to Planet Earth when I told her that Maninder didn't want me to continue with the pregnancy.

Jaya asked me what I wanted. I told her. I heard myself say it out loud for the first time.

"I'd love to have the baby. I'd love to. But it's impossible."

She pleaded with me to tell him how I was really feeling, that I wanted the baby. But I had no strength. I stood outside the clinic crying and talking to the one person I felt I could be honest with.

I hadn't even told my mother.

So I called her and explained that I was in Birmingham with work. Mother asked if I would like to meet up at the station for a coffee and a chat. It was lovely to see her. During our conversation, she suddenly said: "You're pregnant."

I was in shock. I looked her in the eyes, her honest loving eyes. And I lied.

"Don't be daft, Mother, I'm not pregnant. I've only just got married. What made you say that?"

"You're not your usual self around me. And I'm old. Old people know things. In our gut. You would tell me if you were, wouldn't you?" She looked straight at me, almost through me. "You know that if you ever need to talk…"

I felt so guilty for lying to her. I couldn't face my own mother. I made an excuse and flapped my way out of the coffee shop. I walked around the block and then sat on a bench. I was carrying my child yet all I felt was an emptiness inside.

I got myself together, went back to Milton Keynes and called Maninder to collect me from the station. The clinic had called me on my way back to say they could fit me in for the abortion on Monday 9th June. There it was. Like booking a holiday.

I didn't have the energy to talk to Maninder but there were arrangements to be made. I was on a downward spiral over which I had no control. I just wanted to get on with everything until I could understand what was going on with my life. I told him about the appointment; he'd need to take me to the clinic in Birmingham.

"You're expecting me to take you there?" Surely that was the least he could do, I said, especially since I'd organised everything and been to all the appointments on my own. He exploded. "Fucking great. I'll have to take the day off work. Can't you just do it yourself?"

I remained calm. I needed his support. I didn't – I couldn't – do this alone. He had to share in the guilt I was experiencing, the pain of losing my baby.

***

Simranjit Mum got a phone call from her younger sister. Their dad was seriously ill. Kabir Dad got us together to talk about the possibility of Maninder's Simranjit Mum going to Canada to be there for her dad. In the early hours of Sunday morning Simranjit Mum came knocking on our bedroom door. She needed Maninder to book a flight to

Canada immediately. Her dad had become critically ill and was in the final stages of his life. I helped her pack her bags and Maninder booked her flight. Working as a team, we got her organised, took her to Heathrow Airport and on the flight by 10.30am. We were so busy I temporarily forgot about the pregnancy. I knew that in her absence I would have to care for the family, make sure that Maninder's Gran was looked after, cook all the meals and keep the house clean.

When we got back from London we told Kabir Dad that we were going to be busy on Monday so he would have to look after Amritpal *Bee Ji*. Kabir Dad had Monday and Tuesday off work as he worked Wednesday to Sunday, so I needed to make sure that I was the leading lady of the household for those days. Everything had to be done to the same standards as Simranjit Mum expected. I was now the third generation of Purewal women; my duties were clear. I felt that whatever I was going through and however much I was hurting inside, it had to be controlled.

Monday morning arrived. Maninder and I hadn't spoken about what was happening. We drove to the clinic in Birmingham, which was just around the corner from an auntie's home.

I knew that my mother would be hanging out there, as she did most days. When we were outside the clinic Maninder spoke. "This is as far as I can go. You'll have to go alone. People will know I'm Sikh because of my turban. What would they think?" To his credit, he apologised for his behaviour! But what did Sikhism say about the way he was treating me – and did he know that in Sikhism, abortion is completely forbidden? Actions speak louder than words. He could apologise over and over, but if our actions don't change, the words become meaningless. I said nothing.

I got out of the car and went straight to the clinic. God was my only witness with regard to how I felt. He gave me the strength to go through this alone, as a strong woman. Writing about this has been the second hardest thing I've ever done. Living through it was the hardest.

The only advice I can give is to communicate honestly with your partner. If you want the baby, tell them. In the end, you will be the one who either goes through with the procedure or gives birth; you have to be selfish. Before falling pregnant all I ever wanted was a stable relationship, a nice house and a very large and close-knit family. In one way, I wanted this baby. In another way, I didn't. Waiting on my own before the procedure was the longest, darkest ten minutes I have ever endured. All that runs through your head is the guilt and the feeling that you are snuffing out an as yet unformed life. I still couldn't believe I was pregnant so the idea that I was in an abortion clinic waiting to get rid of the baby that I had always longed for was too much to compute. I was losing a life that I had created with Maninder.

I had to have a scan before the abortion and this was what hurt the most. I asked the nurse doing the scan if I could look at the screen. I shouldn't have. This made it all the more real for me. I could feel this little person within me. And now I could see them.

I asked forgiveness from my unborn child for what I was about to do – and made my own peace with myself.

Maninder and I had decided that if we were to have

kids, we would call our first child Ekam, which is derived from the *Gurbani* word '*Ik-Onkar*'. *Ik-Onkar* is the first word of *Gurbani*. It represents the One Supreme Reality and is a central tenet of Sikh religious philosophy. *Ik* means one or more united, *On* means supreme, ultimate, or highest *Bhrama* (God), and the *Atma* (Soul) of the entire universe or system, and *Kar* means without shape or form. **(http://en.m.wikipedia.org/wiki/Ik_Onkar)**

I hoped in time I could forget the pain.

The doctor dispensed the first abortion pill. I swallowed the pill and tried to swallow the consequences. Four hours later I was given the second abortion pill, because I was not able to come back the next day as usually happened. I was monitored and then discharged. I'd been there no more than three-quarters of an hour. Just 45 minutes to shatter a lifetime of dreams.

Maninder was sitting in the car park waiting for me. It was as if nothing had happened. He said nothing. I got in the car and on the journey home the pain started.

When we got home I couldn't look at him. I think he realised how badly he had behaved towards me and decided to change his tune and start supporting me. I couldn't care less. I just wanted to get into bed; the pain was unbearable and all I could feel was guilt at the thought of what I had done. I took painkillers and sleeping pills, given to me by my GP before I got married to help me sleep due to the stress of the wedding. Too many. Not enough to be a worry, but just enough to try and dull the pain I was feeling. And I slept, even though the pain had not been killed....

Maninder woke me up in the early hours of the

morning. I found myself swimming in my own blood and the aftershock of what I'd done. I felt overwhelmed; I couldn't understand what was going on. I was in so much pain. I felt disorientated. Maninder had woken up when he felt my blood drenching the bed. It was a reminder of the deep loss I had experienced. While I battled my grogginess and showered, he stripped the bed and remade it with fresh new sheets; new sheets to hide the evidence of the wrong he had chosen to put me through. When I emerged from the shower Maninder asked me to keep the noise down as Kabir Dad had woken up and asked what was going on. Heaven forbid the truth to be known.

The pain was unbelievable; I could barely walk. From the beginning of this process, I couldn't understand why Maninder hadn't been bothered about what was going on. He was so cold and it chilled me how there was no remorse for the life that was lost. I couldn't control my feelings. It was so hard to try and act normal and the pain reminded me of what I had done. It broke me every time I tried to gasp for fresh air.

Ever heard the saying 'A woman is like a glass bottle'? I was broken and I couldn't be fixed. I was in so much pain, both physically and mentally. Like any other woman I was a fragile being, and this was the moment in my life that the hurt was at its deepest point.

The next morning Maninder came into our bedroom and asked me what time I was going to be getting up to give Kabir Dad and Amritpal *Bee Ji* my presence and show my face. He'd seen I could only just walk and I told him that I was not well enough to get out of bed.

An hour later he popped into our bedroom again and

asked if I minded getting up and cooking Amritpal *Bee Ji* some food. Kabir Dad wanted to know why I had not come downstairs to socialise with the family. I had just lost the life I had created and I felt physically and emotionally drained. And Maninder still didn't show me any remorse.

Despite the pain, I got up, took my time and welcomed the family with a smile. I couldn't believe Maninder thought it was more important for me to be cooking than resting upstairs. Without family, there's nothing to live for. He had made me destroy the root that was going to be the beginning of our family, but all he cared about was his family being fed, not how I was coping with things.

I just couldn't allow this man to touch me or be near me anymore. I had nothing left for him to hurt me with. Everything felt dead and emotionless. But life goes on...

Yes – abortion hurts emotionally like hell! Till this day, it's been hell just to think of a beautiful life lost. I'm getting very emotional just writing this. Counsellors or therapists don't work. If you regret it at the time, you will always regret it. There's no way you can change your mind about something like that, no matter how many people you discuss it with, professional or otherwise. After this experience, I asked myself when the right time to have children was. Is there ever a right time to have a child? You always have to make time and sacrifices, just as our parents did back in the day.

The next morning, I felt even more of a rush of blood trickling down my legs, and the unheard cries of the life that I'd once nourished pierced my heart. They were the cries of shattering trust more than that of pain. I'd lost the strength to stand on my feet. I came face to face with my dead child in the bath, where I allowed the warm water to carry away the pain that had made me numb. I didn't have any idea it would be this gory and traumatic. No one had prepared me for this moment. There was no leaflet given by the GP or abortion clinic either. I'd rather have died than go through this trauma, when a part of my soul was killed. I killed it. He killed it.

THE PHONE HACKING SCANDAL

Amritpal *Bee Ji* came over to me while I was sitting on the sofa and asked if I was okay. Then she asked if I was pregnant, as she'd noticed how many times I had left the kitchen while cooking. Little did she know it was the pain of standing up that was stopping me from getting on with things like cooking a meal for the family. If she'd any idea that I had aborted her great grandchild...

I'd called the clinic to tell them about the discomfort I was having and I had been advised to pop into the local clinic for a check-up. Then I'd called my Derby Ranveer *Mama Ji's* home to speak with my great *Nani Ji's* sister *Bibi Ji.* I was feeling sick and I needed to hear a familiar, warm voice. I was on the phone for about five minutes before Amritpal *Bee Ji* came into the kitchen to keep me company. She started telling me some of the house rules, things I had no clue about. Then she advised me not to use the house telephone as the landline was tapped. I have to admit, I thought she wasn't all there. Who listens in to a home phone line? I couldn't understand why she would say something as bizarre as that. I laughed it off and started talking about things we could do to get her out the family house, get her some fresh air and sort her head out. I really thought she'd lost her mind. But when I found out the truth, it was my mind that would be lost...

I had been warned by Maninder and his parents that she had a habit of playing mind games, but this was a hurtful game she was playing with my mind. Two days passed by. Maninder came home early from work and finally realised I was struggling. I was cooking the evening meal for the family and he came into the kitchen and asked if I would like any help. I asked him to cut the vegetables and we got talking about this and that... I grabbed the moment and brought up the conversation with Amritpal *Bee Ji* about the landline being tapped. He looked at me and asked if I would come into the main living room and sit down as he had something to tell me. I sat on one sofa and he sat on the other and said: "I have to tell you something. Please hear me out and do not disturb me until I've finished talking. Then you can let me know how you feel." I looked at him, feeling very confused. He admitted that the house landline was tapped and explained why. His dad didn't get on with his sisters and wanted to listen in on the conversation that Amritpal *Bee Ji* had with her daughters. I was so disgusted. I couldn't even think straight. I thought Amritpal *Bee Ji* had lost her marbles and was talking gibberish... Little did I know she was looking out for me! The one person I had not even taken much time to get to know was on my side. I did not know a thing about this place I called home. Three other people in this house, who I had taken the time to get to know, didn't have the decency to look me in the face and tell me.

The first thing I asked Maninder was where the hell was this phone hacking or tapping device. He took me into Simranjit Mum's bedroom and showed me a box hidden behind one of the thick curtain fabrics. My in-laws slept in separate bedrooms. She was still in Canada but the device had been left on to record all the conversations so she could catch up on the gossip when she got back. I really had nothing to say. I started to cry. Why hadn't Maninder thought it important to communicate this information to me? Why had he not told me this before our marriage? He knew that I couldn't condone such behaviour. I have had problems with family members, don't get me wrong – we all have our ups and downs within our own families – but this was utterly unacceptable.

I asked him who the mastermind behind this plan was. His mum, of course! That didn't surprise me. She came across like butter wouldn't melt in her mouth and made herself out to be the victim. Before the wedding she told me that her two sisters-in-law were jealous of her relationship with my father-in-law. Over the years they had bullied her but because they were older than her, she respected them. But where was the respect right now? Listening in on her mother-in-law and sisters-in-law's conversations, what was that all about? The same applied to my father-in-law. No one in this household had the right to listen to anyone's private conversation. I felt I had been betrayed. I had no words for such behaviour... I just couldn't believe this was happening. This was the sort of thing you read in the *desi-parades* papers about other people's marriages. If someone listens in to your phone conversation, without your permission, it is a crime punishable by law – as well as a gross invasion of privacy.

It changed my outlook on life. It's funny how we always assume everyone is happier and has the most wonderful life compared to our own. The truth goes untold unless you ask, but even then you're always on the outside looking in. We all have our own hardships and untold horrible stories only we can understand. However, the world continues to look much brighter through someone else's eyes. Everybody was looking at me thinking how blessed I was to have the perfect husband, perfect family and perfect home.

"The grass is always greener on the other side" – until we visit the other side and find something totally different and unexpected: AstroTurf. The obstacles that come with life are ones we all have to juggle. This marriage had definitely brought about some of my most joyous and depressing moments in such a short period of time.

What upset me the most was that I had left my handbag on the train a week ago and when I had informed Maninder he advised me to use the landline to cancel my bank cards. I'd also had a conversation with the GP regarding the abortion. I'd assumed my phone calls were confidential but little did I know, none of my conversations were private. I was hurting and I needed someone to talk to. I called my Pretti *Mame Ji,* asked her to call me on my new mobile and told her what I had discovered. She said I must forgive Maninder and his parents as it was the first mistake they had made, but for some reason I just couldn't get my head around the situation. Normally when someone screws up once I let it go but this was different.

I was feeling unwell and right now was not the time to talk about my feelings. I was dealing with my own issues and trying to hold the family together and no one had given me a manual. I just had to get on with things like a good Punjabi wife...

Maninder and I had a few arguments and I decided at this point I couldn't even look at him or talk to him. I felt that I had been lied to and mistreated.

He couldn't stand getting the silent treatment from me so he decided to let his dad know that I knew about the phone tapping. To be honest, I had egged him on; I wanted my lovely father-in-law to know that I knew about their behaviour. Without his wife, Kabir Dad looked stressed, like a lost puppy. He came into the main living room – which was seeing all the action these days. You'd think it was the stage of the Ricki Lake show! – and I asked him when they were thinking of telling me about the British Telecom secret. His reply: once I had settled into the family home. When was that going to be then? He just looked at me blankly. I then asked him who else in the family knew about the phone tapping and he replied that Gurleen, my sister-in-law knew too. I asked if her husband Loveneet *Pah Ji* knew and he said that Loveneet and his family didn't know anything at all. I was angry. I said: "Well thank you, Daddy *Ji*! You have always said to me, from day one when you met me, that I would live under your roof as a daughter, not a daughter-in-law. Well, you have treated me like a daughter-in-law rather than a daughter by not telling me the truth about the home that I am living in. Your daughter is no longer living under this roof. She left two years ago – so why does she know everything about this household? It's parents like you who treat their daughters and daughters-in-law differently. Rather than advise us on how to build strong relationships, you advise your kids on how to keep information from their partners. You teach them how to lie. What kind of parents are you?"

At this point, he got annoyed with me putting him on the spot and asking him all these questions. But I needed answers. The situation had changed my relationship with every member of this family. They had all taken me for a mug and lied to my face. I loved Gurleen as a baby sister and I had never treated her any different, even though she had with me. I was already feeling hurt from the way Maninder had treated me and this was like salt being pressed into my wounds. I didn't know who to trust or who I could talk to. Yet I didn't want to break my mother's heart because she had been through a great deal with her own marriage and her deepest fear was to see any of her daughters go through the same thing.

I lived with four other people within this family but I had never felt so alone as at that moment. I started to tell Kabir Dad about the abortion but Maninder stopped me and said that we had had a miscarriage. I couldn't even say the word abortion; it had to be brushed under the carpet like a dirty secret. Only one friend and my loving partner knew about it.

Later that evening we got a phone call from Maninder's mum informing us that her dad had passed away. Maninder looked me in the face and said that he would have loved to have said goodbye to his Mohanbir *Nani Ji* and it was only because I was pregnant that he was unable to go to Canada. I was gobsmacked. It's not like he was giving me much support. In fact, I wouldn't even have cared if he had gone. To be honest I wish he had, for it would have been less of a headache for me.

Even though I had been through a great deal these last couple of days I knew that I had to just get on with things and be there for everybody else. I decided to bury my feelings. I took down all our wedding decorations from around the house and spent time chilling with Amritpal *Bee Ji*. It was funny, Amritpal *Bee Ji* was the one person that I hadn't had much interaction with at the beginning and the one person I had not even taken the time to get to know, yet the one person who had been honest with me was her.

I knew that Maninder and his dad were really angry with Amritpal *Bee Ji* for giving me the *chaat* (sauce) to the *masala*. They couldn't believe that she had told me about the phone tapping and they were not making much of an effort with her. I decided to show that I was grateful for her *pyar*(love) and started to spend more time with her. I would sit with her while she watched one of her Asian drama series, or talk away about Maninder and his childhood and other irrelevant topics. I felt so much peace and comfort around her welcoming scent.

Simranjit Mum returned from Canada but for a while, nothing was mentioned about the phone tapping or my health. One day my brother came to visit, and he and Maninder decided to play golf. I just wanted to rest up so I stayed home to relax in front of the TV. Suddenly Simranjit Mum came into the living room and asked me why I had not joined the guys for golf. I said I was resting. She then said, "I gather you've had a miscarriage." I looked her in the face and thought, well, if she'd listened to the phone conversation she'll know it was an abortion, not a miscarriage. She asked me how I was feeling and then switched the conversation to what her husband had told her about Amritpal *Bee Ji* and the phone tapping device. I couldn't even look at her. I thought she must have planned this moment knowing that the boys were going to be out and wanting to have a heart to heart with me. I didn't even want to know what she had to say as I knew she would only open her mouth and allow more lies to come out and fool me. I stared at the TV and said I'd rather not talk about things right know as I wasn't feeling well – thanks to her lovely son and the family secrets I had discovered.

During this period, we had a great deal of people visiting the family home to pay their respects regarding Maninder's Mohanbir *Nanaa Ji* passing away. I started becoming a pro at hiding my feelings... Smiling every time someone came over and hiding the pain I was going through. I didn't allow people to get too close to me; I didn't want them to know the pain that I was suffering.

I returned to work after having some time off and spent a lovely few weeks in my job. However, I never really opened up to anybody about what was going on in my heart or head. I asked Maninder if I could stop over at my Ranveer *Mama Ji's* house for the next few weeks rather than commuting every day from Milton Keynes, as the stress was slowly taking over me. He agreed, especially as I was still bleeding quite heavy, as I needed to rest as much as I could. Sometimes I popped home to stay overnight at my mother's place in Birmingham. While visiting my mother one time, I started getting abdominal pains to the point that I couldn't even walk. I lied to my mother and just said that I needed to get back to Milton Keynes. I hoped she wouldn't notice what I was going through.

I got home to discover more guests paying their respects. After the guests left Simranjit Mum had a friend's birthday party she wanted to attend. We were all going as a family but I could only just about walk. However, I felt under pressure. I knew if I didn't go, the family would start wondering what was going on with me. I informed Maninder that I was experiencing some pain but he didn't take any notice of me and just carried on getting ready for the party. I felt as though I was talking to myself, so I stopped, controlled my tears and got ready.

When we got to the party we walked in like one big happy family. It was a lovely party and I got to meet Simranjit Mum's friends, who I had heard a great deal of positive things about, and met some other friends of the family too. Simranjit Mum asked if I would like to have a dance and I agreed, feeling a little better. While dancing away I did a sudden move and at that point, I knew something wasn't right with me. I could walk but my legs felt like jelly. I knew that I was not going to make it through the whole evening so I found Maninder and told him that I needed to go to hospital. We used the excuse that we needed to check if Amritpal *Bee Ji* was ok. We came back home and I changed into something more comfortable. Then we travelled to A&E and I waited 40 minutes until a nurse checked me over and straight away put me on a drip. She did some internal check-ups and discovered that I had a massive infection.

After realising the state, I was in, Maninder apologised for just dismissing my feelings that evening. I could see he was shocked by the seriousness of the situation. The hospital kept me in until the early hours of the morning. I was finally discharged with a course of antibiotics and advised to have a follow-up appointment with a local GP. Maninder concocted some story for his parents and asked them to give me time to rest. Gurleen and her family were coming to visit and it was going to be the first time I would meet Loveneet's side of my extended family. Maninder informed me that his parents said I should just rest up and not worry about coming down, but I felt that I should make an effort as Loveneet and his family always made time for me and I got a very warm feeling from them. I made it down to see everybody and spent a couple of hours with them. There was time to rest after they left.

OPENING MY LETTERS

I was coming to the end of my contract, so I decided that it was time to start looking for a new job. I signed up with a few agencies and contacted the local design companies in the area. One evening I came home and noticed that my mail had been opened. I brought the issue up with Maninder and he said someone may have opened it by mistake. I know mistakes can happen so I mentioned it to his parents and Kabir Dad admitted that he opened my mail by accident. The letter was about a job I'd applied for in London as a graphic designer; I had not been successful. Then a couple of weeks later it happened again. This time, I couldn't understand why my mail had been opened as there was no one else in this family with a name starting with the letter H or with the first name Harleen. I was a little upset and discussed it with Maninder, who asked his parents who had opened the letter. Kabir Dad laughed and replied that he had mistakenly opened my mail. Again. Maninder asked how, as his name started with the letter K, and he replied that he thought it was for the Amritpal *Bee Ji*. Maninder pointed out that her name started with the letter A. He was annoyed because the explanation we'd got wasn't good enough. He told Kabir Dad not to open my mail again. I was only applying for jobs and I had not yet transferred my bank account or other mail to my new address – and, having had my mail opened twice, I decided not to transfer anything until I felt comfortable with the family. Tapping into phone calls and opening letters – Maninder and his parents must have had some sort of underlying trust issue. This wasn't the ideal home environment to be living in.

Before Maninder and I got married I knew that I wanted to be living in a family unit. I never thought that I would marry into a family with such insecurities and I didn't know what to do, or how I could help sort things out. So many dilemmas, and my relationship with Maninder wasn't good either as we were not sleeping together because of the abortion and the hurt I was going through. It was all giving me an extra headache which was becoming a painful, constant migraine.

Something inside my gut told me that I was paying the price for not getting to know Maninder before I married him. My advice to every girl out there thinking of getting married is to live with your partner and get to know who they are before the wedding! Be a strong woman who can look her parents in the eyes and say "I know the man I am going to get married to and I know what I'm signing up for." I'd stopped believing in fairy tales, love, and romance. Instead, I was watching Bollywood films and listening to music that made me feel good inside. But inside, I was holding back on everything, becoming emotionless. I just did my duty as a good Punjabi wife, a perfect Punjabi wife...

ROUND ONE: HITTING ME FOR THE FIRST TIME AFTER FOUR MONTHS OF MARRIAGE

We were arguing. Again. I hadn't noticed that the nature of the bad feelings between us had increased incrementally. Then, one day, they escalated. Escalated to another, worrying place. Maninder lashed out at me and hit me. I was shocked. He hit me like I was a friend he had fallen out within the playground; it was very strong and forceful. And it came from nowhere. I couldn't believe that I had chosen this man as my life partner. I curled up inside, feeling like I had no control whatsoever. As he went to hit me again I screamed out loud. His mum heard me, came running into our bedroom and asked what was going on. Shaking, I explained that Maninder had hit me. She asked him to leave the room and to leave me alone. She left too, but ten minutes later she returned and asked me to come to a wedding with her. I was amazed. In my view, when you stop a child from hitting without telling them off they are more likely to hit again. Maninder had hit me and all his mother was bothered about was going to a family friend's wedding reception. I was in shock, but she explained that it would help Maninder and me to have some space apart and time to calm down.

My confidence was at its lowest ebb. I was being asked to go to a wedding of people I didn't even know, dress up in a glamorous *saree* and act like I was in one of those Asian drama series where all the women are happily married. But inside I was dying. I was going to attend my first wedding as a married woman without my husband, who had physically assaulted me just moments ago. This was going to be great.

When we arrived at the wedding lots of people asked where Maninder was. My *Saas* (mother-in-law) was on call to answer the questions; she said that he was busy with work and he had exams for his job that he needed to focus on. I felt like I was living the life of my Mother by lying to people about my marriage. History was repeating itself. Simranjit Mum was doing a great job of putting up an old school Punjabi-style appearance with the local community. I remember seeing nine newly-wed girls at this wedding looking a great deal happier than me and with their partners by their side. I didn't get married to attend functions as a singleton – I could have done that when I was single. Nor did I get married to attend functions with my mother-in-law. I had been too many family parties and functions with my mother as a single parent and I wasn't going to start doing that here when I had a husband. I left the function feeling upset. Simranjit Mum's friend saw me crying as I left and told her to check if I was okay. It took someone that I didn't even know to point out that I was upset. Simranjit Mum came out after me and told me to go, as I couldn't let people see me like that.

It said a lot that she was more bothered that people had seen me upset than about being a responsible parent, talking to her son and making him understand that his behaviour was not acceptable. Instead, she chose to run off to another person's wedding to celebrate rather than face up to the situation.

When I got home from the function Maninder came up to me and started talking normally. He didn't once think to apologise; it was too hard for him to man up to what he had done. Yet again I was left feeling more hurt than ever. What had I done to deserve this? The only effort he made was to ask whether I wanted to go to the cinema with him. I refused. I wasn't going to pretend everything was la de da. Why should I keep giving in to him? I didn't get back half of what I gave.

Simranjit Mum got a sniff of me rejecting her angelic son and came to my room to have a go at me. I stood up for myself and told her that I now understood how my mother felt being a single parent. I got married to share the special times with my husband, not be made to feel the way I had today. Why was she having a go at me for refusing to hang out with her son? Why hadn't she had a go at him for hitting me? I guess it's always easy to blame someone else's kids rather than take the time to understand it's your own who are at fault. I refused to socialise with him until he could understand that his behaviour was not acceptable, and I was not going to allow him to think it was.

You would think that Simranjit Mum would have understood how I was feeling as a woman, understood what I was trying to say. Instead, she used the excuse that he had been a bully in his younger days and he would push his sister around. She didn't see that it was not civilised, and not the way to behave towards your life partner.

Good relationships don't just happen. They take time, patience and two people who truly want to be together. Two people who work hard at it every day...

What Maninder's mum needed to realise was that her little boy had now become a man. He had to be responsible for his own life. May his mind be clear, his heart open and his back strong to face the big wide world alone – as a real man – without his "mum". So why was she allowing him to hold tightly onto her *palla*?

This was the first time I took note of her mood swings. I had met many people in my life and every time anybody showed me mood swings I chose never to take them on board. The way I look at mood swings is that the person is taking time out of their life to ruin their mood for the day – not mine – so I allow that person to exercise that process until they can move their mood back to a happier place.

Simranjit Mum had shown me her true colours; everything Amritpal *Bee Ji* had said was true. I loved the way she played the role of an innocent person who had been mistreated by everyone from her in-laws' side of the family.

However, Maninder's parents didn't know what was the right or wrong thing to do; they too were guilty of unacceptable behaviour towards another person living under their roof, without even knowing it. How were they going to teach him the right way to behave? You can only be proud of your parenting skills once your kids know how to live a morally correct life.

Maninder and I continued our passionate arguing now and then. There were times in our relationship when I thought things were getting better but at other moments, I had to pull myself together, be patient and get on with things. I never really showed anyone how I felt; I didn't express my feelings to anyone other than my best mate Jaya.

Jaya would really crack me up with the running commentary she would do while I was dwelling on my problems. She made me see the bright side of life and told me to get on with it because sooner or later it would get better. We laughed about my life being better than a *desi* drama show these days.

I had not invited any of my friends to come and visit me in Milton Keynes. Actually, because of the problems I had not even spoken to anyone since getting married. I didn't know what angle to start talking from and I didn't want people close to me to know about the hurt I was enduring.

***

Since moving in with the Purewal family I had still not been given a set of house keys. I asked Maninder when I was going to be getting my keys and he said I should ask his parents. I should have guessed; it would have saved me asking him. At times, I felt like I had married my in-laws rather than my husband.

I broached the subject with my Father-in-law, and he said I would get a set of house keys when I passed my driving test. I was a bit shocked and didn't really know what to say. I am an ambitious person and I know that I will get my driving licence someday. However, if they thought this would push me to take the test early, they were wrong. I just needed a set of house keys to allow me in and out of the home I was living in, that's all! How would they feel if their daughter wasn't able to get into her new family home? I remembered when we went back to my mother's house the day after the wedding and I gave my mother my keys. She had asked me to hold onto them but my Simranjit Mum said to let me give them back: "May Harleen's new home be a blessing and God bless her new keys." So where the hell were they then?

To get in and out I had to wait on the family and communicate my every move. This was purely and simply about control. Any time I was doing something I had to check if anybody was going to be home to let me in. Amritpal *Bee Ji* was always home, but as she was old and walked at about a mile per hour I couldn't expect to keep disturbing her, so I would have to check in with the other members of the family.

In my family, I would always communicate where I was going and what time I would be back. There was trust between my mother and me. I had lived away from home for five years before returning to Birmingham and then living away with my work. Wherever the job took me, I would go. My mother never really questioned me moving around the UK. She was happy and supportive of my job; she was a very proud Punjabi parent who went to weddings and functions and talked about her daughter, who had a degree and was a designer.

Then I got married and my life turned upside down when I started living with my in-laws and husband, who all had serious issues and loved to keep up appearances with the Asian community.

When Maninder and I got married we took care of all the food shopping for the family as well as our phone bills. I never knew what my husband earned, nor did I ask, but I did know I was paying an extortionate amount to commute every day from Milton Keynes to Derby for work. I had extended my student loan to cover the cost of the wedding, and I put some of my monthly salary into the pot. I would also contribute towards the shopping and other things around the house. I never complained as they were my family now too and I understood you share the costs when living with a family. I had not asked for any help. I would be responsible for myself and mindful of the family.

From the day I married into this family I never allowed there to be issues with household chores or paying the bills. When Maninder's mum made the emergency trip to Canada she gave me some of my *choal* money and asked me to pay off her Barclaycard, and pay the bills with what was left. I added my own hard-earned cash to pay the outstanding bills and until this day I hadn't asked her for the money to be repaid. I believed this was my family home too and I needed to contribute towards it.

But for family to work, they need to enter the contractual arrangement in the same spirit. And they hadn't. Nor would they ever...

But why was Simranjit Mum giving me all the responsibility of the bills and food shopping – but not the keys to my home? Did they not trust me?

GURLEEN VISITS MILTON KEYNES

Gurleen *Pehn Ji* had decided to pop home to spend some time with Maninder and me. When she arrived at the family home she mentioned some things she would love to do while she was staying. My health was still delicate after the abortion, and I knew very well to avoid doing anything heavy... Or wild, for that matter.

The next morning, I got up at eight and prepared for a girly shopping trip with Gurleen. Although it was a lovely day, by midday my frail health made me exhausted, and I had to rest. I tried to hide my fatigue from her, and with a semblance of strength, I carried on until Maninder met us in the afternoon. He suggested we go climbing up the wall at X-scape, and I felt sure he would say something to me to excuse me. How wrong was I! I threw him a confused look but he hardly took any notice; he just continued chatting excitedly about the activity. I knew Gurleen was quite excited about climbing as well, so I did my best to participate and mingle with them. I couldn't care less about competing – my health was more important to me – so I allowed Gurleen to race ahead and climb the wall. She was on a natural high when she beat Maninder and me. After a while, I had to sit down. I knew I couldn't do this anymore and I needed to rest up and renew some of the energy I had lost, so I could again pretend to be strong in the evening.

As soon as we got home, I went straight up to my bedroom. Maninder followed me upstairs. "Are you okay, Harleen?"

What a pleasant surprise! At last he'd taken notice of me. "Well," I said, "I need to rest for some time, and I'll be okay..."

I drifted off. Just then, Simranjit Mum called me downstairs to help her in the kitchen with the evening family meal. The wall-climbing champion, Gurleen, went off to take a nap instead.

Maninder walked into the kitchen. "Where's Gurleen?" he asked his mum.

"She's sleeping, *Puth*..." she replied, while lighting the stove.

"Oh, is she?!" he said, scowling. He rushed out of the kitchen and into Gurleen's bedroom, waking her up. "Give us a hand at the kitchen, will ya?" Maninder barked at a woozy Gurleen, who was rubbing her eyes.

Gurleen came into the kitchen and snapped, "I'm not here to do any housework, y'all got that?" As Simranjit Mum started arguing with Maninder for waking Gurleen up, she nonchalantly went back to bed to resume her nap.

Maninder looked me in the eye. "Harleen, you should take some rest too."

Simranjit Mum decided to let off steam at Maninder for encouraging me to chill out when I should be working in the kitchen like a good, obedient housewife. I was shocked by her hypocrisy. I too was human, like her daughter! I'd been doing everything her daughter had done without a fuss, and now, despite my poor health, I had to be in the kitchen to cook the family meal as well!

Maninder stood outside Gurleen's bedroom door, arguing with her. The siblings looked like two squabbling kids. Maninder went on like a vinyl record with a broken track and Gurleen finally got tired of listening to him and came into the kitchen to help. Much to my amusement, she wore a disgruntled look on her face. I was grateful that Maninder had supported me, but what struck me was Gurleen's attitude. I usually used to overlook it because this was my family home. I lived like a daughter, cooked and cleaned the house, but today I felt the pangs of despair. I just wanted it so simple – to rest instead of standing up for much longer, as I felt the twinges and spasms inside my lower abdomen. I didn't want Gurleen to have to come home and do chores either, but Simranjit Mum treated us girls so differently. Gurleen was her daughter and Harleen was her daughter-in-law – whom she expected to behave in a certain restricted way. Yet it had never occurred to this woman to teach her daughter how to cook Punjabi meals, so she could carry those culinary skills into her future family home. As if, sarcastically, she had the nerve to expect *rotis* from me, perfectly circular as the full moon.

Simranjit Mum's discrimination between Gurleen and Harleen was clearly evident. Here's a list of her double standards:

Rules for Harleen:

- The Dishwasher: Harleen was expected to cook and do the dishes.
- The Bread Earner: Harleen was expected have a well-paid job.
- The Talking Parrot: Harleen had to talk to people the way the Purewal household had trained her.
- The Vestal Virgin: Harleen couldn't hug any male member of the family and was told to shake hands or put hands together and say *'Sat Sri Akhal Ji'*.
- The Vestal Virgin Extended: Harleen was not allowed to meet any of her friends after marriage unless Maninder accompanied her.
- The Vestal Virgin Returns: Harleen was not allowed to wear any dresses, deeply cut tops or garments that revealed any part of her body.
- The Pillion Rider: Harleen was not allowed to go anywhere by herself and was picked up and dropped off everywhere.
- The Guest: Harleen was not given a set of house keys.
- The Stalked: Harleen's mail was opened to check what she was up to.
- The Ceder: Harleen had to surrender her twenty-four karat gold jewellery sets to her mother-in-law as they felt she was not responsible enough to take care of her own jewellery.

Rules for Gurleen:

- Gurleen was allowed out until late in the evening to meet her friends alone.
- Gurleen was given full permission to wear deep-cut backless tops and all other types of revealing ensemble.
- Gurleen wasn't expected to cook, clean or help out around the house before marriage, or even after that, if it had anything to with her Simranjit Mum.
- All of Gurleen's gold jewellery was with her Simranjit Mum in Milton Keynes.
- Gurleen need not find a job as her husband, Loveneet had a well-paying job, and in my in-laws' view, she was the definition of an ideal wife.
- Gurleen was allowed to come and go as she pleased, without having to explain herself every moment, or check in with everybody, unlike Harleen.

You may say I was disgruntled... Of course I was!

SNOWDONIA THE AUGUST BANK HOLIDAY WEEKEND BREAK

After the abortion, Maninder and I weren't getting along well. We were slowly drifting apart emotionally. However, he tried to reach out to me and get us to reconcile our differences and start a healthy relationship as a couple – whatever 'healthy relationship' meant. He felt a change from the monotony would do us good, so he booked a couple of days' retreat in Snowdonia National Park. Snowdonia is the largest mountain in Wales.

When Maninder intimated me about his idea, I agreed at once. I could do with a getaway in the midst of unruffled nature. I had heard that Snowdonia was stunning, and I felt it would heal me physically and emotionally. My idea of a break was to get away from the drudgery of life. Also, I still wasn't well enough to do anything too heavy.

The first thing we did when we got to Snowdonia was put up our tent in the midst of the wilderness. I thought this was going to be the most exciting thing I'd ever done, until Maninder came up with a weird suggestion: "Put on your boots. We're going hiking!"

I was really peeved at this point. My husband had no consideration for my physical condition, and I thought that after all I had been through with him, he would at least have booked us a break where I could relax and not strain my health even more. I blatantly refused his proposal to go hiking or do anything with him that I felt I was not up to.

"You never understand me, Harleen!" he said, his voice started to rise. "I'm an active person and you know that!

But you never support me! You know what?" He took off his boots and threw them into a corner of the tent. "You are lacking in our relationship!"

I was taken aback! I'd just had an abortion and he wanted me to climb up a mountain! If only he'd ever tried to walk in my shoes! He should understand that if I took on activities that I couldn't handle, I would cause irreversible damage to my reproductive system and I might never bear a child again. I was not willing to go through that, and I knew I was the only person who had my best interests at heart. His interests were everything else, except me.

I knew Maninder was not into Bollywood movies; however, I think he was expecting to woo me in the Welsh mountains, just like Aishwarya Rai was wooed in *Ho Gaya Na Pyar* (Love Has Finally Happened) in the 2004 film *Kyan*. There was definitely no Bollywood song sequence happening between Maninder and me. My insides were filled with enough fresh Welsh air to last me a lifetime.

We stayed in the mountains for two days. Maninder was not doing much except hearing me sulk most of the time. The good old Welsh rain started at night and continued into the morning. We slept poorly these two days as Maninder hadn't been able to blow up the inflatable bed correctly. Well, he wasn't good at doing anything! The sleepless nights took a toll on our moods and we were both on the verge of a mental breakdown.

"I never expected it'd turn into this," Maninder said, sipping his black coffee and looking out into the mountains. As for me, I just wanted to get home, take a shower, and relax in the comfort of my own bed.

Finally, Maninder was so fed up he decided to pack up

and go back to Milton Keynes. I know he thought I was being ungrateful throughout this trip, but it was far from that. At times, I wanted to get more involved but I felt physically and mentally exhausted through constantly wearing the mask that manifested my strength.

I just couldn't comprehend what was going on in his mind. Before we got married, he knew very well that I was a lively and dynamic woman. However, due to the physical stress I was in, I was unable to do much right now, and I had been informed by my GP to take it easy as I'd suffered a major internal infection. You would think that would have given my husband a wakeup call. At this hour, we needed to relax and bond together to revivify our relationship through communication, not act like a pair of immature adrenaline junkies.

GURLEEN'S SECOND VISIT AFTER I FELL ILL

A few days after we got back from Snowdonia, Gurleen came down to visit the family. My in-laws were at work and I was in bed, my health still being weak. I thought Maninder would ask Gurleen to help out looking after Amritpal *Bee Ji*. Instead, he walked into our bedroom and asked, "Harleen, can you cook some *roti, sabzi* (vegetables) and *dhal* (lentil soup) for Amritpal *Bee Ji*?" I knew Gurleen couldn't cook this dish – oh, come on, she was no master chef from India – but she could at least have tried to be an apprentice chef. However, that wasn't possible for her lazy ass, either, so I got up and cooked all three of them lunch, even though I was the ailing one.

I was a bit thwarted when it came to Gurleen; I couldn't believe Simranjit Mum hadn't taught her how to cook these simple dishes! I knew she found it difficult to cook for her family in London. On occasion, she would call Simranjit Mum and ask her to cook food for her, and bring it with her when she was visiting. Sometimes, she'd call her before coming to Milton Keynes to ask what dish of the week was being cooked, and if she could bring her some curry. If Simranjit Mum had put a little bit of energy into teaching her daughter how to cook, she wouldn't have had to take food to her daughter all the time...and I wouldn't have had to get out of bed today because she couldn't cook the food that our Amritpal *Bee Ji* wanted to eat.

After cooking the meal, I went back to bed to rest. This little effort had worn me out. Sadly, not once did Gurleen come up to ask if I needed anything, yet I was expected to get up every time and cook meals for the little princess, just like her mother did. She'd often complain about how hard she had found settling into her in-laws'– it was probably because her mum had deprived her of the basic skills. Her parents often used to compare Gurleen with me, and mention how well I had settled into their home. Well, maybe it was because I treated it as my own home, rather than my husband's.

I had put up with a great deal from her brother and her parents but I had chosen to just get on with my life and make the most of what had been bestowed on me. With a fake smile plastered to my face, I tried my best to get on with adversities and tribulations.

Most Punjabi marriages that end do so because of issues escalating from the incongruity with in-laws, pressure of household chores and other mundane things, but my situation was much worse. Still, I never complained. Sometimes, though, however strong I pretended to be, I broke down. As comments were made here and there, my patience and mental endurance failed me. I took each day of my marriage as an impatient countdown. I had heard that the first two years could be difficult but this was entirely at another level. I counted down the days till the second anniversary of our marriage, wondering if things would finally become easier for me. I banked upon hope.

OUR JOBLESS DAYS

Maninder had lost his job three months into our marriage. We had been through a lot together, and now I had no job either. I'd been looking for design jobs but there was nothing available locally. There were jobs in London but when I registered with a few agencies, the first thing they asked was if I was willing to move to London. I would reply with a confused answer. The pay was barely enough to cover the cost of commuting daily, let alone supporting the two of us.

There were some jobs available in Milton Keynes Shopping Centre. I knew Maninder and his parents had explicitly dissuaded me from applying for jobs in the retail sector. Simranjit Mum worked for a retailer, but she wanted her daughter-in-law to have a better job than hers. However, I didn't really have that kind of competitive attitude toward jobs – or towards life, for that matter. I just wanted something that would help bring in some money; if it paid the bills, it was good enough for me. I had never been the typical Punjabi girl who would expect her husband to pay for her.

So I applied for a retail job, and grabbed it in one go! It helped get me out of the house and clear my mind. Maninder was still at home, jobless. At first, I didn't mind him being unemployed, as I thought a couple of weeks' break would be nice. But as the months rolled on, the scenario became worrying. He was still sitting on his ass in front of the television, lollygagging and gaming on the PlayStation all the time, like a school kid in the summer holidays. Neither of his parents ever intervened and I was a bit shocked at this. In my household back in Birmingham, my mother wanted her kids to at least be working part time while we looked for jobs that befitted our qualifications.

However, one day, while Maninder was gaming on his PlayStation, Kabir Dad made a few remarks about the mortgage and bills. I felt something wasn't right and finally I intervened. "Is everything okay, Maninder?"

"Why you always so nosy about me?" he retorted. "It's your fault! Do you ever care about me?" In three sentences, he had turned the situation back onto me and started another argument! I was lost for words. For a moment, I pressed my hand over my mouth in astonishment. When the situation cooled down a bit, I went to bed.

Maninder and I had been sleeping separately since the termination; he'd told his parents he was not able to sleep well. They advised us to look for a larger, more comfortable bed, which would help us sleep better. As the future of our relationship seemed to depend on us getting enough sleep to avoid being irritable, we went shopping for the perfect bed. All I can say is that the further away from me he was going to be in the bed, the better I was going to feel! We both wanted a super-deluxe bed where we wouldn't even be aware of the other person; it was like sleeping worlds apart.

After getting the new bed we still slept separately in our own spaces, but we were certainly sleeping better and we started to get on better with each other too. Maninder would pop in to see me during my lunch break and pick me up from work. Sometimes it was nice; I think he had reached the point where he just needed to get out of the house. When we met for lunch, we would talk about ourselves and nothing else; it was lovely when the conversation focused on us and what we each needed to do to develop ourselves and get along with each other better. I encouraged Maninder to find a job and follow his passion and dreams. He applied for two interviews and got the second job. Well, it certainly wasn't the job that he was looking for the long term, but at least it would help us pay the bills.

He told me he wanted to become a police officer and I said there was a vacancy in the police department, and he should apply for it. His parents didn't want him to apply. They thought he might hear racist remarks because he wore a turban – and admittedly I had noticed people treating him differently because of his long beard and turban. However, I felt his passion for this career more than anything else he spoke to me about. I wanted to direct him in the right way to fulfil his potential, and experience the level of success that he was capable of! Finally, things seemed to be getting better.

Simranjit Mum's 50th birthday and the in-laws' 30th wedding anniversary were fast approaching and I decided I would like us to celebrate with a surprise party. It would be Punjabi in style – a chance to piss the neighbours off with full-on noise pollution and the mouth-watering smell of Indian curry! I felt it was a great opportunity to bring the whole family together. Maninder was meant to be helping me get the people together from his side of the family, but as he didn't really keep in contact with most of them, it became quite difficult to get them to come over. I decided to bring Kabir Dad into the scene and get his support, as I didn't know the family at all other than the few I had met when Maninder's Mohanbir *Nanaa Ji* passed away.

Kabir Dad decided to tell me which members of the family Simranjit Mum would not like to see at this party we were organising! Although the party was meant to be a joyful hiatus from reality, the arrangements were becoming too stressful. Maninder and I were meant to be planning this together, but, woe, here was I, doing everything by myself yet again!

I designed all the invites and asked Maninder to check the spellings of the name of the invitees for me, but for some reason better known to him, he couldn't even do that much. I sent out the invites to my side of the family, only to have my younger cousin *Masi Ji* call, and point out some spelling errors. That really wound me up. I had dyslexia; my husband was a well-qualified man with a decent education, yet he couldn't be bothered to properly check the invites before they went out to our family members; I'd repeatedly asked him to have a look at the names, and he'd concluded there were no spelling errors. So when I got that call, I was so frustrated with him. I felt that I had all the world working against me. Once I knew which spelling errors required my attention, I corrected them and sent the rest of the invites out.

By now I knew what kind of support I would be receiving from my loving husband for the rest of my life, until death did us part.

THE BIRTHDAY PARTY

The good news was that Maninder had bagged a new job. The bad news was he wasn't going to start for another month. I was working part time at a retail outlet. It helped me pay off my bills, yet gave me enough time to myself to recover both physically and emotionally. Despite my meagre salary, I had paid for this party out of my own pocket, with a bit of help from Maninder. I called Gurleen on two separate occasions to ask if she would like to contribute towards the party, or at least towards her Simranjit Mum's birthday present, but I never heard anything back. So I decided to sort out the birthday and wedding anniversary presents, all by myself.

Planning the party invitation lists had become quite a challenge, as there were restrictions on who we could and could not invite. I had imagined it would be great to bring the family together, and try and get everybody to put their differences aside, but it was not to be! Kabir Dad didn't want his sisters to be there, as they had failed to make satisfactory efforts towards our wedding. But Amritpal *Bee Ji* wanted everybody to be invited, including the sisters. This had me all stressed out. For the first time, I wished I had not come up with this plan. Simranjit Mum didn't get on with most of the family members either. In the end, I just sent out the invites to whoever Kabir Dad dictated me to. Not surprisingly, the guest list consisted of my family, Loveneet's family, and some of Simranjit Mum's family. The plan to bring the family together through this party was entirely mine, but, ironically, no one from Kabir Dad's family was invited in the end, as Simranjit Mum did not get on with them.

An Asian catering company in Smethwick was assigned the task of preparing the takeaway and my mother would pick it up before coming to the party. Maninder and his family had bought a large, plain white tent because, being Punjabi, they knew the tent would be used for more than one celebration. This tent would probably outlast my in-laws and witness their grandkids' weddings! But for now, putting the bloody thing up was the issue.

"Can you put the tent up? Can you put the tent up?" I had lost count of how many times I had pleaded to Maninder.

"You are such a nagging wife!" he snapped. "I hate this kind of behaviour, I tell you."

"I have asked you so many times. I've asked you kindly. But you chose not to do it. And now I am a nagging wife? Wonderful!" I threw an angry smile. "What are you doing all day, except sitting at the PlayStation?"

Maninder walked out on the job and rushed out of the house without saying anything more. I felt really stressed out with his behaviour and asked Kabir Dad to have a few words with him. I waited hours for him to come back. By this point I had not eaten for about six hours and my blood glucose levels were plummeting rapidly, and I could sense that. Maninder never cared if I had eaten or not, but I'd never deprive him of a fresh meal. I thought to myself, why on earth did I think about doing this whole malarkey?

Kabir Dad was trying to get Smranjit Mum out of the house so we could prepare for the surprise party, but it was becoming an even bigger job than anticipated as they never did anything separately. She started asking questions to see whether he was hiding anything. This process helped me understand better why they could not allow either of their kids to just get on with their married lives as they themselves had never done anything alone. Eventually I had to help him get her out of the house and after that I had to sweet-talk Maninder into putting up the tent. I knew by then that an argument or grown-up request would not work. Sweet talk was the only way.

Finally, things started to fall into place, and I felt a wave of relaxation as the twilight deepened. Most of the people we had invited turned up, and as the evening rolled on, the party turned into an exhilarating one, full of surprises and fun.

But Amritpal *Bee Ji* was clearly disappointed when she realised that no one from her side of the family had been invited. I noticed the gloomy face and chagrin in her actions. She told my side of the family that she took offence at her daughters not being invited, and soon she left the party and went into her room. My mother tried to talk to her about it, but she was evidently apathetic to any sort of explanation.

I could understand her displeasure. If my family hadn't been invited I, too, would have been upset – but this wasn't my house, nor my rules, and I explained to her that my hands were tied. I'd had to listen to Kabir Dad and Simranjit Mum.

"I expected that you'd give me that respect where you'd invite my daughters and help turn the conflict between the two families to peace. I hoped at least this much from you," Amritpal *Bee Ji* said grimly.

"Look, Amritpal *Bee Ji*," I tried to explain, "I have

already tried my best. I pleaded to Kabir Dad, who was organising this party with me, to invite your daughters, but he was not allowing me to. He knows that Simranjit Mum will not be happy. Wouldn't that be awkward, because I was selflessly trying to make everyone happy here? If this were my home, I'd have my door open for everyone, Amritpal *Bee Ji*. But it's not my home... it's your son's."

"Whoa..." She took a step back. "I expected at least you'd fight for me and take my side." That was hard on me. I wasn't there trying to take anyone's side, but help bring peace to the whole family by filling up the potholes. I just hung my head. She sensed my disappointment. "This is my home too," she said, "but I never got any respect or support from any member of the family before you came along." She ambled towards me. "You want me to talk to your Kabir Dad?"

I knew Amritpal *Bee Ji* would be dismissed when she tried to state her opinion. They would accuse her of being a troublemaker – which she wasn't; she was just honest, that's all. She believed in telling the truth and nothing else.

Maninder and I had another fall out due to him not being a Superman and putting up the tent. We stopped talking, but by now this was nothing new to me. I had mastered the art of burying deep my feelings and getting on with life. We were just five months into our marriage, and I had become a master at faking.

This was the first party I had organised, and I wanted it to be perfect. I wanted to make sure everyone mingled. So I was running around, checking with everyone if they needed anything, smiling ear-to-ear, and trying to make everybody happy. When I am the host of the party, I like to create pleasant memories for everyone. Grabbing Gurleen, we danced a silly dance together. Then I danced with everyone.

Maninder was watching from a distance. All of a sudden, he came to me and dragged me to a corner of the room. "What's the problem with you?" he barked. "You are not giving me attention as your husband while you are fooling around with everyone else! Who do you think you are?"

I shook my hand from his grasp. "What do you mean by that? I'm just enjoying myself at the party we've organised. What's your problem?"

"My problem is you and only you!" Maninder walked off.

My heart skipped a beat. Quietly, I walked out of the room and back into the tent. I was worried that someone from our family was going to notice how unhappy we were, so I decided to get everyone up dancing. This was one of the things I was good at and I would keep on dancing, no matter how angry or upset I was inside. I would dance until it had banished the woes inside me with its moves.

Among my family, I had a reputation for being the centre of attention at any party, and I wanted to uphold that reputation here at my in-laws'. I used to get a lovely, warm feeling in my heart every time I saw people laughing and enjoying each other's company. Creating great memories like this was hard work, but I felt it was worth every drop of sweat.

At the end of the evening, I secretly hoped Simranjit Mum would thank me for the scintillating evening. Instead, she dragged me into the kitchen, and yelled, "Where did you get the *Mithai* (sweets) from, huh?"

I looked down and replied, "There is a catering company near my mother's house in Smethwick. I ordered a takeout."

"Do you have any idea how embarrassed you made me tonight?" Simranjit Mum ran off and brought the box of Indian sweets "Look here! There is mould on the sweets! Have you even tried to check them before ordering, huh?" Honestly, I hadn't; I had been busy hosting the party. I agree, there was just one sweet that had grown a mould, but what was with all the drama? "And why have you given me a card with just yours and Maninder's names in it? Where are Loveneet and Gurleen's names, *huh*?" she continued to grumble.

I felt she would never realise how much I had tried to please her, and how much Maninder and I wanted to make this a party special for her and for Kabir Dad. She knew neither of us was working full time, and we had been struggling emotionally and financially, but all she could do was complain and grumble about things that were not up to her standards. I had to ignore her to preserve my sanity.

Living with the in-laws, I had realised one thing about Maninder's mum. No matter how perfect you tried to make the situation for her, she would find a fault. I could see how good she was at it. I also witnessed how she would say spiteful things and then try to cover them up by saying she had been feeling depressed and hadn't thought when she spoke. That was obviously an excuse in my view, and an opportunity to be as mean as she could.

That day, we all stayed up until late into the night, and

after the party wound down, we watched home movies in Amritpal *Bee Ji's* room, so that she was involved too. It was an attempt to allay her disappointment. I loved the way she would randomly remember stories from Maninder and Gurleen's childhood and start sharing them with me. After the movie had played to the end, she asked if we could put on an older one from their mischievous days as kids. Oh, did we have some more stories flying around the room, redolent of nostalgia! I knew this family wasn't perfect in any way, shape or form (indeed, none in the world is) but that was the first moment I felt like I was a part of the family, and that made the aura perfect – all of us sitting in one room, laughing over stupid memories and speaking our hearts out. It was a short but lovely moment that I knew I had to enjoy as, like every beautiful moment, it would be as evanescent.

"Okay, okay," Simranjit Mum clapped, "it's bedtime! Everyone to bed!" Damn! Simranjit Mum killed it!

It seemed as if Simranjit Mum couldn't stand Amritpal *Bee Ji* and me getting on with each other, as she had never got on with her Mother-in-law. I could see how much she hated our closeness, hated how Amritpal *Bee Ji* complimented me on everything I did. It used to make her blood boil like tomato paste sauce in a pan hung over the inferno of hell. It upset her that she didn't share this intimate relationship with her mother-in-law or her daughter-in-law. Simranjit Mum would just walk out of the room and into the kitchen like a *desi* wife, and chain herself to the kitchen sink.

A couple of days later the in-laws' wedding anniversary arrived. I gave them their presents and cards from

Maninder and me, and again Simranjit Mum made a comment about it being just our names in the card.

At that moment, Kabir Dad came into the kitchen and asked whose idea it was to get Simranjit Mum tickets for the upcoming Jagjit Singh Live Concert. Jagjit Singh was a prominent Indian *Ghazal* singer, songwriter and musician. Known as the '*Ghazal* King', he gained acclaim together with his wife Chitra Singh, a renowned Indian female *Ghazal* singer in the 1970s and 1980s. "In 30 years of our marriage," Kabir Dad said, "we have never done anything without our better halves, and now why have you got a ticket for her to go with her friends? Why haven't you got two tickets so that I could join her?"

One day, Simranjit Mum had told me that she had not been to any of her work Christmas parties as her husband wouldn't allow her to go. Now I could see where Maninder got his genes from! I wanted to change that and help my husband see that we and his parents could do things separately as well as together, and still have fun. You don't have to live in each other's pockets to be in a happy relationship, and I wanted to prove that.

Simranjit Mum came into the kitchen with a face like thunder. "I want to go to the concert with him! Why haven't you got two tickets?" she yelled. I wondered why I was trying so hard to please these people. I pretended to take no notice and offered her some *Mithai* (sweets) to celebrate their wedding anniversary.

Soon, Simranjit Mum's friends arrived to pick her up. After she had gone, Kabir Dad started skulking around the house. It was as if he was waiting for one of his kids to come in from a night out.

Finally, Simranjit Mum returned and all she could do was complain about the whole evening: the singer was not up to her standards, the atmosphere was not great, and the people at the concert were not the kind of people she would ever hang out with. I'd hoped she would enjoy the company of her co-workers and watching someone on stage she loved to listen to on CD. Instead she complained about everything – and this was the story of her life and what she was happy doing. She had this habit of looking back at the past, pondering about the mansion surrounded by a big garden and the business that her sister-in-law and brother-in-law had bought off them and still owed them money for; she would always turn it back to herself and complain negatively about her life, all the time.

Everybody was at fault through her tinted glasses. But she never saw any fault in her own demeanour towards others because she was Mrs. Perfect Purewal. Yet she never got on with her own in-laws, my family or Loveneet's family either, and she was always complaining that Gurleen was not put on a pedestal like a princess.

Where did all this bigoted thinking come from, I wondered. I knew she was from India, but come on! What happened to the woman who had been portraying herself to me as a modern-day mother-in-law before I got married? Was it all a masquerade? Why was she expecting her daughter to be treated like a princess, but not showing nearly the same level of respect towards me?

KEEPING UP APPEARANCES IN THE PUREWAL FAMILY HOUSEHOLD

Maninder and I were still not sleeping together. One morning, when we were alone at home, he came into the kitchen and said, "Why don't we try for another baby, Harleen?"

I felt a stab in my heart, and the shocked look on my face showed how I felt about the subject. I blurted out, "I can't see me having a baby with you for at least five years! You want your freedom, independence, and all the materialistic things like a car and a house! And you wanted it all rather than a baby!" My voice started to rise. "I am not a baby making machine, that you can choose to get babies from whenever you want. Nor am I a genie, here to grant your wishes! You know what, Maninder? Some things come easy in life, but character and trust take time to build. We need to build our relationship over again. You must know that your decision not to keep the baby has wounded my soul indelibly, and I've already made the decision not to have kids until we are set up in life with a house, car and every little thing you want!"

I didn't want to have a child until we were stable and strong in our relationship, too. The next time I told my husband that I was pregnant I wanted him not to ask me to terminate the pregnancy, but to celebrate our relationship and step forward into a fresh new chapter. I continued, "I'm not like a lotus. You can't put me into murky water in the early months of our marriage, and then expect me to be a pure and faithful flower ready to say *"Haan Ji"* (yes, please) all the time, and give birth to all the children you want when it suits you!" And when it didn't, I'd silently walked into an abortion clinic...

He snapped at me, "You're so selfish! Now you're trying to get your own back on me!" He punched the kitchen door and left a hole in it

When my in-laws came home they noticed the hole. Simranjit Mum sprinted straight into the living room so quickly she'd have beaten Usain Bolt in a race. She barked, "What have you said or done to annoy my son?" Rather than sitting us down and talking to find out what the problem was, let alone trying to solve it, she stood straight in front of me and started using me as verbal punch bag, throwing question after question at me. In their view, Maninder was never wrong. They always chose to overlook his faults; everybody else caused him the big *desi* problems.

I slumped on the floor, thinking to myself, "If you want your son to yourself then why get him married in the first place and ruin both of our lives? At the end of the day, I'm this girl who has left everything behind to come and be a part of your family – so why torment me like this?" The mother-in-law had a daughter of her own. She at least should have understood that no girl should have to go through such mental and physical torture. It's plainly unfair.

I got up from the floor and walked away. I just couldn't be bothered with her and her son – my so-called husband.

My best friend, Jaya, was getting married and her wedding present was going to be wedding napkins I was making for her. It took me a day to cut them all up and a few days to sew them up. As I was making the napkins in the garage, Simranjit Mum came inside. "Harleen, can you cook dinner for us? Let me sew some of those napkins, while you are at it." At the same time, Kabir Dad offered to mend the kitchen door. But not once did they ask Maninder to apologise for his behaviour or at least explain why he had behaved in such a way. This was something my in-laws were great at doing – covering things up and letting the rest of the world look at their perfect home and think they were such a perfect and normal family, when in fact, all they did was poorly patch up their broken home, and pretend and lie to people. They never knew how to sit down and have a healthy conversation as a family about what could be bothering them, or asking about their mental condition. They only communicated to others by demanding what they expected from them. It wasn't my job to change the people I lived with, but I did want them to understand that such demeanour couldn't be tolerated forever.

Once she worked out I was not talking to them, Simranjit Mum kept offering to help me with the napkins, perhaps out of guilt. My legal husband just sat on the couch and started at the television, while his parents covered his ass.

This was another reason why I didn't want a child with him now, or in the future. He just wasn't a responsible man. He hadn't taken any responsibility in our marriage, so what responsibility would he take when it came to children? He never tried to fix problems; he left everything to other people to sort out. What kind of role model would he be for our kids? What kind of a father would he be? He would leave it up to his Kabir Dad and Simranjit Mum to deal with everything and pick up the mess, while he kept on lollygagging.

JAYA'S WEDDING

My best friend Jaya was getting married in Wolverhampton. As we were going to be near Birmingham, we decided to stop over at my mother's place for the weekend. Maninder's mum suggested that we could pick up our wedding DVD while we were there. Maninder and I had a busy day ahead of us anyway, and we had to take a detour to the *desi* video maker's house. By the time we arrived at Jaya's parents' home, we'd already had a few tiffs in the car and again, like immature children, we were not talking to each other. It was the first time I'd seen Jaya since my wedding, and the first time her family would meet my husband, Maninder. Jaya's brother-in-law introduced Maninder to all the men there, and they all shook hands with him, and started their manly chit-chat. Maninder seemed to be enjoying himself; he was grinning, and mingling with everyone so perfectly and I was glad to see my best friend Jaya smiling and enjoying her family's company.

Later that evening, we drove to Birmingham and met up with Maninder's cousins. I warmed to these girls straight away, but Maninder was displeased with one of his cousin's because it was the first time she had met me and she was fairly drunk. I couldn't care less; she was merry and, most importantly, she was happy, at least at that moment. But I was aware that Maninder felt she didn't help him keep up his dominating attitude.

The next day was Jaya's *Vatna* and again Maninder and I spent a few moments in the day bickering. It was as if a day couldn't end without a squabble issuing between us.

And again, we went into silent mode towards each other for the evening. Jaya noticed and mentioned it to me whilst we were dancing, but I pushed everything – including my emotions – aside, and went on dancing. When I looked over I could see that all of Jaya's family and the men were making an effort to get along with Maninder. He'd got up to dance, which made me smile instinctively. He started to calm down and chilled out with everybody. I finally felt at ease as I watched him relaxing.

On the wedding day, we both had a great time. Before the weekend, Maninder had mentioned that he was not looking forward to Jaya's wedding as he thought I would not give him enough time and attention, and that Jaya's family wouldn't either. But as it turned out, her family made him feel more loved than he felt at his own family weddings, as everybody was warm and welcoming towards him. He saw me looking over his way every so often to check if he was alright. With my affable personality, I could get along with anybody, but Maninder was the opposite. He did not find it as easy to talk to people, but surprisingly he got along fine that weekend.

My best friend's full name was Jaya Gandhi and for some reason, Simranjit Mum had a thing about her surname. She'd kept yapping on about it, which made Maninder feel ill at ease around Jaya. "During the 1984 riots that erupted across India," she started lecturing, "following the murder of Prime Minister Indira Gandhi, Hindus took their revenge on Sikhs, who were blamed for the assassination." She continued: "Indira Gandhi, the Prime Minister of India, was killed by assassins in New Delhi. Mrs Gandhi was thought to have been walking through her garden on the morning she was shot. The initial reports suggested the two attackers were guards at her home but it was believed the pair were Sikh extremists acting in retaliation for the storming of the Sikh holy shrine of the Golden Temple in Amritsar in June 1984. Indira Gandhi had been receiving death threats since the attack on the temple in which a thousand Sikh people died."

Simranjit Mum made it clear that she would not like to meet my friend simply because of her surname! She didn't stop with this antipathy, and kept trying to plant seeds of evil in Maninder's head too, which had really started to disturb me. Her bigoted thinking was now manifesting beyond the walls of our house!

Jaya and I had many cheerful memories of our mischievous university days together. University friends were for life! I wanted Maninder to be part of that friendship. I knew that he felt insecure when I went on and on about my friendship with Jaya, and I wanted him to come together and not feel left out. He knew how much I loved Jaya; she was like a sister to me. It meant so much to me when Maninder met her for the first time at her wedding. He actually told my in-laws that he'd had a great time at Jaya's wedding. Simranjit Mum was not at all excited about this. Her face portrayed her shock.

Many of Maninder's friends were Muslim's, and I, too, had friends from all walks of life. Unlike Simranjit Mum, I never judged people by religion or surname or social background. "And don't ever make me meet Jaya again!" she reminded me, even though Jaya had now married a Punjabi-Sikh man and carried a Punjabi surname. She just didn't care. That she had been 'Gandhi' as a maiden was excuse enough.

TRIP TO INDIA

Maninder had finally started his new job, and I was still working part time as a sales assistant at Karen Millen. He'd met me a few times for lunch, when we had mundane conversations, but my guard was up. I was not opening up my bruised heart to him. He, too, had noticed that I wasn't myself of late.

While I was at work one day, Maninder and his parents had talked to him about a trip to India as our first family holiday. They wanted me to meet their family out there and check out their properties as well. Maninder told me about the trip as soon as I returned home from work. I said we could not afford it and asked how we were going to pay for it and he told his parents my concerns. The in-laws called a family meeting – though of course Amritpal *Bee Ji* didn't get an invitation. She might be the oldest member of the family, but it was my father-in-law and mother-in-law who had their names on the property, so what they said was final. I expressed my concerns to them and explained that the timing wasn't great as Maninder had only just started a new job and I was working part time. We simply lacked the funds to take this trip.

"Harleen," Maninder's dad suggested, "we will pay for the whole trip, but when you get back and get a better job, you can pay us back the money you owe us as a loan..." He looked over his glasses. "You needn't pay any interest."

"What the...!" I whispered. The proposal was quite degrading for me. Had I left my family home, my Mother and my siblings, to marry a bank that gave promotional offers? "I'm sorry, Dad." I kept my voice as low and polite as possible. "I think I'll pass..." I knew I wouldn't enjoy the trip knowing that I was clocking up a bill with my in-laws.

Simranjit Mum put up a permanent grimace for a couple of weeks, and put herself in a zero-communication mode towards me. Maninder was also in a mood with me, as he wanted to go to India and thought it'd be a great time for us to take a break, as we were getting along better. He believed the trip would help transcend our relationship to a better level. But I had upset the applecart for him. He wanted to go to India during Diwali as it was the best time to be out there and experience the culture. I felt it wasn't a good idea, and stood firm to the decision I had made.

A couple of weeks later, Kabir Dad called another family meeting on the same subject, as he thought I might have changed my mind. I again expressed the same views; I would not change my mind, no matter how moody they got. Finally, I realised the three of them had made their minds up about taking this trip to their motherland, and my opinion didn't matter. How classy of them; they thought they could bully me into going. I stood my ground with them all. Forty-five minutes into the fight, Kabir Dad insisted Maninder leave, as he had a meeting at the *gurdwara*. "You go," he said. "I'll deal with her." The tone of Kabir Dad's voice suggested he thought I was an imbecile off the streets. What the hell did he think he was? I wouldn't allow my own father to talk to me like that!

He turned to me and said, *"Meh thenu bundhi banoundha."* ("I'm gonna sort you out now. I'll make you into a man!")

It was incredible to think that Maninder was once a helpless little baby, but now he was an overgrown helpless man, one who got his parents to deal with his wife as he couldn't!

"Kabir Dad," I said, "my relationship with you is through Maninder. I'm no longer having this conversation if he is not here! You are not my real father! I only have a relationship with you because of your son," I emphasised.

"Get back here!" he yelled. "How dare you walk out on me!"

I wasn't some woman who'd give in so easily. It would take more than three of these Purewals to control me! I held my head up high, walked up to my bedroom and locked the door behind me. Kabir Dad and Simranjit Mum stood outside my bedroom door yelling cusses at me, and calling me an uneducated person. I had learning difficulties in my childhood because of my dyslexia, and they thought they could target my weak point and bully me into changing my mind!

I tell you again, I was not a woman who would wave the white flag! Every insult thrown through that door consolidated my willpower, and made me even more determined to stand up to them, be firm and loyal to myself, and reject their decision. If they could behave like this in a country where there are laws in place, how would these people behave towards me in a country where anything is acceptable? I would not allow myself to be put in that situation. I didn't trust either of them – or the man I married.

Who gave them the right to talk to me like that? Who was he going to be teaching a lesson to? Me? Got to be joking! I wouldn't allow my biological father to talk to me like that. Who the hell was my father-in-law to me? I was only related to these two loonies through their son – my so-called husband – who never grew a backbone.

They hollered Maninder back into the house. He came running inside, and banged on our bedroom door. "Harleen, open up!" I could hear him yelling. "Come on out and join us downstairs!"

I knew he wanted to finish off the conversation that he had left, following his parents' orders. He had abandoned the meeting at the *gurdwara*, as he actually wanted to talk things through. By now they had all realised that their bullying was not going to work on me. I came out of the bedroom and joined them. Simranjit Mum kept her mouth shut and didn't say a word; I knew Kabir Dad had instructed her to stay quiet. Instead, Maninder took the lead. "Are you going to India or not?"

"I have already told you, I'm not! We have just started work, and we just don't have the funds!" I turned around and walked out of the living room again. This time it was Maninder who hurled a few cusses at me. I clenched my teeth and started mumbling my Mool Mantra in an attempt to ignore his swearing. (The Mool Mantar (also spelled Mul Mantra) is the most important composition contained within the Sri Guru Granth Sahib, the holy scripture of the Sikhs; it is the basis of Sikhism. The word "Mool" means "main", "root" or "chief"; "Mantar" means "magic chant" or "magic potion". Together the words "Mool Mantar" mean the "Main chant" or "root verse". Its importance is emphasised by the fact that it is the first composition to appear in the holy Granth of the Sikhs and that it appears before the commencement of the main section which comprises of 31 *Raags* or chapters. The Mool

Mantar is said to be the first composition uttered by Guru Nanak Dev upon enlightenment at the age of about 30. Being the basis of Sikhism, it encapsulates the entire theology of Sikhism. When a person begins to learn Gurbani, this is the first verse that most would learn. It is a most brief composition encompassing the entire universally complex theology of the Sikh faith. It has religious, social, political, logical, martial and eternal implication for human existence; truly humanitarian and global concepts of the Supreme power for all to understand and appreciate. This Mantar encompasses concepts which have been evaluated and proven over many eras (or yugs) and are known to be flawless beyond any ambiguity whatsoever. The rest of Japji sahib that follows this mantar is said to be a elaboration of the main mantar and that the rest of the Guru Granth Sahib, totalling 1430 pages, is a detailed amplification of the Mool Mantar.

(http://www.sikhiwiki.org/index.php/Mool_Mantar)

I went up to my room and lay on my side of the bed. My brain mechanically switched to daydream mode. I conjured up visions that I was in the most perfect marriage, and I was happier than ever imagined. I fantasised of the most amazing life that could ever be lived.

Building castles in the air helped me to disconnect from the realities of my marriage and the people with whom I lived. I used to do this often when I was a child and needed to switch off the noises downstairs, or I was asked to spell a word that I had no idea how to spell. My ability to shut things off often helped me move on with life, when in reality it was falling apart. This time I was using my power of imagination to create make-believe games in which I was living the perfect marriage with my Prince Charming and his parents – the most honest and cooperative parents I've ever met, who always protected me against evil. Well, I was living the lies of a fairy tale, but it helped me get through the hardest days of my life. From that day on I chose to forget the hurt and pain, and not be a slave to fate. I thanked God too, and recited my *Mool Mantra* in my head and heart whenever things got tough.

From that day on, Simranjit Mum decided that she was not going to talk to me and she started playing subtle mind games, like intentionally not making any food for me. Also, when I had put the clothes on the washing line outside and asked her to take the clothes off, she would pay no heed to me and ignore me. The best way to deal with this was to not take on board her attitude or mood swings and just get on with things, and show her that she was not bothering me at all. Pretending not to be a victim takes the power out of your enemies. I would cook my own food and Maninder's as well, and then ask her if she would like some, to make her realise how immature she was, behaving in this way.

What she didn't realise was that I was a lot stronger than she thought, and this kind of behaviour wasn't going to break me down, but only make me stronger. I was determined to build a castle with the stones she threw at me. I was grateful for my job as a part time sales advisor, which gave me a break from them and helped me maintain my sanity during these difficult times.

No matter how unacceptably they treated me, I never drooped down to their level. I knew deep in my heart that I was better than these people. Every time I was mistreated, I offered a compassionate listening ear to their sorrows. I had been hurt by every one of them and did not want to let them get close enough to hurt me again. So I decided to get on with life and not allow myself to get carried by emotions, and just quite simply stick to righteousness.

On the day they were leaving for India, Simranjit Mum asked me to pack Amritpal *Bee Ji's* bags. I obeyed her. They had not told Amritpal *Bee Ji* she was going to India until the night before, as they didn't want her telling her daughters – which I believed was wrong. I decided not to get involved, and asked Amritpal *Bee Ji* what she would like to take with her on her exciting, adventure-filled trip to India. The first thing she asked me was if I was coming along too. I told I wasn't, because I had to stay behind to keep an eye on the builders. Milton Keynes council had paid for the building of an extension so Amritpal *Bee Ji* could have a shower fitted downstairs. What was surprising was that Kabir Dad was going around telling people that he had paid for it, because he was the caring, supporting and loving son – which was clearly all lies. He should thank the council for that £20,000 extension!

I packed Amritpal *Bee Ji's* bags and booked her insurance online like a good, dyslexic daughter-in-law. No one was talking to me yet, but somehow, they all got me to do their chores. I didn't know why Simranjit Mum couldn't book her Mother-in-law's insurance given that she was an educated woman who always thought she was better than me! After I helped them out, Kabir Dad softened up a bit, and started talking to me normally. But Simranjit Mum still held on to her ugly attitude.

Just then, the main door slammed open. Maninder had

returned from work. He was going to be dropping his parents and Amritpal *Bee Ji* at the airport; Gurleen and Loveneet were going to meet them there. I decided I was not going to play 'happy families' when no one was bothering to talk to me. I told Kabir Dad that I'd not be coming with them to the airport as I did not want to spend the ride towards the airport in an awkward silence.

"Are you okay, *Puth*?" he asked. "Are you totally sure?"

"I've never felt surer about anything in my life," I said, confidently. I went up to Amritpal *Bee Ji* and Simranjit Mum to see them off and wish them all happy holidays. Maninder just looked at me vacantly and walked away. Why should I sit in their company when they had no respect for my feelings at all? Also, the thought of riding in the car on the journey back from the airport would have killed me more, as Maninder and I were not talking, either. Besides that, I'd have to deal with him for three and a half weeks alone. This was the first time in our marriage that we were going be alone and have no one else to come home to. This was going to be challenging, given that we were not even communicating.

After they had left, I reached for my mobile phone and called my best friend, Jaya, who was not a bachelorette anymore. We cracked jokes about the situation and shared a laugh. I got something to eat, enjoyed some 'me time' by watching a film, and finally went to bed.

I had just dozed off when Maninder walked in through the bedroom door. He got changed and climbed onto the super king-size bed. We slept on our own separate sides and didn't say anything to each other. I was not going to apologise for anything as I had done nothing wrong and he had to learn that his behaviour was not acceptable.

Next morning the builders arrived and started on the extension. I made them rounds of tea, offered them biscuits and snacks, and kept up the appearance as the Purewals' daughter-in-law. To kill time, I decided to register with a few agencies in London and apply for a few design jobs. I was really enjoying the peace and tranquillity, as I was finally able to focus on myself.

Every evening before Maninder came home, I cleared up all the mess that the builders had created during the day, and cooked dinner for us both, like a good Punjabi housewife. Gradually, we started talking again. I asked him to cook at least two nights a week, as I wanted to chill out and I felt he should make some effort. He still seemed bitter that we hadn't gone to India.

On the first night that he cooked dinner for us, he told me about a letter he had received from the Metropolitan Police, a few days before my in-laws went to India. He'd been invited for an interview through the first stage of the selection process. He said he'd told his parents but, shockingly, he had never informed me until today! Yet it was I who had encouraged him to pursue his dreams and apply for the post.

From that day, we started communicating more if any part of the conversation went sour. I filled him in on the agencies I'd joined, and he started talking about his new job and about the people he worked with.

OUR FIRST DIWALI TOGETHER

On our first Diwali together, I decorated the front entrance and the hallway with candles, to allow light into our home and hearts. I prepared some special Indian sweets and Maninder's favourite *Chilli Paneer* (a spicy dish with cottage cheese), but he arrived home in a bad mood. I couldn't make out what was going on. We started getting ready for the *gurdwara*, but my running a bit late vexed him. Finally, I was up and ready – like a cheerful Indian bride – and we showed up at the *gurdwara* to wish our peers a happy Diwali. We got there just as the service was about to end, and this irked Maninder even more. I could tell by the look on his face that he was boiling like the curry inside one of the saucepans in the *gurdwara* kitchen.

I tried in vain to improve his mood by cracking a few jokes. When we arrived back at the house, the home phone started ringing and Maninder went to answer it. It was the in-laws from India, wishing us a happy Diwali and *Bandi Chhor Divas.*

(https://en.m.wikipedia.org/wiki.Bandi_Chhor_Divas).

They probably started going on about how they wished we were there with them. This piqued Maninder even more. He handed the phone over to me and I wished Simranjit Mum and Kabir Dad a happy Diwali and then asked where Amritpal *Bee Ji* was. They said she'd stayed back in Daddy *Ji's* village while they went to visit Simranjit Mum's village and ended up stopping for the night.

'So,' I said to myself, 'they went all the way to India to celebrate a family Diwali and dumped Amritpal *Bee Ji* elsewhere while they enjoy themselves! What an exciting treat this will have been for Amritpal *Bee Ji!'*

Later that evening, the home phone rang again, and I answered it this time. It was my own mother wishing us happy Diwali. Maninder started playing up by speaking over me, so I put the call on speaker phone. "Oh, Mother, don't you know? Sikhs don't celebrate Diwali!"

Maninder started being rude to Mother, talking down to her as if he was more educated and had more life experience than her. Yes, he did have an education; however, the life experience he didn't have. "Us Sikhs don't celebrate Diwali, Mother," he said. "You should know that by now, with your life experience."

Mother's tone turned serious. "Why?" she asked him. "If you knew that much, don't you know how important Diwali is for Sikhs? Sikhs do celebrate Diwali, Maninder. We celebrate *Bandi Chhor Divas*, where our *Guru Hargobind Ji* was released in 1619AD from the Gwallior fort and he also helped free other 52 *Rajas* (kings) from life imprisonment. The celebrations were held when he arrived at the Golden Temple of *Amritsar*. Also, haven't you even read *Gurbani*?" Maninder fell silent. She continued. "The *Gurbani* says that the purpose of celebrating Diwali is for us to pray for our liberation from worldly attachments, and follow the *Guru's* path of enlightenment. Light a *diya* (candle), Maninder... not only in your home, but also in your heart. It's symbolism for lighting your mind with divine knowledge and enlightenment."

My husband had no answer to that, and he escaped by running out of the room. I was really pissed off, as his parents had done so many rude things to me but I never stooped down to their level or was rude back. Who'd given him the right to talk to my mother like that? What was he trying to prove to me? Or was his thought that he was the boy's side of the family, so he could get away talking to his in-laws like this?

ROUND TWO: HITTING ME FOR THE SECOND TIME

I came off the phone and asked Maninder what his problem was. And he exploded! He grabbed me by the neck and pinned me against the wall. "You are my problem, you stupid cow! You!" he roared.

"Maninder, you're...hurting me..." I was choking, and I struggled to catch a gasp of air. I grabbed his hand and tried to push him away from my neck. Suddenly, a fit of rage came over me, which instilled a superpower within me and I pushed him off me. Wheezing and coughing, I ran up to my bedroom and picked up my mobile phone to call my mother. Maninder rushed inside, grabbed my phone and threw it across the room. Then he grabbed my hair and dragged me across the floor, like a lion dragging its prey. But I was not his prey – he had forgotten that. I was the lioness! I pushed myself up, pushed him away from me, and ran out of our bedroom and back downstairs. I tried to grab the kitchen phone, but Maninder had got there first, and he smashed the phone into pieces on the kitchen floor. Then he slapped me across the face for trying to call. I had two choices: to try to get to the dining room phone, or run upstairs, barricade myself in the bedroom and try my mobile.

So I went back upstairs, locked the bedroom door behind me, and moved the set of drawers against it to stop Maninder from coming in. I found my mobile phone on the floor, shattered into pieces... just like our relationship. It was one in the morning. I picked up the pieces of my phone, as I did with my life when everything seemed to go wrong, and reassembled it. The phone magically booted up, although the screen was cracked. I called my mother. Sobbing, I told her what had happened. She was shocked. Half asleep, she asked me to stop crying, like she used to do when I was a little girl. "Now take a deep breath," she said. When I had calmed down a bit, she asked me to explain what had been going on between Maninder and me. "Where is that scoundrel now?" she yelled over the phone, when I finished.

"He's still in the house and I have locked myself in our bedroom."

She hung up on me and called the home phone to talk to Maninder. I don't know to this day what she said to him, but later she called me back and asked if I would like her to pop down that evening with my brother. I said it was okay, as I was in my bedroom and I was not going to allow Maninder back in; he could sleep in one of the other rooms.

More women should stand up for themselves against physical abuse and domestic violence. It is not acceptable from anybody, least of all at the hands of your partner or husband. Domestic violence is not tolerable in any shape or form. It is not only an insult to one's dignity, but also constitutes a criminal offence. Don't ever suffer thinking that you're alone. There are special government institutions and services that will help you come out of the nightmare, and ensure you're protected from any repercussions taken by individuals seeking revenge.

Just because you are male doesn't necessarily mean you are a man. A man who hits his wife because she doesn't agree to be his puppet, and finds violence the only way to express his facade of power, is a coward in my view. My father was a coward, and now Maninder had proved himself to be a coward too.

At this point, I had the opportunity to call the authorities. However, I chose not to this time, as it would further embitter things between Maninder and me. Maninder's parents were also away, and I wouldn't want them coming home to such a situation. What would everybody think?

The following morning, I heard a knock on the bedroom door. It was Maninder. He asked me to let him in. Shakily, I opened the door, silently praying he wouldn't grab me or hit me again. He came into the bedroom, gathered his work clothes, got ready, and left for work. I got myself up, and cleaned up the mess from the previous night before the builder arrived. It reminded me of when I was a kid and my father would beat my mother up; the days of cleaning up his mess. I just wanted to stay in bed all day, but I couldn't. That day, I didn't have the urge to offer any of the builder's tea and biscuits; I didn't want to pretend everything was fine. I wanted to wash away the night ... but how would I wash the scars off my soul?

My mother called me early to check on me, and I explained everything to her calmly. She said she knew we'd been having problems when she wished Maninder a happy Diwali and he was so rude to her. She asked me again if I wanted her to come up and stay for a couple of days, or whether I wanted to go home. I explained to her I couldn't, as the building work would be in progress for the next couple of weeks. I came off the phone thinking of the pain my mother would have felt when she got the call last night and heard what I was going through. This was the day that my mother had always dreaded, and now here she was facing it: one of her daughters living through what she had lived through in her marriage.

Maninder returned home that evening with some flowers for me to say sorry – but no amount of flowers could erase those indelible scars he'd given to me, and our relationship. He had been pushing me from the moment I agreed to marry him, chipping away at my self-esteem and confidence. I'd been pushed by him and his parents on so many occasions and I was sick of it all. They had debased me by saying that I couldn't do any better than him, and my self-confidence had fallen so low I was finally holding onto to him in desperation.

I couldn't imagine going through this process without my *Guru Ji* (God) on my side. The only thing that kept me going was praying for the sun to come out and the rain to stop pouring down on us. I prayed every day with all my heart, hoping that things would start getting better. Like the lotus flower that is born out of mud, we must honour the darkest parts of ourselves and the most painful life experiences, because they are what brings out the most beautiful version of ourselves. Finally, after six months of marriage, that moment had come about!

A recruitment agency offered me an interview for a job as a formal shirt designer in Nottinghamshire, working for a supplier of Marks & Spencer. I didn't care a bit about the amount of travelling and decided at once to go for the job, to get myself out of the house. I passed the first interview, and was told I had secured the second. I didn't even think about how far it was from Milton Keynes or what the family was going to say about it. I just wanted to stay inside my own bubble, and begin to live again. I'd still not been given any keys to the house; I'd been using Kabir Dad's keys while they were in India. So I decided to get a duplicate set cut. Once I had my own set of keys, I could come and go as I pleased, without having to worry whether someone was going to be home to open the front door for me. Now I could gain access to my own home without relying on others.

OCTOBER 2008: MANINDER'S BIRTHDAY

Three days after my interview, it was Maninder's birthday. I had organised a private dinner with his side of the family and some of our mutual friends, even though we were not talking or getting along with each other. I had started planning for this occasion during the period when the relationship between us was somewhat smoother. I knew we needed to start talking, or else others would start noticing. It reminded me of my parents' situation, when my mother would lie to the family about her relationship with my father. I felt that I was walking in my mother's shoes, worrying about what the neighbours, friends and family thought of my relationship. Before I got married, I never worried what people thought about me and what I was doing. But after becoming a Purewal daughter-in-law, I always had to fake the appearance of a happy Punjabi wife. It was almost like one of those Indian melodrama scenes you would watch on the television.

My brother wasn't planning on coming over until my mother told him what was going on. After hearing about my situation, he made a conscious decision to attend the dinner party to show Maninder that I wasn't alone, and I had the support of a brother.

Maninder's birthday fell on a weekday. In the morning, I gave him a greeting card, put his birthday present on the living room table, and cooked him breakfast. He left the house quietly, but later in the day, I got a text on my cracked mobile phone saying thanks for everything and that he couldn't believe I'd done all that for him considering we hadn't been talking to each other.

That was the thing he never really understood about me – that I always put his and his parents' feelings before my own. Rather than being thankful, most of the time he would be very unappreciative and hurtful; so much so that I had started to question why I bothered with him at all. I loved him so much at the beginning of our relationship, and even after the hurt he had caused me, I had not stopped loving him, but he was making it difficult for me to continue with this marriage. I'd begun to have visions of leaving him. But I didn't have the strength to walk away as I was worried about everybody else.

Maninder came home from work and apologised for his behaviour earlier in the day and we talked to each other open-heartedly for the first time in a while. I hoped that finally, things were going to start going well, that we were going to put our best feet forward, together.

Maninder's top-secret get-together plan was going to materialize the coming weekend. He had the Friday off work and he helped me around the house, and we worked as a team. It was like we were breathing new life into our marriage once more! I helped him knock down a wall in the front garden. We also went to see my Guruleen *Massar Ji* together and chilled out at my mother's place in Birmingham.

On Saturday, the invitees met up with Maninder at the golf range in Milton Keynes to play a few friendly games before the birthday dinner. I joined the guests just before they left for the restaurant; I had to drop off his birthday cake and another cake for Kamalpreet, Loveneet's cousin, who had turned 14 the week before. I had a thing for the kids. I loved them like my own, and interacted with them all. The children in Loveneet's family had shown me a great deal of respect and love, for which I was humbled and grateful.

At the golf range we acted like a bunch of overgrown kids and we all enjoyed the day and our birthday dinner. Most of us didn't want the night to end, as we'd all had a great time, so Maninder and I proposed our guests head back to our place and continue enjoying the rest of the night.

We all came back to my in-laws' house for coffee. The lads all chilled out in one room, playing on the PlayStation, while we lasses were in the other room yapping about girly thingies. It felt like a resurrection of old-school Punjabi family moments from the 70s and 80s!

Maninder and I were not wild and bohemian, but sometimes just doing basic things was a challenge at his parents' house when they were around. Even just having everybody back at our place would be a big deal. Gurleen reminded me that her parents wouldn't like it at all if they found out we'd invited so many people back to their place. The people Gurleen was referring to were just family and friends. No outsiders. She could be such a *Bibi Ji* (Grandma) at times.

It was satisfying to have Maninder's relatives and friends come over to our house and not have the in-laws dominating the evening. It also gave Maninder and me a chance to explore what it would be like to have a place to call our own. There would be many welcome changes: no phone tapping, no one opening my letters, and I knew that we would work as a team all the time and over all situations. We had struggled at the beginning after his parents went to India, but to be honest, Maninder and I didn't really know each other, or what it was like to be just the two of us. We had to get to know each other again and start afresh, which would take a while.

After the weekend had passed, we were still getting along well. I heard back from the company I had applied for a job with, and what do you know? I had bagged the job!

I called Maninder to let him know about my success, and he was over the moon for me. Not once did he mention anything about the location, or say anything negative about the job at all. To celebrate, we went out for an evening in London with a friend, and it was overwhelming. We had fun and we came back home without the stress of us falling out, or the parents having a go at us. We were harmonising so much better, though we were still not being intimate together in bed; instead, we just shared the bed and lay next to each other every night.

The day before the in-laws returned from India, my mother called me to ask if I would like her to sit down with them and bring up the topic of Maninder's hostile behaviour. As we were synchronizing so well right now, I didn't want her to rock the boat so I asked her to hold back for now. Maninder had also specifically mentioned that he would not like Kabir Dad, Simranjit Mum and Amritpal *Bee Ji* to know about the big argument we had in their absence, and though I was sure he was just trying to sugar-coat me by being nice to me, I decided not to say anything or get my mother involved. I had lost myself in a culture because of this relationship; pleasing society had become more important than my own feelings. There was a level of respect I wanted to show to everybody around me, by not letting them down by letting my marriage fail. I decided to stop questioning things and carry on with it all like a puppet, especially since I was looking forward to starting my new job.

By the time Kabir Dad, Simranjit Mum and Amritpal *Bee Ji* returned from India, the extension in the house had been completed, and Maninder and I had put our own money into decorating the shower room. What the council was going to do with the interior sounded very clinical, and I wanted the room to feel homely and cosy, so I had decided to take charge of the decorating and modify some of the choices that Kabir Dad and Simranjit Mum had made. A pathway up to the house had been also completed and Maninder and I had saved them some £400 by knocking down the wall ourselves! Simranjit Mum made a few remarks here and there, but overall everyone was pleased with how things had gone.

When Kabir Dad and Simranjit Mum heard about my new job, they were annoyed at how far away it was. Simranjit Mum asked Maninder if he knew that I was looking for a job and asked him why I had found another job in the north rather than in the south. They were also not happy about a trip I was going to be taking to Florence with the new company; they felt Maninder should accompany me.

During the next couple of weeks, we attended a wedding, a birthday party and a *roti* service at various immediate relatives' homes. I was trying to settle into my new job, commuting every day for the first couple of weeks, until Maninder suggested I find a place to stay in

Nottingham during the week, and then travel back to the family home at weekends. Of course, it was easier said than done. We had to have a very big family meeting to allow me to make this move, and I was quite surprised that Kabir Dad and Simranjit Mum couldn't understand why Maninder was supporting me in my career. Maybe they could see that I was supporting him as a wife, and he needed to support me as a husband so we could take our relationship to a higher level.

We found an apartment in Nottingham for me to stay during the week. Maninder would drop me off late on Sunday and spend the night with me. We started to develop our relationship again as a couple on every healthy level. The space and time apart gave us time to understand each other, miss each other, and appreciate each other's presence more.

Some weekends, Maninder would come up and chill out with me. It was nice to have our own hideout from his parents where we could do whatever we wanted – even if they did call us ten times a day to check if we were okay! Ironically, when we were home, they didn't really bother with us, but when we were away, they couldn't wait to have us back just so that they could know what the hell we had been up to without them. They couldn't bear it if we'd enjoyed ourselves, and they bristled at why they weren't allowed to share the fun.

FIRST CHRISTMAS WITH MY IN-LAWS

I wanted to put up a Christmas tree in the main hall of the house on Christmas Eve, so I brought up the conversation two weeks before Christmas. Maninder and his parents politely but firmly reminded me, "We are Sikhs, not Christians. In case you didn't know, Sikhs don't celebrate Christmas!"

I got upset, went into my bedroom and sat solemnly on the bed, my dream of a Christmas tree vanishing into thin winter air. Maninder walked into the room and sat on the opposite side of the bed, as if to balance out my weight. He asked me why it was a big deal for me to have a Christmas tree, especially as I didn't want to buy presents. I turned to him, held his gaze, and said, "Christmas is something that makes me hold on to my childhood. It's a turning point in my life from darkness into light, and the Christmas tree, for me, represents hope. Its roots and branches spreading out represents a family growing and spreading out. We decorate and nurture the tree, like we do with our families. All of us doing that together symbolises the cultivation of our relationship. And when's a better time to start than Christmas?"

It was officially my first Christmas with my new family; however, they didn't really have much interest in the holiday that the whole world waited for with bated breath. I'm not a Christian, but I love Christmas and the spirit it heralds.

I continued, "As a child, I grew up watching my father come home blind-drunk and beat my mother up, especially during the festive seasons. In the first Christmas after my mother and father got divorced, when it was just the five of us for the very first time, my mother took us all to the local marketplace to buy a Christmas tree. The one we chose was three feet high, thin, and bottle-green. Mother bought some cheap but scintillating decorations to adorn it, and we kids spent the afternoon decorating it, as my mother cooked *Chole Bature* (spiced chickpeas and fried bread) and *Samosas*. Our home smelled like an Indian takeaway. The living room painted the scene of a perfect family, whistling and singing and decorating the tree like Santa's little helpers. We all pleaded with Mother to buy this silver angel, and I remember her putting the angel on top of the tree. It was as if the angel epitomised Mother, our angel, who had driven the darkness out of our lives by leaving her husband. This was our first Christmas celebration, and it looked like a bright and hopeful one. We didn't care if we got Christmas presents or not, but it did matter a whole lot that we had a peaceful Christmas, filled with gaiety. That Christmas turned out to be the best ever for us all. I remember that particular Christmas as if it were yesterday."

I stopped abruptly, and walked into the bathroom. Sitting on the toilet seat, I finally broke down in tears, as I had never before shared with anyone my Christmas memories and the emotions it evoked. I turned the tap up for the water to dull the sound of my sobs from Maninder. Since the very first moment we met, and more so in the first few months of getting to know each other, I had accepted that our upbringings were quite different, but I only fathomed the extent of that difference after getting married to him. He was the only son of his parents, who had everything handed to him on a plate with a silver spoon – or one of pure gold, in his case. Let me be crude. During the short period that I lived with him, he was a true sufferer of OPS: Only *Putar* (Son) Syndrome. On the contrary, in my upbringing, I had to share food with my siblings, and we worked hard as a team to get where we had as a family. Teamwork ran through my veins. I wanted to marry a Punjabi guy who was living with his family, so that when we had kids they would be able to feel the love of their grandparents – both sets of grandparents, not just on one side of the family, as was my case, unfortunately. My Amirjit *Nani Ji* would visit us from Canada and stay with us for six months every year to help my mother out. We understood the values of every relationship through our Mother's side of the family. Sorry to say, we didn't know anybody from our father's side, nor were they invited to our weddings, but that was a choice we had to make.

By the time I came out of the bathroom, Maninder had gone downstairs. I got into bed and dozed off. Now I felt even worse for having shared my feelings, as I found my husband to be quite cold to the warmth that I cherished in my heart.

As I travelled back home from work on Christmas Eve, I knew in my heart I was not looking forward to this Christmas, as it would be the first time I wasn't going to have a Christmas tree waiting for me at home. I would not have any hot chocolate to drink, either. I remember when I was a kid, my Amirjit *Nani Ji's* cousin's sister would always brew me hot chocolate before I went to bed on Christmas Eve. It was a special smooth and creamy hot chocolate that smelled sweet, and the mug would warm my numbed palms. I love hot chocolate at any time of the day; it bolsters my spirits, however blue I might be feeling.

That evening, Maninder called to inform me that Simranjit Mum was going to be picking me up from the train station. I walked out of the warm station into the freezing winter night looking out for Simranjit Mum. I spotted her in the queue of cars waiting to get into the pick-up spot. I waved at her and walked over to the car. It was warm and cosy inside the heated cabin and she drove us home to the Purewal residence. As I entered the house, I dropped my bags in the hallway. I was taken aback when I walked into the main living room to find Maninder decorating a six-foot tall tree with red and gold decorations! I had the biggest smile on my face, like a child whose Christmas wish had finally come true! I welled up with emotion. I couldn't believe that Maninder had actually been listening to me that day. I felt like this was going to be another amazing Christmas, to be remembered till the grave. Okay, Maninder didn't get an angel for the tree, but he'd got a gold star in its place, and left it for me to put it on. My husband was my Christmas star for listening to me and getting me the tree. I stepped on a stool and proudly put the star on top of the tree. Simranjit Mum brought in some tea and snacks for us. We both cuddled, sitting before the tree and looking up. As he held me in his arms, Maninder turned to me and said, "See, I do take note of what you say. I understood why you wanted a tree but I still think it's funny we have a tree but no presents under it."

"It's not the presents, my dear," I said, "it is about the wonderful people I am going to share my Christmas with!"

We had a lovely semi-Punjabi family Christmas. A Quorn turkey with all the trimmings, along with desserts, were brought in for dinner. I've got to say that there was one thing that I had in common with Kabir Dad: a sweet tooth. We watched Elf, a funny but expressive Christmas-themed film. For the first time in what seemed like ages, we all sat in the same living room, all five of us: Amritpal *Bee Ji*, Kabir Dad, Simranjit Mum, Maninder and me. It was a great day full of love, laughter and Christmas miracles. Three generations enjoying a Christmas meal together. What more could I ask for? No one could have given me a better gift like that moment, which would forever echo in my heart.

We went out for a walk in the evening. As we walked down the streets, I kept looking through the windows at other people's trees, with their flashing lights and decorations. I smiled, knowing that my tree was the best. I had become a part of this family tree and they had become a part of my world, even with all the ups and downs.

After New Year, we both returned to work. One day during the first week, my phone started buzzing away in my coat pocket. I took it out to find it was Maninder, calling to ask what I would like to do on our first wedding anniversary. Honestly, I had no idea. At this point I was very busy; I had a great deal of work to complete before heading off to Florence for the business trip. I rushed the conversation and said I'd talk to him when I came home over the weekend, and we could plan something then.

That Sunday Maninder and I sat in the study talking about our jobs. We were now earning enough money to start thinking about getting a place of our own, and I mentioned that we should start looking as it would take time to find an ideal house. Maninder tried to switch the subject a few times and I asked him why he was ignoring the idea of moving out of his parents' place. It was like I was pulling him out from the branch that he was attached to. He explained that he didn't like the idea of moving out at all. I was disheartened. We aborted our baby because he said he wanted us to have a place of our own first, but now I knew he didn't ever want to move out.

I was confused and annoyed with him at the same time. He came out with this bullshit about how he was their only son and that was why he couldn't move out and leave his parents on their own. I kept my patience and just listened to him as he tried to play me, thinking that I was going to fall for it. I walked out of the study and into the living room, muttering that he must think I was a fool! He didn't want a baby; he didn't want to move out of his parents' place. So what the hell did he want? He'd been controlling me and lying to me from the start, and I couldn't take it anymore. I felt, once more, as if I had been beaten up so many times in one of those never-ending boxing matches.

While I was away with my job during the week, Maninder called to have a catch up and happened to mention that he and his parents had gone to look for an apartment in the city centre. I was a bit pissed off: Maninder had refused to look for a place of our own when I suggested it, but as soon as his parents accepted the idea, he was happy to go along and join them in their search for real estate. Turns out his parents' idea was for us to invest our money in real estate by buying an apartment and letting it out. I didn't want to buy a house to let it; I wanted to move out of the Purewal household due the circumstances I was living under.

At times, Maninder and his parents would irritate me so much that I'd decide not to go back home for the weekend and do some overtime, just so I didn't have to bother seeing them at all. This way I got more time to myself. Maninder could be so selfish towards me, so why should I go home just to clean up his mess, wash his clothes, and cook and clean for his family? My work was the only thing that allowed me to escape from this nightmare!

That weekend, I stayed in Nottingham alone, without having to run around after Maninder and his family. It was a welcome break. I chilled out in bed watching TV, and went out for a four-mile run. I enjoyed doing the overtime at work and coming back to quiescence.

THE IN-LAWS VS. THE BUSINESS TRIP

The weekend before my trip to Florence, Kabir Dad and Simranjit Mum were not happy with me going abroad without Maninder holding my hand. A family meeting was held to suggest that Maninder accompany me on this trip. If anything, this didn't shock me as much as it amused me. Yes, he was my life partner but I didn't need nor want him to hold my hand and help me through everything in life! I was fully capable of taking this trip alone. My in-laws went as far as suggesting that the company I worked with should pay for his flight and insisted I talk to someone at work about it on Monday.

I just sat on the sofa, thinking I was not going to allow this to continue. "We are in the middle of a credit crunch, the worst since the Great Depression of 1929, and my company would not be willing to pay for my partner to tag along!" I retorted.

"Then we will!" they agreed unanimously.

I stood up. "I am going to be working 10 hours a day, doing research and collecting ideas for the coming season. In the evenings I will be networking with other designers and buyers. I simply won't have the time to spend with Maninder, either in the day or the evening!"

His parents gazed at me blankly for a moment before Simranjit Mum concluded with, "We'll let you know if you'll be allowed to go on the trip alone."

I couldn't believe this was happening. The company I worked for was making cutbacks in every department because of the credit crunch, and now my in-laws were trying to cut me off from a business trip I desperately needed to take to advance my career. You had to be kidding me! Where the hell were those people who were proud of their own daughter, Gurleen, before she got married, happy that she had an amazing job, where she could travel here, there and everywhere? What happened to those people? Who the hell replaced them with these older folk?

I didn't care what the outcome was going to be at home, as I had already made up my mind that I would be going on the business trip with my executive. I called up my mother and told her about the situation. She went mad. She was especially annoyed as she had put me through university to get a degree and make a good career for myself, and now my in-laws were stopping me from realizing my ambitions. My mother couldn't believe my in-laws were doing this to me. She advised me that if they had a problem with me travelling alone, she would intervene and insist that they allow me to take the trip. They didn't really have the power to stop me from going on the trip; however, I knew things could get difficult at home. I'd gone through a great deal with them already and I didn't want the added stress. All I wanted was for them to accept my chosen profession and allow me to go on this trip.

All day Sunday I ran around the house like a *desi* princess bride, just so they'd allow me to go. Finally, before I left the house that evening to head up north, they called me into the kitchen as if it were some sort of *desi* Gordon Ramsay show. They said they were about to give me the verdict on whether or not I could go.

"*Owww balla balla*," they said, "*Haan Ji* (yes)... as long as you promise to call and text home every day!"

That was the deal! I did a *Bhangra* dance in my head. I couldn't wait to get back to my flat to shake a little booty in my room. Maninder seemed really excited that I was allowed to take the trip, and also a bit disappointed that he wasn't going to be able to join me. I was happy that he wasn't able to come, as I needed to build relationships with my new team, and not babysit him.

FIRST LOHRI WITH MY IN-LAWS

The day I was due to fly out on the business trip to Florence was also the day of my first *Lohri* with my new family. Thank you, *Waheguru Ji*. *Lohri* is the festival of harvest for the Punjabi culture, and its origin is as old as the legends. It marks the end of the cold, chilly winter, and welcomes the arrival of spring and *Vaisakhi*, the Punjabi New Year. After *Lohri,* the days become noticeably longer and the nights shorter. *Lohri* is celebrated to commemorate and eulogise Dulla Bhatti, popularly known as the Robin Hood of Punjab, who led a revolt against the Mughals under the rule of King Akbar. Like the legendary Robin Hood, Dulla Bhatti would steal from the rich and distribute the stolen wealth among the poor. He was a hero among the local Punjabi's, who loved and respected him. Most *Lohri* songs are sung to pay tribute to Dulla Bhatti. *Lohri* marks the movement of the sun northwards towards Punjab from its winter solstice. The festival brings together family, relatives and friends to meet and exchange gaiety, love and, of course, lots of sweets.

Lohri carries a great significance for newlyweds and new-born babies. The newlywed bride wears her wedding bangles, her new clothes, and embellishes herself with colourful *Bindi* on her forehead and *Mehendi* on her hands. She tries to look her best to show that her husband is the centre of her world. Newlywed husbands dress up too, and wear colourful turbans. I knew Kabir Dad and Simranjit Mum would gift me new clothes and another twenty-four karat gold jewellery set – like I didn't already have enough stashed away in Simranjit Mum's bedroom drawer. She was like an Indian money-snake, sleeping on sparkling gold jewellery – both mine and Gurleen's. Yes, her own daughter was not excepted from this situation.

I was done with having to act like a newlywed bride. The way I looked at it, the loving family I married into had taken the colours out of me and put me through nine months of hell. Kabir Dad and Simranjit Mum were too nosy, and at times downright manipulative. Simranjit Mum played the victim before every member of the family, and Kabir Dad only spoke once his wife had given him a run-through of what she wanted him to tell everybody, while she played the role of the silent wife. Kabir Dad was her voice. Not to mention, they had no respect for the older members of the family, like Amritpal *Bee Ji*. How did they expect me to show them any respect? What hypocrites! And my invertebrate husband needed to grow some balls and make up his own mind about what he wanted out of life, rather than living in his parents' shadow.

In my case, my career had become the centre of my world, rather than my spineless husband. I just wanted to live my life in peace and quiet, spend at least half my time away from the family, and busy myself with my work. I was so happy that I was going on this trip with Kelly-Marie, my executive, rather than Maninder, my husband. Kelly-Marie was a 38-year-old single lady who was like the Iron Woman, Maggie Thatcher, in my view. "Work hard and play hard," Kelly-Marie would say. She made sure I worked hard. She also made sure I cried to let out the grief built up inside me. She was someone I would definitely invite to my dinner parties and I had some amazing conversations with her. I was happy to work all the hours under the sun to please her, rather than being with my family at home.

When I got back home after the trip, Simranjit Mum tried to do the whole *Lohri* procedure on me but I calmly refused by saying that the moment of significance had passed. I was also a bit annoyed at her that she had not passed on to me a white *Lohri* suit my mother had brought down at New Year. Before I got married, it was explained to me that I couldn't wear anything black or white coloured suits until a few months after our wedding. I loved the bright colours I wore, but I also loved the simplicity of white outfits and the elegance of black, which made every overweight woman look slim.

After *Lohri* came the busy season of weddings, parties, and other festive occasions. Every other week it seemed there was one or another occasion to attend, more often for family friends rather than actual family members. If it weren't a *Lohri* party, it'd be some other distant relative's wedding. Maninder's family hadn't been invited to most of the parties but they would shamelessly call up the person who'd be throwing the party and start talking about the occasion so the other person would feel obliged to send them an invitation.

Kabir Dad wasn't even invited to his nephew's wedding, and he said he wouldn't allow Amritpal *Bee Ji* to attend unless they invited us all. Before my wedding, they made sure they had a wonderful relationship with most of their family, and when the idea of getting married in India was suggested by my mother and me, they politely declined, as they said they wanted all their family to be there for the wedding. Ironically, this younger *Pua Ji* (one of

Kabir Dad's sisters) and her family, for whom we didn't get married in India, never even came to our wedding! I would rather put my energy into developing my career and relationship with Maninder than attending random *Pendoo* (luxurious) family functions where I would meet most of the population of Milton Keynes.

Sometimes Maninder and I would be busy doing our own thing when, out of the blue, we'd be told to get dressed for a family friend's celebration. I had never before been to so many random strangers' parties! The in-laws bought me heavy decorative Punjabi suits to wear. However, as heavy suits were only worn to family functions, and I had no family that they really got on with, I didn't have anywhere else to wear these traditional clothes.

THE DESI, BIG BROTHER SHOW

The Purewal castle had a CCTV camera connected to their TV so, with the flick of a button on the TV remote, they could see who came to visit while they were all out at work. The camera was also put in place to spy upon who came to visit Amritpal *Bee Ji* behind their backs, and also so they could keep an eye on her and the rest of the family. Early on, I'd made my feelings known to Maninder that I didn't feel comfortable living like I was being watched all the time, much like the Big Brother reality show, and I wouldn't be surprised if our conversations were being recorded. The only thing missing from the reality show was the diary room and the funky furniture.

We should not be living like this! Was there no love or trust left amongst the people in this home? I felt choked knowing that they were trying to control me and everything around me. You just can't live like that; controlling everybody and every situation was not the way to move forward. Not even prisoners are watched around the clock! I was not brought up like this, and I couldn't live with these kinds of activities. What was so wrong with Amritpal *Bee Ji's* daughters visiting her while my in-laws were at work?

Every time I tried to find a solution to the problem, there was always an excuse for why it wouldn't work. If there was no excuse to be found, Simranjit Mum would start acting up by getting upset.

Everyone did what Simranjit Mum said and she was the Queen Bee of our hive. If you did what you were told, you enjoyed the taste of the honey. Otherwise, you were just a worker bee with no respect, toiling till the end of your life. All these issues made it hard for me to open up to Maninder and allow him into my world. The distance between us started to grow even more, and I felt it was pointless talking to him with an open heart and professing my true feelings for him.

I never forget this one trip we took as a family when my father was around. My father and mother bought my siblings and me one gift each. I remember picking up a glass house, just like the one I am living in today. It was very beautiful, and looked as if it were so delicate and perfect.

Yes, my husband was perfect, my house was perfect, and my life was perfect to the outside world. However, deep within, my soul was being devoured by the snakes of the Purewal household. Well, no one's life is perfect, I admit. But my life was devastated.

The glass house from my childhood was on display in the drawing room. Every Punjabi home has a spacious drawing room, where everything pretended to be so perfect. Your prized possessions were kept on display as a silent brag to your guests. As kids, you were never allowed in that room, and when we were old enough to enter that room, we weren't allowed to touch anything, or our parents would give us the dreaded Punjabi look that could turn you into ash if you didn't turn away from those trophies at once.

I had overstayed my welcome in this home. I wanted to move out with Maninder and get a home of our own, so that we could start to build a perfect, simple and normal life together. The camera was never going to retire. I was surprised that the Milton Keynes BBC news station didn't yet contact the Purewal household to get the evening news coverage!

The camera, its infra-red LEDs faintly glowing twenty-four seven, was upsetting my soul and making me feel pissed off that I had to live like a guinea pig in a laboratory experiment, being watched around the clock.

THE TAPPED PHONE

One weekend when I was home, Amritpal *Bee Ji* received a call from one of Maninder's aunties, who lived in London. I spotted Simranjit Mum sprinting up to her bedroom so fast, she'd put Elaine Thompson to shame! I followed her, tiptoeing up to her bedroom, and peeked in. She was by the phone tapping machine behind the curtain. We'd had a family meeting during which Kabir Dad, Simranjit Mum, Maninder and I unanimously negotiated a protocol that this tapping device would no longer be used in the Purewal family home. Now I was shocked to discover Simranjit Mum breaking our family protocol. It left me fuming. Feelings tumbled through me like knotted telephone cables and the hurt stabbed into my heart like sparks of electricity. She thought I wouldn't know anything, as I was living away from the family home in Nottinghamshire.

I didn't say anything that day, but the hurt made me snap at Maninder over petty issues. "Why are you being so moody tonight, darling? What is it that is bothering you?" he asked while driving me to Nottingham.

I explained what I had seen, and added that I was disappointed with him and his parents. He called Simranjit Mum and she admitted that they had been tapping calls again. He was as shocked as me. He didn't know that his Simranjit Mum was still using the device when she felt like it. We headed back to Milton Keynes at once, and called for a family meeting without Amritpal *Bee Ji*. At the meeting, my in-laws argued that it was their house and they could do whatever they wished. Maninder lost it with them for the first time. He exploded at his parents and told them they were being unfair and unethical. He argued that it was not going to help his wife feel more settled when they were clearly not respecting her feelings and wishes. The meeting went on until late in the evening, and then Maninder drove me back to Nottingham. I was so grateful that he fought my corner about the eavesdropping situation. I knew his parents weren't happy with how he had spoken to them. I loved him for not accepting that kind of behaviour any longer, and protesting against their immoral deed.

BOOKING THE FIRST WEDDING ANNIVERSARY TRIP

Maninder brought up the topic of our first wedding anniversary over the phone that week, while I was in Nottingham. This helped take my mind off the eavesdropping subject. "What special thing would you like to do that day?" he asked, excitement in his voice.

I thought for a moment and suggested, "I would like to spend some time alone with you...just the two of us." I was smiling to myself, even if he couldn't see me. We were getting along much better, and surprisingly, the distance between us was helping us grow closer.

We both agreed on booking a five day trip to lovers' paradise – Paris. Maninder booked tickets for Eurostar and a hotel. I agreed to cover our spending money when we got there. This was the first time in our relationship that he had asked for my opinion and we had completed a task together without fighting. There was clear communication between us, as well as a newfound mutual respect. Our first year of marriage had been hard – like the beginning of a battle. But that day, I was feeling very positive about things between us, regardless of what we had been through. I kept thinking of all the positive reasons why we had decided to be together, and the happy times we had shared. I had an amazing cheerful feeling about life, as if life had breathed new life into itself.

On the first Valentine's Day after our marriage, Maninder sent me flowers at work and he came up to Nottingham to spend the weekend with me. We decided to meet up with my university friend, Charlotte, and her boyfriend in Manchester. On the way, I yapped away with Maninder about my university days and told him stories about each place we visited. It seemed we were becoming more patient and understanding with each other. As we shared stories and laughed at insignificant little things, I knew I was finally opening up to him.

WEDDING ANNIVERSARY IN LOVERS PARADISE

Shortly before our first wedding anniversary, I lost my job because of the ongoing recession. It was shocking and upsetting for me. However, Maninder advised me to live in the present, enjoy the trip to Paris, and then come back and worry about things later. For once he understood my feelings, which helped me get out of my blues. He even said, "I care about your feelings and want to know what you want to do." Man, how I needed that!

The night before the trip, Simranjit Mum and Kabir Dad came into our bedroom and handed me a white envelope that felt like it was full of cash. I placed it on the music system, but they insisted that I open it, as there might be something important in it for us to take to Paris. I explained that it was not our wedding anniversary until Monday, so until then we would not be opening any presents.

They also offered to host a small anniversary party for us, but I turned them down. I knew it would be all about them and nothing about us. Eventually they left us alone, and we finally got into bed. The following morning, while Kabir Dad was dropping us off at St. Pancras International in London, he decided to attempt one final push to get us to open the envelope. Why couldn't they just give it a break, leave us alone and choose to respect our decision, like adults?

When we arrived at the station, I was getting butterflies in my stomach. This was the second time we were going to be alone – just the two of us together – without any work to worry about, or the in-laws constantly interfering; the first being our honeymoon. I didn't know how everything would turn out. I trusted in my *Waheguru Ji* (supreme, divine being) and hoped it would all be positive.

On the way to Paris, there was a family of three sitting opposite us in the train – Papa Bear, Mummy Bear and Baby Bear. Baby Bear was sitting on his mother's lap. I could see something was bothering Maninder, as his mood started to change. "Are you okay?" I asked him.

"This kid keeps kicking my knee," he whispered. I was puzzled that an unknown kid could kick Maninder and he would not do anything about it other than complain to me, when he had never failed to throw his weight around me and other family members.

We arrived in Paris and checked into our hotel. It was a pleasurable week, but once again I noticed that Maninder had our itinerary all mapped out. Well, I liked things to be planned, but what I enjoyed much more was living in the moment and having spontaneous fun—something Maninder never did.

Here we were in the romantic city of Paris, but we didn't need a tour guide as apparently my husband was one! He had been to Paris a few years ago with his family, and he kept going on about that trip. This was my twelfth time in Paris, for I had been here many times as a student and as a young professional. No part of Paris was new to me. I was familiar with the underground, the streets, and the walkways too! I loved Paris, and every inch of its fashion, culture and people. This trip made my soul come alive.

We both had our own experiences of the city, but to

come here together and create our own magical moments was a rejuvenating experience. We visited the Eiffel Tower, Louvre Museum and Pyramid, The Notre Dame Cathedral, Sacré-Cœur, Arc de Triomphe, Jardin du Luxembourg and La Grande Arche de la Défense. We got on really well, like when we were young lovers, though we did occasionally have our moments of frustration.

The evening before our wedding anniversary, Maninder gave me tickets to a Gurdas Maan concert. I crafted him a handmade paper card with an embroidered heart on it – as the first wedding anniversary gifts are traditionally made of paper. I was going to give him a certificate confirming we'd made it through the first year without killing each other, but after deeper consideration, I realised it wouldn't go down well – so I gave that thought a miss. We spent the evening in Starbucks, where we sipped cappuccinos, watched the world go by, talked, and wrote postcards to send back to our families. When we got back to the hotel, we made love, which was a silent expression of how much we cared for each other and hoped everything would work out for the good.

BACK TO MILTON KEYNES

On our return from Paris, the in-laws were once again like two anxious school kids waiting for us back at the house. Maninder and I had grown so much closer and I was feeling special because he made me feel important. His parents gave me the envelope, as well as another twenty-four karat gold jewellery set. Maninder could read my expression better now. "Everything okay?" he asked. "You don't like the design of the jewellery?" Observing my silence, he continued, "My parents bought this necklace and earrings some eight years ago for one of my cousins, as her wedding gift."

"What's the point of giving me all this jewellery when they're just going to let me keep it for a few hours and then put it back in Simranjit Mum's bedroom drawer?" I said, finally. I was never allowed to hold on to my jewellery. However, Gurleen was younger than me by a year and her in-laws trusted her with all her jewellery. Her mother, our Simranjit Mum, never told her to deposit her jewellery with her Mother-in-law. Then it struck me – they were giving me jewellery that had been rejected by Maninder's cousin! Man, I could really feel the warmth of love from these two loving parents! It was like twenty-four karat gold: shiny and pure on the outside, fragile on the inside! I didn't want anything other than for them to treat me fairly, respect my wishes as a human being, and understand that I too had emotions – just like their own children.

When Kabir Dad and Simranjit Mum discovered that Maninder had bought us two tickets for the Gurdas Maan concert, but not for them, they expressed their infuriation in no vague way. They finally realised that he had taken the time to find out what I would like to do, and arranged it just for the two of us, rather than having them join us.

MARRIAGE COUNSELLING

On the weekend of the Gurdas Maan concert, we went home to Birmingham, stayed at my mother's house and chilled out with friends and family. Though Maninder and I were getting along just fine, I decided to talk to him about seeing a marriage guidance counsellor so we could talk through some of the problems we were having. I had been contemplating this idea since the beginning of the year, and now it had started playing more on my mind. He didn't seem to be over the moon about having to attend counselling sessions, but he compromised, and asked me to go ahead and book an appointment. I found a marriage counsellor in our locality, who seemed okay on the phone. I booked an appointment with her and let Maninder know that we would be attending.

When we arrived for our first appointment, Maninder was not happy because the counsellor was an Asian lady named Asha. Asha was affable, and I liked her. The first session was great to start off with. She started with how we met, and as each of us talked, smiles growing on our faces, she was certain we loved each other.

She told us that she could see how much we cared for each other, and then delicately moved the conversation on to why we were there. I open-heartedly expressed my feelings to Maninder for the first time, hoping that he would hear me crying inside and understand the pain I was going through. It seemed like there were times when he would understand me, but then there were other times when he'd dismiss my feelings or say, "Harleen, I don't have time for this." I was deeply hurt by the termination of my pregnancy and I wanted him to understand that. And I was upset about all the family rules I couldn't live with. I wanted us to move out and have a home we could call our own. I knew that our own home would definitely not have phone tapping machines and I would not open other people's letters. I would have a key to my house, and I would allow all our family and friends to come and visit us – none of this picking and choosing who could come. The in-laws had made it clear at the last family meeting that it was their home and we needed to abide by their rules. I couldn't live with that anymore.

But this time too, Maninder ignored my feelings. He made up his mind that we were never going to leave the family home and he would always live with his parents. Although I had agreed to marry Maninder knowing that I wanted to live within a family unit, I never realised that the family I agreed to live with would be this insecure within themselves, and antagonistic towards their newlywed daughter-in-law. It simply wasn't something I could compromise on or adjust to. I had asked them to make changes, but to no avail. I knew I couldn't continue living with them.

We'd been attending the marriage counselling sessions for six weeks by then. However, Maninder never paid attention to the counsellor. One day, when I called her to arrange our next meeting, she asked me to meet her on my own. She sounded serious on the phone, so I agreed to meet her in the evening. I was shocked when she informed me that Maninder had turned up at her family home one Saturday afternoon and threatened her in front of her husband! I was dumbstruck! He'd had the nerve to go behind my back and tell her to stop influencing me towards becoming more westernised. I realised all Maninder and his parents wanted to do was control and manipulate me. I had wrongly thought that by attending marriage counselling, it would help us improve our communication pathways, which in turn would help us become more understanding towards each other. I was starting to see the conniving and insecure side of Maninder.

After I got back from the appointment, we all – including Gurleen, who was visiting us for a couple of days – went to the *gurdwara*. I was fired up with what I had learnt earlier in the day. As we approached the entrance of the peaceful *gurdwara*, we saw a beautiful woman with her lovely little daughter. This young woman welcomed everybody – Kabir Dad, Simranjit Mum, Maninder and Gurleen – as if she had known us for ages! As Maninder and I were walking up the stairs towards the *Darbar Sahib* of the *gurdwara*, he gave me the lowdown. The woman was one of the older *Pua Ji's* (father's sister's) daughters – the daughter who ran away from the family and married a white slice of bread. Because of that, her family had cut her off. While she was organising her master getaway, she'd planned on breaking into Maninder's parents' safe. Maninder had mentioned this to me in a passing conversation a while ago. So this was the girl who stole from their safe, and ironically, she was getting so much respect from them all between the four walls of the *gurdwara*!

I was always dropped off and picked up from everywhere. I wasn't even allowed to walk to the nearest letterbox to post letters, and Simranjit Mum had transferred everything from the safe into her bedroom, and started sleeping on top of her valuable possessions. While sitting in the *Darbar Sahib*, I got quite worked up thinking that I had never done anything wrong to my family, so why was I treated unfairly because of others' mistakes?

I was annoyed with them all for being sweet as pie in front of the woman, only to slag her off behind her back. I hate people who talk behind others' backs. While we were having *Langar* (a free meal) at the *gurdwara*, I sat between Gurleen and Simranjit Mum. I turned to Simranjit Mum and asked her why she didn't think it was important to introduce me to Maninder's cousin. "Harleen, you're not going to be socialising with her. So why does it matter to you?" she replied.

I was really pissed off by this reply. "Then why were you all hugging her and welcoming her, as if she has given you so much respect?" I snapped.

Gurleen cut into the conversation. "Well, Harleen *Phabhi Ji* (sister-in-law), we were all shocked to see her here today...we were not expecting her."

Before she could finish her sentence, I cut her off. "I didn't ask you the question! I asked Simranjit Mum the question – so why are you answering for your mum? By the way, Gurleen *Pehn Ji*, you're married in your husband's home, and this is my home, not yours!" I gave her a taste of her own medicine. "This also reminds me of the phone-tapping situation," I smirked.

Gurleen began to realise that she needed to keep her nose out of my business. This was the first time I had stood up for myself in front of her, and told her where she stood, as well as making her aware that I knew about the phone tapping and everything else that went on in the Purewal castle. (Loveneet wasn't aware of anything that went on.) Simranjit Mum and I got into a tiff, as I was not allowed to talk to her darling daughter like that. However, they were all allowed to talk down to me as though I were just a piece of dirt off the streets.

Following this argument, I reached a point where I decided to call my first family meeting with Kabir Dad, Simranjit Mum and Maninder. I'd asked Gurleen to keep Amritpal *Bee Ji* company, as she wasn't in the *gurdwara* with us that evening, and Gurleen was married and no longer a part of this family. I'd lost count of the amount of times my in-laws would tell me that Gurleen no longer lived here, and I shouldn't try to judge why they were treating us differently.

I sat them all down and told them upfront that I didn't want to live with them anymore. Anything I'd communicated to my in-laws with an open heart went unheard or was dismissed, just as Maninder did when we spoke as a couple. Maninder and I needed a place of our own where everybody was welcome, and telephone lines were not tapped, and there was no camera spying on our every move every second of the day. I told them I was upset by Simranjit Mum's mind games and I wanted to live in an environment where respect and trust was given to each person without having to question each other's behaviour.

We went round and round in circles, just like the roundabouts in Milton Keynes town centre. Simranjit Mum told me she was not going to take on board anything I suggested. Rather than them listening to me and understanding why I wanted to move out, the meeting created even more issues, and simply escalated Simranjit Mum's animosity towards me. I had hoped that by telling them the truth about why I couldn't live with them, this would help them shift a change in their behaviour towards me, or at least make them understand why I couldn't live under the same roof as them. But Simranjit Mum's behaviour after we had this meeting left me with even more issues playing on my mind.

The next day Kabir Dad was in the kitchen, cooking Amritpal *Bee Ji roti* for lunch. I asked him why he hadn't asked me to cook Amritpal *Bee Ji* her lunch. He replied, "Harleen *Puth,* you've got work to get on with."

"Dad I don't have a problem with cooking your food or looking after you all. I just don't agree with the way you run your home!" I said.

He looked at me, smiled sweetly and said, "Harleen, you have a clear heart and you're just honest. I know you have no bad feeling towards us. Your Simranjit Mum and I were talking after the meeting, and we thought you had a problem with us. However, all you really want is for us to change our habits."

I felt better knowing that Kabir Dad had taken the time to talk to me. I got the feeling he understood that I didn't want to hurt him or Simranjit Mum; I just didn't agree with the way they had gone about things with regards to the phone tapping and other issues.

HOLIDAY TO CANADA AND FAKING ILLNESS TO GET ATTENTION

One day, Simranjit Mum and I were home alone with Amritpal *Bee Ji*. We were expecting a guest. Simranjit Mum had cooked a meal for us, and was being over-friendly. I couldn't quite make out what was going on, but I could sense she was up to no good. Before the guest arrived, she told me that she would love to go to Canada on a vacation. She and Kabir Dad had been talking about this lately, and he had advised against it because the last time she went to Canada, when Mohanbir *Nanaa Ji* passed away, Amritpal *Bee Ji* had opened up to me about the family's secrets. So Simranjit Mum wanted me to talk to Kabir Dad to assure him that I would be okay, so that she could take the trip.

Simranjit Mum had been nothing but a thorn in the side of my already failing marriage. She had been playing mind games with me for the past few weeks. So why should I now support her to take this vacation? I didn't get her support when I needed to take the business trip to Florence earlier that year. As soon as she finished talking, I walked away.

Two minutes later, she asked me to join her to pick up the guest of honour from India, the *Chacha Ji* (Kabir's dad's younger cousin's brother) who was coming to Milton Keynes for one of Maninder's cousins' weddings.

We arrived at Milton Keynes coach station at midday, and spotted a tall slim guy in his mid-forties, wearing a very bright orange turban, a tightly tied beard, chequered shirt, casual jacket, semi-flared trousers and tan-coloured sandals. He was carrying an overnight bag as if he was going to be stopping for the night, but my in-laws had not seen him for a quite a while now and were not sure about him spending the night at our house. He seemed to be lost, but when he recognised Simranjit Mum, he threw a warm and jovial smile. Simranjit Mum started to walk him towards the car. I got out from the front seat of the car to welcome him, Punjabi style – *"Sat Sri Akhal Ji!"* – and then climbed into the backseat.

Once we entered the house, Amritpal *Bee Ji's* face lit up to see her nephew. He told her about how all the family were doing back home in India. While everybody was running around this new *Chacha Ji*, my phone rang. Following my redundancy, I had been searching for a new job and I'd called some recruitment agencies earlier in the week regarding a design job. The call was from one of the agencies so I broke off from the family reunion for a moment and emailed over my resume.

After I finished, I returned to join the rest of the family. Simranjit Mum was ranting to *Chacha Ji* about how hard it was living with Amritpal *Bee Ji*. She explained that Amritpal *Bee Ji* was very bossy and could upset the environment of the household within seconds. She tried to explain how Amritpal *Bee Ji* had caused problems between all of us. I couldn't believe my ears! Simranjit Mum was putting the entire blame on an innocent, sweet old lady, when she herself was responsible for the reprehensible acts of phone tapping, eavesdropping, spying with cameras, opening others' letters, ever since I'd been married into the family! She was the vile leader of the pack, who guided everybody.

"I so want to go to Canada, you know. But I'm scared! The last time I went to Canada, this old haggard messed up my relationship with Harleen!" she said. But not once did she explain about her own deplorable acts! She walked out of the room laden with crocodile tears, and I just sat there watching the drama unfold right under my nose. This was like a drama on an Asian TV channel! I didn't say a thing. This new *Chacha Ji* looked over at me, and I grinned with embarrassment.

A few minutes later, I went to check on Simranjit Mum and found that she had worked herself up so much she was having a panic attack in the kitchen. "Mum, sit down here, and stop over-thinking things," I suggested.

She looked up at me from the stool. "Thank you for joining me to the coach station to pick up your *Chacha Ji*. I didn't want to go alone and have him sit in the front seat of my car."

Nothing surprised me now.

Kabir Dad came home and welcomed his first cousin. Simranjit Mum got up to join them all. She sat there seeming normal, but half an hour later, she disappeared upstairs, and Kabir Dad soon followed. I couldn't make out where exactly they had gone. They'd left me alone with his new *Chacha Ji*, who I had only known for a couple of hours. I excused myself to check out what was happening, and where everybody had gone.

I found Simranjit Mum in her bedroom, groaning. She claimed that she was having severe chest pains and pain in her left arm as well. Kabir Dad panicked. He thought she might be having a heart attack. Without hesitation, he dialled 999. He went to tell the guest of honour that he would have to drop him off at the railway station, as we all had to go to the hospital. It all happened too quickly for me to process, and I ended up in the wee-wooing ambulance with Simranjit Mum, an oxygen mask covering her mouth. I called Maninder to let him know what had happened, and that his Simranjit Mum would not be able to pick him up after work.

Kabir Dad locked up the house so no one could get in or out, leaving Amritpal *Bee Ji* all alone in the mansion. Then he dropped off *Chacha Ji* at the railway station, picked up Maninder, and drove straight to the hospital. Before they arrived, I was asked a few questions about Simranjit Mum's health. I answered them to the best of my knowledge, and explained that I felt she might have been having a panic attack earlier in the day. They asked me to elaborate on the cause, and I told them about the holiday to Canada.

When Maninder and Kabir Dad arrived, they rushed over to Simranjit Mum like she was the queen bee and they were lost without her honey. Maninder asked me if anything had happened in the day that could have caused her stress, and I filled him in about the argument over the trip to Canada, which he had no idea about. No surprise there! I also mentioned my suspicions about this being a panic attack; I knew very well that this was not a heart attack, but I didn't want to say too much, as they might think I was being insensitive.

Kabir Dad called Gurleen and successfully managed to get her into a panic attack (At this rate the whole family would be taking up the beds in the hospital ward!), thinking that her Simranjit Mum was indeed in danger. I felt Kabir Dad was enjoying playing the hero, like Amitabh

Bachchan of *Sholay* (Bollywood film). He and Simranjit Mum were blowing the whole situation out of proportion without knowing the facts. By this stage, we had been in the hospital for a few hours, and I was the only one worried about Amritpal *Bee Ji*, who had not had anything to eat, and was locked up inside the house. So I suggested that we should get going. Just then one of the doctors came into the room to confirm that Simranjit Mum had not had a heart attack, but she might be suffering from a trapped nerve. Kabir Dad insisted that she stay the night in the hospital, and then made a big deal out of the situation – he asked them to check her over thoroughly, and went on to mention that something major had happened to his wife and she was now getting pains in her stomach. Kabir Dad should have been a doctor rather than a truck driver! Well, aren't most Punjabis self-proclaimed doctors? He might as well walk around carrying a doctor's briefcase! The issue was simple, but he wanted it to be something serious. They were simply wasting the NHS's money and time.

When we finally got home, I went straight into the kitchen, prepared some food for Amritpal *Bee Ji*, wrapped up some more, and took it back to the hospital for the in-laws. I didn't get back home till one o'clock in the morning, and went straight to bed, but was back up at four o'clock to cook breakfast for Kabir Dad and pack his lunch box, as Simranjit Mum was still in the hospital. He was very grateful. He knew that neither of his kids would ever have taken responsibility like I did. As he thanked me for the lunch, he patted me on the head.

I went back to bed for a while but finally got up at eight in the morning to cook Amritpal *Bee Ji* some breakfast. We went back to the hospital to find Loveneet and Gurleen had arrived to see Simranjit Mum. Gurleen was so tense she had failed to get a good night's sleep.

While we were all there, the doctors finally confirmed that Simranjit Mum was doing all right. There was no trapped nerve, and her stomach was fine too. Loveneet and Gurleen came back to our house from the hospital. On the way back, I asked Maninder to get some groceries, while I cleaned the house and made some late lunch for us all. Loveneet and Gurleen had gone to B&Q to look for something for their home. I badly needed some sleep, but I was happy doing the chores if that helped everyone. While Maninder and I were in the kitchen, I explained to him about the panic attack and suggested that we should talk to Loveneet and Gurleen about what had happened to get their advice. However, Maninder was more worried that his brother-in-law would find out about the phone tapping and would not agree. He knew Loveneet would not condone it. Since discovering the house landline was tapped, I'd managed all my communication through my personal mobile phone. If I did answer the house phone, I would keep my conversations to a minimum.

When everybody had finished eating, I went to do the dishes, and again asked Maninder to talk with them both. His mood quickly shifted, and an argument ensued. To my utter disbelief, he slapped me across my right cheek. I surrendered to quiescence, and was on the verge of tears. I had been running around after his family and making sure that everyone was looked after, and all I got in return was verbal abuse and assault!

I ran out of the kitchen, straight upstairs, and into my

bedroom, and got into bed. My right cheek felt heavy, and my heart, heavier. I lay in bed holding my cheek till I fell asleep. A few hours later Maninder came up to the room to ask if I was going to cook dinner for the family. "Ask your sister to cook the family meal," I grunted, "or you do it. It's your family, not mine!" Finally, they ordered a takeaway. Loveneet hollered to me to come out of my bedroom, but I refused to go down and join them. The hospital called to say Simranjit Mum had been discharged, so Kabir Dad and Gurleen went to bring her back.

When Maninder came to bed, he left me a note of apology. The following morning, he was being quite nice and polite to me. I couldn't make out why, as normally when I stood my ground, he would teach me a lesson by being a real asshole towards me. I got my answer as soon I looked out of the window. Loveneet and Gurleen's car was parked on the driveway, and they were still inside the house. Maninder didn't want them to know what had happened, and that was why he was being so nice to me. I, being the 'good Punjabi wife,' kept the pretence up, and fanned the flames of his charade.

I helped Simranjit Mum make breakfast, while Gurleen looked on. Loveneet was reading a book in the living room. Simranjit Mum pretended to be quite weak, and while we ate our croissants and fruits, we all suggested she go to her bedroom and get more rest. I have never seen her move so quickly – she was like a rat up a drainpipe. Clearly she was feeling better, even though she was acting as exhausted as someone who had just run the London Marathon.

Loveneet and Gurleen left after breakfast, and Kabir Dad, Simranjit Mum and Maninder set off for a committee meeting at the Milton Keynes *Gurdwara*. They wanted me to join them, but I couldn't be bothered with a meeting, nor with these people and their infused drama. What had happened to Mother-in-law's poor health and her needing more time to rest? She was all dressed up as if she was attending someone's wedding! Who'd imagine she'd been rushed to the ER two nights ago? While they attended the meeting, I stayed at home and did some comprehension for a forthcoming English exam. In the afternoon, they came home all excited about a situation that had cropped up at the *gurdwara*. The police had to be called to calm the situation down.

Over the course of time, living under the Purewal household, I started to notice a few things about Maninder's Simranjit Mum, especially her unaccountable mood swings. One minute she was saying she didn't feel well, next minute she'd be all fine. During public appearances and meetings, she would always be on top form and at the forefront of things. All the local Indian cameramen were on first name terms with her. If she didn't get her own way, she wouldn't get out of bed and would claim she was feeling depressed. I knew she had suffered from depression many years ago but now I often found her depression coming to visit her when it suited her. She knew how to play that game. Hats off to her.

I THINK I CAN FORGE HER SIGNATURE

One morning, a letter came for me from the *gurdwara* asking me to explain why my signature didn't match a form I had submitted a year ago. Simranjit Mum was standing next to me as I opened the letter. "Who the hell has been signing on my behalf?" I asked her with a scowl.

"Harleen, I am going to burn down the house of the person who tries to cause any problem within our home!" she retorted.

I looked back at her in shock and asked her again if she had signed the form on my behalf. She didn't reply but just walked out of the room. I didn't say anything more, and I forgot to bring it up with Maninder that evening. The form was for me to become a committee member of the local *gurdwara*; however, I wasn't a member of the Purewal family, so how was I going to become a member of the local *gurdwara*?

The next morning, I received another letter. This time, it was from the local council informing me that another form had been filled out on my behalf, and again the signature didn't match mine. This time I lost it. I found Simranjit Mum and asked her if she knew anything about this second letter, but she denied any knowledge of either of them. This was plain illegal!

When Maninder came home from work that evening, I showed him the letters and asked him to explain what was going on. He approached his parents and asked them who had forged my signature. Finally, Simranjit Mum admitted to forging both forms. I was infuriated. This was another atrocity to add to the list – as if they hadn't hurt me enough by now. First they had opened my mail, and now they'd forged my signature!

When Maninder told me about Simranjit Mum's confession, I was fuming. I couldn't believe she had the nerve to look me in the face and lie to me twice! The *gurdwara* form had been filled out while she was faking her illness. I decided to go to the *gurdwara* and declare to the committee that Simranjit Mum had forged my signature. While I was there, the entire community of local Uncle *Jis* and Auntie *Jis* filled me in on what had happened at the *gurdwara* committee meeting. My 'very ill and weak' Simranjit Mum had mouthed off to a few people at the *gurdwara* and then had the time to fill out this form on my behalf. What a sweet lady! She behaved in front of Loveneet as if butter wouldn't melt in her mouth, and then had the nerve to ask me to join them. Thank goodness I didn't. Their behaviour didn't seem to shock me anymore. I had seen all the colours of the rainbow in them and their son – actually, come to think of it, they were more like all the colours of hell's darkness than those of a rainbow.

This bothered me for a while and I decided to discuss it with Maninder. However, I knew both he and his parents would think this was not an issue, and it would be brushed under the carpet. Yet again! Every time they did anything wrong towards me, it was seen to be no big deal. I should have challenged Simranjit Mum, or forged her signature and seen how she'd like it. Maybe then she would understand that what she was doing was wrong. I didn't have the time to play their games; I was trying to live a simple life. I just wanted to be happy, not complicate my life further.

MANINDER'S COUSIN'S WEDDING IN MY HOMETOWN

One of Maninder's cousins got married in Birmingham, my hometown, and we had a pleasurable time during the wedding ceremony. However, my in-laws started putting pressure on Maninder to assist with the wedding. They explained that his cousin didn't have a maternal brother so Maninder and I needed to be there on time and be on top of everything, and play the role of a good brother and sister-in-law. The bride's family had planned every inch of the wedding, and had mentally assigned everyone's roles. We couldn't just walk into someone's wedding and start imposing ourselves on people, but that was what my in-laws were doing.

Kabir Dad was troubled because Simranjit Mum kept yapping on and on about how she was disappointed because they hadn't invited us to the pre-wedding party at their family home a week before the marriage. Kabir Dad pointed out that if they had invited us, he would have had to give the bride a gold jewellery set – a twenty-four karat one, of course! Well, if he really did care that much, he should have given the bride a gift, regardless of whether they got an invitation or not. I never really saw my in-laws offering any help or support to this family before the wedding, and yet they expected them to run around us. I felt we should enjoy the wedding and offer help and support if it was needed, but not get in the way and go on irritating people. I know this much about Punjabi weddings: real families care about helping out with the preparations, but pretentious, fake people just want to play happy families on the day and try to be the cynosures of the ceremony.

Even though we were travelling from my mother's place in Birmingham, which was only 15 minutes from the bride's parents' house, we had to be up at stupid o'clock to get ready for this wedding. My in-laws wanted us to be there bright and early. Kabir Dad called Gurleen to get her assurance that they were going to be there at stupid o'clock as well. This was a way of life for my in-laws; they always made sure that they got on well with people, but they didn't really have any people skills to enable them to do things the correct way. They just put pressure on people and demanded respect. Why didn't they understand that you have to give respect to receive it? Respect is earned, not coerced.

MANINDER'S COUSIN'S DAD'S PASSING

I came home one night to be told that Maninder's cousin, who just got married, had called. Her Dad was seriously ill. We all went to Birmingham to visit the *Fuffar Ji* in hospital, but a week later he passed away. We went to visit his family, but for some reason I haven't understood to this day, we went in two cars; Maninder and me in one, and his parents in another. Ours was not a two-seater Lamborghini!

Before we left home, I had asked Simranjit Mum if I needed to take anything but she just ignored my question. We were halfway towards Birmingham when she called Maninder on his mobile to ask him if I had a *chunni* with me. At once I felt annoyed. Why couldn't she have answered me when I asked if I needed to bring anything? Why had she called Maninder to make it look like I hadn't thought of asking her? No, I didn't have a stupid *chunni* on me. So I called my own Mother in Birmingham, explained the situation, and said I would pop around with Maninder to pick up a *chunni* on our way to pay our respects to the family.

When I came off the phone, Maninder started bickering with me about why had I told my mother that his mum wasn't communicating with me like an adult, and how she'd been rude to me. I'd said that she was playing mind games with me and had given my mother examples of what she'd done in front of Maninder, and what level of meanness she displayed to me.

"What is your mother going to think of my mum now?" he asked.

"Your mum has been playing mind games on me for the

past few weeks. If you want to turn a blind eye to that, like you always do, that's fine!" I yelled over the noise of a pile driver by the roadside. "But I am not going to ignore it or cover it up anymore, and from now on, I am going to be vocal about it to my loved ones!"

We stopped at my mother's house to pick up the *chunni* and she noticed the rising tension between us. "Are you two okay?" she said, shifting her eyes between us.

"Yeah, Mother, we are all fine!" Maninder said, coolly.

I managed to get my mother on her own in her bedroom and told her more about what was happening. "His mum is causing a lot of problems between us. I just can't take this bullshit anymore!" I pressed my fingers against my temples and shook my head.

"You are doing your best, Harleen." Mother caressed my hair like she did when I was a little girl. "Would you like me to talk to them now?"

I didn't really know if her trying to talk to them was going to make matters better or worse. So it was left up in the air.

We arrived at Maninder's cousin's house to pay our respects and help them out. Simranjit Mum and I were still not talking, and Maninder and I argued a little. He had another go at me in the car on the way back to Milton Keynes.

ISSUES WITH MY DRESS

Maninder had booked us tickets for the London Motor Show, where everything from classic and vintage cars to the latest designs would be showcased. I got dressed in a casual denim dress and ballet shoes, which was, in my view, very acceptable. There was nothing wrong with this outfit and I had seen Gurleen wearing something very similar. When we went down for breakfast, Simranjit Mum greeted us but she had a funny look on her face. I thought nothing of it that time, and went on with my breakfast.

After breakfast, I went back up to my room to finish off my make-up. Suddenly Maninder burst into a fitful rage. He was as furious as a snorting devil. He screamed at me to take off the dress I was wearing, as Simranjit Mum hated it.

"No." I looked him in the eyes. "I am not wearing anything wrong, and I have seen your sister wearing dresses very similar to this. And anyway, when we were dating, I used to wear shorter dresses!"

He argued for a while, and then decided to give me the silent treatment; his weapon. As we left the house, the mother-in-law was still giving me looks to say that she was disappointed but I couldn't care less. I hadn't done anything wrong!

Maninder and I were still not talking when we caught the train to London. I tried a few times to break the ice, but he wouldn't allow me in. I gave up. Once we got to London, he started talking to me normally, and we got on with our day.

While we were at the Motor Show, Gurleen called and arranged to meet us for dinner at a fancy restaurant on the banks of the River Thames. We enjoyed the meal, and had a lovely time laughing together, until Gurleen and I went to the ladies' room, and she made a rude remark about my dress and how short it was. The denim dress covered me fully. The only problem was that it stopped above the knees, but I was wearing tights underneath. I didn't see what the issue was. "Why are you so shocked?" I said, raising my brow. "Your brother married me knowing what I wear, and I would never wear anything to disrespect him or the family. Anyway, I have seen you in clothes that show off more flesh than mine."

I knew in my heart that this wasn't Gurleen talking; Simranjit Mum had put her up to this. I had gotten to know this much about Maninder and Gurleen: they didn't have minds of their own, and they were always misled by their parents. They both had too little life experience to know any different, though I didn't consider myself to be better than them. I loved Gurleen, but I had noticed that she wasn't as strong as she made herself out to be. She was strongly influenced by her mother, and I could clearly see that in her eyes.

ME, THE SLUT

We had been invited to Maninder's friend Nav's birthday dinner, and most of his friends were going to be there with their girlfriends and female friends. My in-laws didn't think much of Maninder's friends who had girlfriends before marriage. Gurleen had turned up to tie a *Raksha Bandhan* (a sacred thread **https://en.wikipedia.org/wiki /Raksha_Bandhan**) on Maninder's wrist, and joined us for the meal. I wore a fitting pair of black jeans and a sequin top with a plunging neck and back. As I went to say goodbye to *Bee Ji,* Simranjit Mum came running up to me to tell me that my top was unbuttoned. I looked over my shoulder and replied that it was just the style of the top. She gave her signature funny look and said, "Are you going out dressed like that, Harleen?"

"*Haan Ji*, Mum." I nodded, walked straight out of the door, and jumped into my husband's car to go to London for the meal.

Simranjit Mum didn't have the opportunity to say anything to Maninder before we left, but the next day she told him she was disgruntled with what I had worn, and that he should not be taking me out with his friends, most of whom were Muslim and *Chamar* (people belonging to low castes). Both his parents filled Maninder's ears with crap about not trusting your friends around your wife, and how I could be titillating his friends by the way I was dressed. The next thing I knew, Maninder burst into our bedroom brimming with fury. He told me that I couldn't wear any clothes that showed off my figure. He'd like it if I didn't wear anything tight-fitting or revealing! I had not worn anything revealing, and I couldn't believe I was being spoken to like this, as if I had lifted my dress for the world to see. Why was Simranjit Mum planting seeds of evil into his head and saying stupid things to get him all fired up? Why didn't he trust me?

I'm not demeaning anyone, but honestly, not one of Maninder's friends was my type. It shouldn't even have crossed his mind and he should have known how much I loved him. What was he saying – and what did my in-laws think of me by even bringing up such a topic? Maninder and I had another argument over Simranjit Mum stirring the pot in our relationship. I'd had such an amazing time with his friends, their partners, and Gurleen, but within a moment, everything had been turned upside down.

DOMESTIC VIOLENCE: ROUND THREE AND BREAKFAST GATE

I'd been persistently applying for jobs and finally got an acceptance letter from a retail management company for a part time temporary position. I woke up on a fresh, bright morning knowing it was the first day at my new job, and I was looking forward to it. But before I could get all pumped up to meet my new colleagues and my new cubicle, I had to get my husband's breakfast ready. I was working around the clock like a clockwork machine. This soon became my regular schedule:

7am: Get up and run to cook breakfast.

7.30am: Finish preparing breakfast and check in with all the family to see if they would kindly oblige having the breakfast. Serve them.

7.45am: Pack His Majesty Maninder's lunch for work, like a good Punjabi wife must do, and run to the shower.

8.15am: Ah, finally! All dressed up, looking like a princess.

8.20am: Get back to the kitchen to have my own breakfast. But the breakfast was nowhere to be seen! I checked in vain the microwave and all the cabinets of the kitchen.

On the first day of my new job, my breakfast just disappeared into thin air. It was now 8.30am, the time I needed to be in the car with Maninder, and on my way to work. I got into the car feeling confused. I tried to work out where and how my breakfast could have vanished. There was only one possible culprit: Kabir Dad, who had a stomach like one of those Dyson vacuum cleaners. He must have eaten it!

Maninder looked over at me. "You okay?" he asked, pushing the key into the ignition.

"You know, my breakfast...it just disappeared!"

He burst into laughter. Simranjit Mum thought it was leftovers and she packed it for me to have during break time. Well, sometimes I get hungry in the afternoon." Mystery solved, but my hunger wasn't!

I couldn't believe it. Maninder's mum made such a big deal about me getting up every morning to make sure her son had breakfast before leaving the house, as she didn't want him to go to work on an empty stomach. But she didn't think about my stomach with the same emotion! Had she not noticed that I had eaten nothing that morning? She stood in the kitchen watching me cook breakfast, and she saw I hadn't eaten anything! I had even explained to her that I was leaving my breakfast on the shelf while I got myself ready for work. So why had she packed my breakfast for him?

Maninder told me not to make a big deal out of such a trivial issue, and that I should just open his bag, get the lunchbox out, and enjoy my breakfast. At this point, fuelled by hunger and frustration, I felt hurt as I realised that no one cared whether I had eaten. No one had any regard for my feelings. A sudden burst of anger overpowered me, and I yelled, "Your mum is a bitch!"

I saw Maninder's eyes becoming bloodshot as he glared at me for a few moments in numbing silence. He broke the ice by slapping me hard across the face and punching me in the leg.

I was so shocked that every sound from my howling heart was deadened in its tracks. I sat pressed my palms against my face, which burned like the flames of hell. I couldn't believe he had hit me again! And this time, in a car, amongst other people, on the streets.

I felt cold tears quelling my burning cheek. Maninder pulled the car over into the car park and I opened the door and ran out. Walking to a corner of the car park, I called my mother. I explained what had happened and admitted that I called my mother-in-law a bitch. My mother gave me a good telling off – but then she affirmed that my husband had no right to hit me.

I had decided that I would no longer travel with Maninder in the car; I'd rather walk. After work I was ten minutes into my walk when Maninder called to ask where I was. I told him that I was walking home and I was not going to get in the car with him again. He drove up to where I was walking, wound down the window and begged me to get into the car. I refused, and I was stalwart in my decision. Eventually he drove home alone, waited by the street in front of the house, and parked in the driveway just as I walked up, making it appear as if he had picked me up. He was so manipulating! I went straight up to my room, got changed, and climbed onto the bed.

He followed me into the bedroom. "What the hell is your problem, Harleen?"

I couldn't believe it. What was my problem? What was his problem, assuming he had the right to hit me whenever he felt like doing so? Did he feel like a man by hitting me? I'd made up my mind that I was not going to take anything from him anymore. I would stand up for myself, and would not allow this egocentric and abusive husband to keep assaulting and dominating me. This was the third time he'd hit me in 14 months of marriage. This was the last straw and I wasn't ever going to allow him to abuse me again. I ignored Maninder and made it very clear that he was not to come over to my side of the bed, touch me, or be near me either.

The next morning, I got up extra early to cook breakfast so I would have time to walk to work. Simranjit Mum insisted that I get a lift with Maninder, but I politely refused and walked out of the door.

Later that day I got a text asking me where I was and what time I would be getting home. Maninder finished the text by saying that it was his duty as my husband to find out where I was, and it was my duty as his wife to let him know. Where was his duty as a husband when he was hitting me? Where was his duty when he never supported me in my time of distress? I ignored the text. When I got back home, I made myself some soup, and went to our bedroom.

That night, his parents acknowledged that we were not communicating and that I was no longer willing to sit with the family and interact with them anymore. Simranjit Mum was still playing those irksome mind games and ignoring me, but she was starting to smother Maninder even more by constantly running around after him and using our falling out to her advantage.

I had an English exam coming up and the stressful situation at home was making it impossible to study. I didn't want to fail these exams. I was taking them to prove to Maninder and his parents that I was not stupid. They were not dealing very well with me being dyslexic, and Maninder couldn't understand how I had got myself into university when I hadn't even passed my GCSE English at school. I'd mentioned I wanted to become a teacher of art, and he kept on reminding me that I would need to pass GCSE English. Yes, I was dyslexic and I would make spelling mistakes – but that didn't mean I was dumb! Sometimes Maninder would disdainfully call me "Dumbo". I knew he thought he was more intelligent than I, as he had had private schooling. This did not make him any brighter than me – or anyone else. He'd even challenged me one day to take my GCSE exams and see if I could pass with better grades than him! I wasn't that bothered about proving a point or passing with a higher grade; I'd be just as happy to pass with a C grade. Anyway, in my view a really intelligent person is someone who takes the time to handle things maturely, explain things to you, encourage you, and not put you down.

Once I'd asked Maninder to check my essay, and even that was made into a big deal! He talked down to me like I was an idiot. Sometimes I'd ask him to check things and he wouldn't give the correct answer. He'd just let me look stupid – like when I asked him to check the invitation card I'd created for Simranjit Mum's birthday party. Instead he allowed me to post the cards out, only to have my auntie calling to point out all the spelling mistakes I'd made. I was embarrassed – and Maninder revelled in my embarrassment. That was his victory, letting his wife down once more.

That evening I told Maninder that I would be going home for a week, as I had not visited my mother for a long time and I needed a break from all the mental and physical abuse, and also from the stress. The next evening, I told my in-laws. They looked baffled! They couldn't understand why I was going. Simranjit Mum gave Kabir Dad a look across the room, and it was not the romantic type, but the one that shouted out that somebody was going to get hurt very soon. They questioned me about why I was going home. They never took responsibility for their son's actions; all they were good at was ignoring and concealing it all.

I packed my bags and decided to take the laptop for a revision of the lessons. Maninder snatched the laptop bag off me, and declared I couldn't take it with me. I left it and picked up the bag with just my clothes. Then he had the nerve to offer me a lift to the station, in front of his parents – yet behind closed doors, he was being an obnoxious bully. I'd walked to and from work all that week. What made him think I was going to get into the car with him now? We had a tiff in the hallway and I walked out of the front door with my overnight bag. The railway station was only 20 minutes' walk.

I caught the train to Birmingham New Street. Mother came to pick me up and I broke down in the car as soon as I saw her. I filled her in on the way Maninder had been towards me, though I held back a lot of information. I was protecting him. After all, he was still my husband. I also told her I had applied for another job, but I wasn't sure about going for it. She encouraged me to go to the interview as it was a full time, permanent position.

Next morning, I went back to Milton Keynes to attend the interview. Immediately after, I bumped into Maninder in the city centre. He looked at me in confusion, as if he was not sure whether he'd seen me or had a hallucination. He came over to me rubbing his eyes, and asked, "What the hell are you doing here?"

"I came back for an interview," I replied.

"And you told me nothing! What do you think you are doing?" His voice rose, making the public crane their necks to gawk at us. Who was in the wrong here? Why was I being made to feel like I'd done something wrong yet again?

After the interview, I went to my twin sister Jasleen's house in London, where I stayed overnight. I came back to Birmingham on the Saturday morning to get on with revising the notes for my first exam, which was the following Tuesday.

For some reason, I decided not to follow through with my pact, and I called Maninder. "Do you want to go to Cambridge for my birthday?" I asked him. "You could also come up to Birmingham, and we can have a day away from everybody."

"I don't give a shit about your birthday!" he shouted over the phone. "I don't want to do anything with you!" He hung up.

The following day was my 29th birthday. In many ways it was a hard day for me, as I remembered that I had been pregnant on my 28th birthday, and I could have been a mother by now. It wasn't a surprise that Maninder wasn't there for me again. I revised my notes during the morning, and in the afternoon I met up with my best friend Jaya for dinner. We had a good catch up, as we had not seen each other since her wedding day. It felt lovely, being able to talk to her again in person rather than on the phone. We talked and giggled for a couple of hours, but I knew I had to get back to my revision. It felt good just to talk and laugh off every sad moment. Jaya told me to look forward to a bright future ahead.

I got back to my mother's house to find my in-laws had called. Mother handed over the phone and my mother-in-law said, "I thought you went home to revise for your exams. How come you were out relaxing?"

"Come on, Simranjit Mum," I said, "today's my birthday and I've only been out for a couple of hours to have a break." Finally, after giving me a lecture, even though she didn't have her English GCSE, she reluctantly wished me happy birthday. Kalbir Dad came on the phone to give me birthday wishes and enquired what I had been up to at my mother's place. Then Amritpal *Bee Ji* came along to convey her *Dish Vaadtha* (birthday blessings). She told me how much she was missing me, and added that the house was too quiet and no one even talked to her when I wasn't there. Then she asked me when I would be coming home. The one person I was scared of at first loved me the most today. I was expecting Maninder to come on the phone but Amritpal *Bee Ji* ended the call. It was my birthday and my loving, caring husband couldn't even wish me a happy birthday! Surely his parents hadn't brought him up that badly, had they? I asked my mother if Maninder had called while I was out with Jaya, and she said he hadn't. She asked if he had called or texted me at all that day. I shook my head.

I felt upset. At this time last year, he had stopped talking to me the moment I told him that I was pregnant, and then forced me to go through an abortion. This year, he had hit me for the third time two weeks before my birthday, and then he had the nerve to show me his attitude when I'd done nothing wrong. His parents were playing mind games on me by calling my mother's place rather than my mobile phone to wish me a happy birthday, but not even trying to make their son realise what he was doing wrong.

I went up to my bedroom and called the landline at the Purewal residence. Simranjit Mum answered the call and I asked her how she had brought up her son, and why she had taught him so few manners that he couldn't even wish his wife a happy birthday. She defended him. "Whatever, whatever, Harleen. If he saw you as his wife, he would have done it. But he doesn't, does he? So no birthday wishes for you... Anyway, it is not my problem that he hasn't called you." She too hung up on me.

I was fuming by now. A few minutes later, Maninder called me on my mobile to wish me a happy birthday. Now wasn't that a pleasant surprise? Like his Simranjit Mum didn't have anything to do with it. I asked him why he had not called earlier, and he brazenly replied that I hadn't bothered to call him, so why should he? The only reason he was calling was because his Simranjit Mum had told him to. I hung up on him and wept. At the beginning of the year I thought things were getting better between us, but that was the calm before the storm.

Even when he mistreated me I never took it out on the family, but this time, I had to put my foot down, or he was going to keep taking the piss out of me for the rest of our married lives. His parents needed to stop interfering and getting involved in things between us. After feeling down for a while, I swept the hurt to the back of my mind and continued studying until the morning of my exam.

I went back to Milton Keynes, completed the exam, and then returned to Birmingham. I felt confident that I had completed the paper to the best of my abilities. Having time out in Birmingham to study my notes was refreshing and free of stress, and nothing was going to stop me from passing these exams. I had worked hard regardless of all the crap I was going through with Maninder and his parents. But now I kept focussed on my coursework and exams. This family needed to digest my new GCSE. It didn't matter that I had already got a degree and a good job; they just needed a piece of paper to prove I was not dumb and that I amounted to something. What did it say about their son for marrying someone like me then? It hurt my feelings every time Maninder and his parents talked down to me for being dyslexic or called me stupid. I knew there was a part of them that wanted me to fail these exams so they could continue their condescension. When someone wants to be evil, he or she always finds a pretext to do so. I was not going to allow that to happen. Especially since I knew Simranjit Mum was hoping I would fail. She had been studying for a GCSE in her first year of marriage when she fell pregnant with Maninder and gave up her dream of pursuing a degree. She had used that as an excuse all her life. If she really wanted to get the GCSE, she could have taken the course later. But she didn't.

The environment at my mother's house was the opposite. She would push me to do well in my education and would wait anxiously for the results to be announced. She was confident that I would do well. She always believed in me.

Before appearing for my last exam, which was on Thursday afternoon, I returned to the house in Milton Keynes to drop off my belongings and called a taxi. Simranjit Mum was overly nice to me, and after the way I spoke to her on the phone that day, I couldn't understand why she was being so helpful. It didn't feel good. For a moment I wondered what was going on, but I couldn't be bothered finding out, as I had this exam to focus on. After the exam, I came back to the Purewal residence, and everybody was being extra nice to me. I couldn't quite put my finger on it, but something felt off-kilter. The family were sugar-coating something, it seemed.

Maninder woke me early next morning and asked if I would be joining him at his friend's wedding. I didn't answer. In the evening, he asked me the same question and I replied in the negative. I was sick of playing happy families and didn't care about his feelings anymore. He explained that he would like me to be there with him, as all his friends and their wives would be there too.

"Just like you have always been there for me, like the caring husband you are?" I said, smirking. I made it clear to him that I didn't care, and he could go alone. I was starting a new job on Monday, and I wanted to prepare for it. I told him I didn't have the time for his luxuries, when he never cared about my feelings. I stayed in my bedroom all weekend, reading through and filling out all the documents I needed to complete for my first day at work.

Maninder seemed to enjoy attending his friend's wedding as a single man. I had gone to some weddings with just Simranjit Mum, and now it was his turn. It was funny; I was up in my room all weekend and the in-laws never once came up to ask what I was doing or why I had not gone to the wedding with their dear son. I don't know why, but something just didn't feel right.

I sat on my side of our bed enjoying the view out of the window. This room had known more pain than joy, and we hadn't created any treasured moments here, but there was something about the bedroom that I liked, something that made me feel comfortable. I looked around the room, scanned everything, and felt a funny feeling in my stomach. Something still didn't feel right. It was as if someone had been in our bedroom. Well, who could it be other than Simranjit Mum? She probably came to get some more of her things from the walk-in wardrobe. I'd be happy when she moved herself out completely from our bedroom.

The following day, I started my new job. I was going to complete my training at the Milton Keynes branch over the next week, but I had Thursday and Sunday off. I'd also booked an appointment with a gynaecologist, as I was still having some problems with my periods since the abortion.

THE KEYS DO NOT FIT THE LOCK ANYMORE

Maninder and I were still sharing the same bed but communication was at a minimum. I was just happy to get on with things, and enjoying my new job. I woke up on Thursday morning and Simranjit Mum offered to drop me off at the clinic, which was around the corner from the house. As I was leaving, she explained to Amritpal *Bee Ji* that she needed to get out of bed so she could let me into the house when I came back. I didn't understand why she was bothered about that, as I always carried the set of house keys I had got cut while they were away in India. I told Simranjit Mum I was happy to walk as it only took 15 minutes and I could do with the fresh air to clear my head. At the gynaecologist's clinic the doctor asked me to go through some medical tests. They were all done by early afternoon and I walked back home.

When I got to the front door I inserted my key in the lock, but it wouldn't turn. I gave it a few more attempts and wondered what the hell was going on. Tired of trying, I knelt down on the top step, put my mouth to the letterbox and shouted, *"Bee Ji! Bee Ji! Open the door!"*

"Who?" Amritpal *Bee Ji's* voice came faintly from inside. "Who is it? I can't hear you! Who's there?"

"It's Harleen! Please open the door!"

"Harleen who?"

"Oh, great..." I muttered to myself... "Harleen! Your granddaughter in law!"

"Oh...wait, I'm coming."

Amritpal *Bee Ji* was having a bad week and not doing well so it took her a good fifteen minutes to get to the door.

As soon as she let me in, she asked, "Why didn't you have the house keys with you?"

"Oh, I left them behind," I lied.

I didn't want her to know that the lock had probably been changed. It was lunchtime, so I prepared some lunch for Amritpal *Bee Ji* and then sat with her for a while, watching Asian TV. An hour or so later, she said she'd like to have her early afternoon *chai* (tea). I brewed some tea for her, and decided that I would vacuum the floor carpets, clean the kitchen, and cook dinner for the family before Simranjit Mum and Maninder got home, so I could chill out later in the evening.

I searched for the vacuum cleaner, which was normally kept under the stairs. But today it wasn't there. It wasn't in the study, either. I thought perhaps it was in Amritpal *Bee Ji's* bedroom upstairs. Since she'd stopped sleeping there it had become a bit of a storage room, but the hoover was not there either. Confused, I double checked all three rooms again, but couldn't make out where the vacuum cleaner had flown away to. Then it struck me that Simranjit Mum vacuumed her room two days before, and it might be there. I went up to her bedroom but the door was locked. This was strange, as she had never locked her bedroom door before. I tried Kabir Dad's bedroom door, and that too was locked. What the hell was going on?

I remembered that when I joined the family and was given my grand tour of the house by Simranjit Mum, she showed me that all the interior house keys were kept in the airing cabinet upstairs. I walked over to the cabinet to get the keys. I pulled them off the little tack they were hanging from, and inserted Simranjit Mum's key into her bedroom door but the lock still wouldn't turn. An alarm went off in my head. Kabir Dad's bedroom door wouldn't budge either, and I realised that something was terribly wrong. I tried all the keys in the doors they used to belong to, and none of them fit the locks anymore. The only door that opened was our bedroom. My heart started racing and I began to feel sick and dizzy, like the actors in those dramatic climaxes of a Bollywood film. I sat glumly on the floor for a while, and went off downstairs to find my house keys. They were resting on the desk. I picked them up and tried them, but they wouldn't unlock the front or back doors.

I thought I was going insane. I called up my best friend, Jaya. Panicking like a fire alarm had gone off in the house, I started crying as I explained to her that something was wrong. At first, she joked around with me, asking if I was sure because, after all, I was dyslexic. I told her that I was serious; all the door locks had been changed without anyone telling me. She advised me to call Maninder and ask him if that was the case.

I called him at work and he said that his Simranjit Mum would explain everything when she came home. At this point I felt nothing but rage clouding my senses. I shouted the question down the phone once again and demanded an answer, but Maninder told me to wait for his Simranjit Mum to come home. Then he hung up on me.

I had put my keys of happiness in another family's hands, and now that family had decided to steal something as materialistic as the house keys. I had never felt more of an outsider in this house as much as I did at that moment. I had in my hands a set of house keys that didn't fit any of the locks of the house that I lived in. The bright and colourful keychain reminded me of the person I was before I got married. And now I had become as rusty and obsolete as the keys themselves.

I walked slowly back to our bedroom. Over the weekend something had seemed funny and I couldn't put my finger on it, but now I knew that someone had been into our bedroom. I opened the door to the wardrobe where we kept the safe box. It was empty! Then I opened the second door, where I kept my gold jewellery, but it was no longer there! Now I knew for sure this was turning into something grave. It felt like this family had stripped me of everything I had ever had. There was nothing more left they could do to me. I felt like I was choking from the shock of realising this.

I called my mother, but it went straight to voicemail. I then called my Pretti *Mame Ji*, who answered the call. I could only just get my words out; I was so broken inside, I was gasping for breath. Pretti *Mame Ji* tried to listen to me but found it difficult to understand, as I had crashed emotionally, and was sobbing and blabbering disconnectedly. Then my Ranveer *Mama Ji* grabbed the phone off Pretti *Mame Ji* and asked why I was crying so much. In his deep, soothing voice, he asked me to calm down before I tried talking to him. I took a moment to myself, and tried talking without sounding like my world had been turned upside down.

This was the first time I had told a male member of my family about the reality of my marriage. I didn't hold back. I couldn't care less what they might think of Maninder, and I knew that Ranveer *Mama Ji* would want to break his legs. I was not going to stand in the way of anyone doing any damage to him. I was not going to protect him like a good Punjabi wife anymore!

I filled Ranveer *Mama Ji* in about the door locks, telephone tapping and countless altercations. "What were you doing before you discovered the locks had changed?" he asked, concern in his voice.

"I was going to clean the house."

He advised me to continue cleaning and cook dinner, and pretend everything was normal, while he took some time to think about what he should do.

I forced myself to calm down, followed his advice, and started cooking. I tried to stop thinking about what I had just discovered, and focus on cooking the family meal. I wept over this meal as I prepared it for them. I had always put their feelings and my love for them first. I had put myself on the back burner by being a wife and daughter to this family.

I called my Ranveer *Mama Ji* back and asked him to sort things out that evening. I also added that if he didn't, I would be walking out of the front door of this so-called family home. For the first time, I had called out for help, and if it was not forthcoming, I'd be happy to be a strong woman who'd take the necessary steps to get herself out of this situation. I had never felt so sure in all my life as I was about walking out of that door to the house that seemed strangely alien that evening.

I waited in the living room for Maninder and Simranjit Mum to come home and as I heard a key in the lock, I walked over to the front door. As the door opened, Maninder looked at me and then looked down at the floor at once. Simranjit Mum followed him. Without giving her a second to settle in, I went straight up to her and asked her why the door locks were not opening with my set of keys, or the keys in the airing cabinet. Ignoring me, she headed upstairs. I asked her again and she replied, "I will talk to you when Kabir Dad gets home."

This time I got mad. "I will talk to you all when my family turns up!" I yelled.

"Whatever. We will see," she said, indifferently.

"I'd like you to explain to my family why you changed the locks without telling me!"

She ignored me again, and went up to her bedroom. I noticed that Maninder and Simranjit Mum both had shiny new sets of keys. Normally they would leave their keys lying around, but this time they didn't. They put them away in their pockets. While Simranjit Mum was getting changed, and Maninder and I were arguing like two fired up lawyers, I called my Ranveer *Mama Ji* back to tell him that I would like him to come up to Milton Keynes.

My Ranveer *Mama Ji* asked to speak to Maninder, and I was shocked by the way Maninder tried to justify everything and act as if it were all my fault, that I was dramatizing and blowing things out of proportion for no reason. If he and his parents hadn't done anything wrong, why was he panicking when I told him that my family would be turning up? Why was he trying to stop them from coming? My Ranveer *Mama Ji* asked to speak to me again, and asked me what I wanted to do. I told him that I'd like him to come up that evening and find out why the hell the locks had been changed. He promised he would.

I started to pack my bag, but Simranjit Mum asked Maninder to follow me around the house and keep an eye on me while I was packing. I picked up a few clothes and some papers relating to my job, and left my bag by the front door. While I was packing, Maninder started yelling at me, trying to demotivate and belittle me. He said I was brimming with ego, and that no one would want to be with a person who had terminated a pregnancy, who was dyslexic, who couldn't satisfy her husband, and who didn't respect her husband and in-laws. I stood up for myself and asked him where my respect would be if he kept on treating me like a doormat!

"I had respect for you all, and had more to offer than you think!" I told him. "Women can be strong without a man, and I am going to show you what I have in me: someone who is driven, focused, grounded, intelligent, caring, emotional, sincere and trustworthy. I know my value, but you people have made me lose my confidence. No more!"

Amritpal *Bee Ji* heard us arguing and spotted my bag in the hallway. "Harleen *Puth*," she said, "this is your house. You're our daughter. Why have you packed a bag? You can't go anywhere – this is your home!"

"Shut up!" Simranjit Mum yelled at Amritpal *Bee Ji*. "Go back to your room and keep out of this, I warn you!" She was an ironic example of keeping out of things. All Simranjit Mum had done was get involved with every inch of my relationship with her son, like two tomcats fighting over a queen in the locality. Amritpal *Bee Ji* pleaded with me not to leave the house and said that however complicated it was, we could sort it out as a family. Then she shouted at Simranjit Mum, asking her what she had done to me that I was packing up a bag. Simranjit Mum again warned Amritpal *Bee Ji* to keep her nose out of this, and threatened that when Kabir Dad came home, he would sort her out. Usually they were great at controlling and dominating people – 'sorting out', in their words. But I was no more going to be the victim. I had had enough of them.

Simranjit Mum stayed in the kitchen until Kabir Dad came home. No guesses to what she was doing there – filling him in over the phone. Kabir Dad looked at my bag by the door. Seeing me sitting on the couch, he welcomed me in an over-friendly manner. "Hi Harleen, how are you? Going somewhere nice?" I glanced at him but otherwise ignored him. He came to sit on the couch next to me and said, "*Sat Sri Akhal,* Harleen."

I greeted him back. "*Sat Sri Akhal,* Dad." Then I went silent on him. I was reciting my *Mool Mantra* in my head, while waiting for my Ranveer *Mama Ji*, Mother and Pretti *Mame Ji* to turn up. If I had to wait for my in-laws to come home before Maninder would talk to me, now they could all wait until my family arrived.

Kabir Dad tried as hard as he could to get me to talk, but I wasn't going to. Eventually he had his dinner alone in the kitchen. After his stomach was full, he decided to take out some of his frustration on Amritpal *Bee Ji* by asking her who the hell she thought she was, why she was getting involved with our situation, and why she was trying to stop me from leaving the family home when I was not their daughter to hold back. Again I heard Amritpal *Bee Ji* say: "But she is my granddaughter and also your daughter! What have you done to her for her to pack her bags today?"

"You, old woman," Kabir Dad threatened her, "don't try to interfere when Harleen's family turns up here! Or else I will make you a homeless old woman, got it?"

Just then, there was a knock on the door, and I could see from where I was sitting that it was my family. I got up to let them in. Simranjit Mum had not come out of the kitchen all evening; it was as if she was chained to the kitchen sink. Kabir Dad had been running around the house like he had more important things to do. Maninder sat on the furthest chair in the room, as far away from my family as possible, as if he knew that he was going to get a thrashing for what he and his family had done to me. I don't think they had anticipated me ever picking up the phone and complaining about them, or asking my family to deal with the situation rather than allowing them to bully me all over again. In my heart, I knew that I needed my family to come over that evening, and not give my in-laws time to cover up their tracks, as I had seen them do with others, pretending they were the victims themselves.

Now my family were here, my in-laws were nowhere to be seen. Ranveer *Mama Ji* asked Maninder where his parents were, to which he whimpered like a schoolboy, "Kabir Dad's is doing some important work, and Simranjit Mum's doing the dishes."

Ranveer *Mama Ji* looked straight into Maninder's eyes and said, in his deep, chilling voice, "They need to get in here now. This situation is far more important than doing dishes or finishing your so-called important errands!"

Maninder took off like a bat out of hell, and brought his parents into the living room. It had been the scene of many meetings in the past where they had bullied me but this was the first time that they were being brought together and asked for an explanation.

Kabir Dad got up from the couch to shake Ranveer's *Mama Ji* hand. My Ranveer *Mama Ji* held out his hand, but didn't get up from his seat. Kabir Dad threw him a petrifying look, and sat down on the couch once again. Simranjit Mum came in with water dripping from her hands, and sat down without greeting anybody. I was shocked to see that she was still inflated by her ego. Ranveer *Mama Ji* spoke first. "We have heard Harleen's version of the story, and now we would like to hear yours. I want to know why all the locks of the house in which Harleen lives have been changed."

Kabir Dad started attacking me personally. "Look at the kind of clothes she wears!" He pointed at me. "They are not appropriate! They're too westernised!"

"Is that why you changed the door locks?" Ranveer said, calmly.

Kabir Dad tried in vain to sound serious. "She forgot to wear a *chunni* to cover her head at my cousin's house, can you imagine that?"

Simranjit Mum added her two pennies. "They are not even sleeping together!"

"So that must be the reason why you changed the door locks on her!" said Ranveer *Mama Ji*, in a 'Eureka!' voice and with a smirk. Finally, he snapped. "Maninder, do you and Harleen even get on?" he shouted.

"Yes, we do," Maninder whimpered.

"Then why don't you two move out and try to make your marriage work?"

"Have you come here to pull our family apart?" Simranjit Dad barked.

"I just want an answer to one simple question – why

you changed the door locks to the home my niece lives in! And for one hour, all I've heard is your nonsense! You have no grounds to justify your actions, do you?

"She also called my wife a bitch! Now can you justify that?" Kabir Dad yelled.

Ranveer *Mama Ji* glanced at his watch and looked over at my mother. Turning to Kabir Dad he said, "*Pah Ji,* you haven't given me a good enough reason for any of your condemnable actions." Then he turned to me and asked, "Now what would you like to do, Harleen?"

I stood up and announced, "I just want to go home!"

THE HOMECOMING

I didn't care what anyone else said, I just wanted to get out of this family that I had never been allowed to be a part of.

"Harleen's family can't just turn up like this at our house!" My mother-in-law tried her last means of defence. "This isn't the correct protocol!"

The word 'protocol' rang as a joke in my ears. Where was the protocol when your son got me to terminate the pregnancy? Where was the protocol when your son hit me? Where was the protocol when you were recording my phone conversations? Where was the protocol when you opened my mail? Where was the protocol when you forged my signature? Where was the protocol when you were dominating and controlling me? Where was the protocol when you removed my jewellery from my safe? Where was the protocol when you changed the door locks on me? Help me understand the word protocol, please.

Maninder stood up and declared, "Harleen, if you leave today, everything will be over – there will be no more of you and me!" As I heard the words come out of his mouth, my heart skipped a beat and I realised that I didn't want to work on my marriage anymore. For the first time, I was not going to be the perfect daughter, a good wife, and an obedient daughter-in-law. It was about time I did something for myself, and put myself first. For once, I was not worrying about all the other people in my life. I didn't care about their feelings; I didn't care how much hurt I was going to cause them. I thought about how I felt, and the hurt I had allowed them to inflict on me for all these months. I felt emotionally stripped by my current surname, and wanted to go back to my maiden surname, where I was the pristine and innocent Harleen, who was once full of life, shimmering with all the colours of the rainbow.

I feared the Harleen who was an insecure and hurt woman. I didn't want to look back at her anymore; I wanted to look forward to the vibrant Harleen yonder. I had been hurt so much that I was numbed to emotions. I just wanted to walk out of the door my keys no longer fit.

Just then, Maninder got a text from my friend Jaya : "You have hurt Harleen today, and if you don't admit it and take some responsibility for your relationship, she is going to walk out on you. So please fight for her."

My Ranveer *Mama Ji* turned to Maninder. "I think it would be best if we took Harleen home for a few days, as your family seems very heated," he suggested. "You should clear your heads, and decide what you all want to do, after you have all calmed down." Throughout the evening Simranjit Mum had been quiet. The money snake was not biting me now my family was here, otherwise she'd have taken every opportunity.

I walked over and picked up my bag. All of a sudden Simranjit Mum found her tongue and announced, "Stop! Not so fast! We need to check her bag. She might have stolen all of her wedding jewellery!"

I couldn't believe the audacity of the woman! I unpacked the bag that I had packed in front of her son. Even after she'd emptied my bedroom and stripped it all out, she had the nerve to say that I had stolen the jewellery. I just wanted to slap her across the face with the very *Belan* (rolling pin) I had used to make round *rotis* for this family, and sing the song *'Ni Main Saas Kut Ni'*. But, somehow, I resisted and walked out of the door. Leaving felt like a new life was welcoming me.

My family had only scratched the surface of my world of pain. They hardly knew anything of what I had been through. I wished the very walls had voices to tell them what I had gone through in this house, with the people they had trusted me with. Their delicate little doll had developed so many scars. I wanted them to know that those very people who pretended they cared about me actually never loved me as their own or allowed me to become part of their family. Each brick was cemented together to build a house, but there was no warmth between these walls and the people that lived within them. All they knew was how to humiliate others.

At this point in my life I was the only thing that mattered to me – and the love that my family had shown me by turning up and rescuing me. I had a clear sense of direction in my life, of walking through the door to freedom.

HOME AGAIN!

"Considering what you have been through over the last 19 months, you only called her a bitch!" said Ranveer *Mama Ji* glanced away from the road to look at me as he drove through the empty streets. "If I were you, I'd have slapped the bitch long ago!"

By the time he dropped my mother and me back in Birmingham, it was one o'clock in the morning. I could see the stress on my mother's face. I had work in the morning and had only slept for two hours. At five a.m, I could hear my own beautiful mother walking around the house. A part of me thought it was all a pleasant dream.

My phone started vibrating under my pillow. It was Jaya, calling to check if I was alright. I told her I felt like a burden had been lifted off me. They couldn't hurt me again and I was safe at home, back with my mother in my old bed, where my life was simple and uncomplicated. I had been pushed to the limits by Maninder and his parents' domineering and manipulating behaviour. These people thought they could chip away at my self-esteem and confidence by telling me that I couldn't do any better than him. No, they were not going to come across another daughter like me – someone who would put up with their son and their loathsome and degrading behaviour. My confidence was so low that I had been holding onto him and the very legal contract that had joined us into one soul. I had loved him and tried to love his family. I kept putting their feelings before my own. I had to make a decision for myself for the first time in a long time. I was not going to allow them to control and dominate me anymore. I felt as if

I could breathe again. I felt betrayed by them all and now I was happy that I had made the choice to leave. I had no regrets. Jaya was shocked as I told her this. She had no idea that was how I felt about my relationship.

I went downstairs with a full-hearted smile on my face. From what I could remember, my mother was a very strong woman during her separation from my father. She played the role of a mother and a father throughout our childhood.

The following Friday evening, Ranveer *Mama Ji* called to invite my mother and me to Derby for a family meeting. He wanted to know all about my marriage and I decided to tell him every fine detail, everything I had been through, and not leave any stone unturned.

Mother and I arrived in Derby on a pleasant Sunday evening. Ranveer *Mama Ji* and Pretti *Mame Ji* were waiting for us. I sat at the centre of the room. As I started opening my bag of hurt and pain, I crashed emotionally, physically and mentally in front of my loved ones. My Ranveer *Mama Ji* said that if I were one of his daughters, he would never put me back in that house. The family said that the decision was mine and they would respect me regardless of whatever I chose. I said that I would never go back unless Maninder agreed to move out and could explain why they had changed the door locks.

I had lost everything I knew. One day I would wake up feeling strong, but the next in complete despair. Seeing what I'd done to my loved ones was much harder than dealing with my own situation. By holding everything back from my family until the very end, I had broken them too.

EPILOGUE

Maninder and I had been separated for a year and a half. We had been through mediation sessions with my family, my in-laws, Gurleen and Loveneet, who all had mediated throughout the counselling. Nothing had changed other than the fact that I felt I had got a few answers for their unacceptable behaviour, but nothing that really explained anything. In fact, their behaviour took a turn for the worse once people outside the family saw their true colours.

My family were not going to allow me into their home as everybody in their social network now knew what had happened. My in-laws cared more about what their social community thought of them and this started to overpower their common sense. For once they didn't try to make an effort to apologise for their actions against me or give Maninder any support to make our marriage work. Maninder didn't have a backbone, nor was he capable of standing on his own two feet without his parents' chequebook.

There was a part of me that wanted to work at the marriage. I didn't want people to think of me as a lonely divorcee. I still didn't know the true value of myself until a few more months had passed. It took me time to regain my confidence and self-respect. I had lost a great deal of myself in this marriage.

After being separated for months, I took a holiday to India and Pakistan, and came to the realisation that life is short. The relationship was truly destructive and I had embarked on a one-way trip to nowhere. Now I felt as if I were in a fabulous place in my life, filled with positive energy and on a natural high. I no longer wanted to strive to work on this relationship.

Time and experience had gifted me a clearer sense of purpose. It was too late to go into questions of blame. What mattered now was my future and I could decide whether it was going to be a miserable one or a happy one that I was content with. I chose the second. That would always be my choice.

I simply requested a divorce. I decided to walk away. There was no reasoning behind the way my husband and his parents treated me or played games with my feelings. I learnt the hard way that I cannot always count on others to respect my feelings, even if I respect theirs.

Seven years on, I have burned the bridges to my past, and have never looked back. Life is too precious to be with people who belittle you, play with your emotions, dominate you, strip you bare and, ultimately, destroy you. Life is short, and should be lived, not compromised.

I'm surprised I've held up as well as I have, considering some of the madness that has gone on in my marriage. I have learnt one very important thing: that I can forgive more than I ever thought possible. After going through this whole situation myself, I wanted to hear and understand the reasons my parents had a divorce and why my father had decided to take that route. I asked questions, listened to what he had to say and asked him how he felt now, knowing what I had gone though – and I got advice from my father from his own experience. Today I have my father in my life. If someone told me that I would lose my relationship with Maninder and gain a relationship with my dad I would never have believed it but today I've seen him a lot since Maninder and I separated and divorced. My father is a changed man; a man who respects women, takes the time to understand and is caring. I'm glad to have this relationship back.

I'm taking no regrets or negativity with me so I can start again with a fresh, healthy blank slate.

FINAL WORD

Here's some food for thought if you're the parent of a daughter or daughters.

What would you do if this story happened to your daughter?

How would you have coped with the situation?

What would your advice be for Harleen?

Please leave your thoughts and comments on my website.
www.kalbirbains.com

AN IMAGE AND A POEM THAT DESCRIBE MY JOURNEY

No one falls in love to get hurt
No one gets married to get divorced
No one falls pregnant to end a pregnancy
No one loves another person's family to be treated unfairly
Not everyone loves another person's daughter as their
own...
that's why
You're NOT OUR DAUGHTER!
The true story of a daughter-in-law

Kalbir Bains

ACKNOWLEDGEMENTS

With gratitude to my dear family and friends, who have loved me and supported me through the hard times and the writing of this book. The book became my passion, a journey that I wanted to share with the world. Thank you to you all; you know who you are for your love, support and encouragement of an idea that has become a reality.

Special thanks to:

Alison Thompson
Brian Would
Caroline Ann Michael
Hardeep Singh Kohli
Jag Lall
Jagdeep Riana
Jasbir Sohotha
Kavaljeet Singh Bhamra
Maryam Ali
Peter Michael
Soumyadeep Koley

KALBIR BAINS

Birmingham's where I was brought up. It's where my heart
is and where I got the inspiration for most of my story.
Please visit my website for more details:
www.kalbirbains.com

34141723R00234

Printed in Great Britain
by Amazon